89753

D1001923

Brothers at War

Making Sense of the
Eritrean–Ethiopian War

TEKESTE NEGASH &
KJETIL TRONVOLL

James Currey
OXFORD

Ohio University Press
ATHENS

James Currey Ltd
73 Botley Road
Oxford
OX2 0BS

Ohio University Press
Scott Quadrangle
Athens, Ohio 45701

1 2 3 4 5 04 03 02 01 00

British Library Cataloguing in Publication Data
Negash, Tekeste
  Brothers at war : making sense of the Eritrean-Ethiopian war.
  - (Eastern African studies)
  1. Eritrea - History - 1993 - 2. Ethiopia - History - 1974 -
  3. Ethiopia - Foreign relations - Eritrea 4. Eritrea -
  Foreign relations - Ethiopia
  I. Title II. Tronvoll, Kjetil
  963'.072

  ISBN 0-85255-854-6 (James Currey paper)
  ISBN 0-85255-849-X (James Currey cloth)

**Library of Congress Cataloging-in-Publication Data is available
from the Library of Congress**

  ISBN 0-8214-1371-6 (Ohio University Press cloth)
  ISBN 0-8214-1372-4 (Ohio University Press paper)

Typeset in 10/12 pt Baskerville
by Long House Publishing Services, Cumbria, UK
Printed & bound in Great Britain
by Woolnough, Irthlingborough

Contents

List of Maps and Tables

Preface

At the beginning of May 1998 the relationship between Eritrea and Ethiopia took a new and surprising turn as military forces from the two countries clashed in some disputed border areas. After four weeks of intense fighting, hostilities ceased, but flared up again in February 1999. During the lull, both countries mobilised huge forces along their common border and each spent several hundred million dollars on new military equipment – ranging from Kalashnikovs to advanced jet fighters.

Outside observers may find it difficult to weigh up the official statements and proclamations issued by the two governments on the conflict, given their polarised content and fervid mutual denunciation. It is therefore important to study the context of the conflict closely, so as to achieve a balanced understanding of how a new war between Eritrea and Ethiopia could develop so fast and unexpectedly.

This book does not aim at presenting an exhaustive picture of the conflict in order to identify and denounce an aggressor. Instead, we have focused on some important contextual aspects in order to explain the growing discord between two former friendly governments.

In preparing the project, Kjetil Tronvoll visited Ethiopia frequently between August 1998 and December 1999, doing studies in both Addis Ababa and Tigray. He also went to Eritrea (Asmara, Zalambessa and Badme) from 29 September to 14 October 1998. Tekeste Negash visited Ethiopia (Addis Ababa) for three weeks in September 1998, and undertook archive studies in the Trevaskis collection at Oxford.

Our book does not present the full history of the war, since the Eritrean–Ethiopian conflict is not yet settled. Since the mediators are still engaged in reconciling the two governments, it is also too early to make definitive statements on reconciliation and preconditions of peace.

We have documented the history of the conflict until December 1999, however, and we have attempted to examine it from various angles. In particular we have dealt with historical relations between the two countries from the late nineteenth century. The complicated relations between the major liberation fronts – the Eritrean People's Liberation Front (EPLF) and the Tigrayan People's Liberation Front (TPLF) – are also addressed, based on secondary research and structured interviews with the leaders of the two organisations. The history of the border issues is closely scrutinised to shed light upon the local understanding and practice of the borders. The chapter on economic relations is supported, *inter alia*, by hitherto inaccessible documentation made available to us by the Ethiopian Ministry of Foreign Affairs.

As regards the effects of the conflict, the book identifies ethnic deportations as the most negative effect, followed by decline in economic development, in addition to the thousands of lives that have been sacrificed on the battlefields. This book has also noted the undermining impact of the politics of destabilisation that both countries are still conducting. We thus express a certain amount of pessimism as regards prospects for a speedy normalisation of relations.

We have also closely documented and analysed the peace initiatives that have been attempted so far, and the book voices a sharp criticism of the manner in which mediation efforts have been carried out.

In conclusion, we synthesise the information addressed and offer interpretations of why the conflict between Eritrea and Ethiopia erupted.

In the course of writing this book we have benefited from the support of colleagues and friends. We wish to enter on record the generous cooperation of Ato Sebhat Nega of TPLF and Ato Yemane 'Jamaica' Kidane at the Ethiopian Ministry of Foreign Affairs, and of the Ethiopian embassy staff at Stockholm. We would also like to thank Ato Yemane Ghebreab of EPLF's People's Front for Democracy and Justice (PFDJ) and Ato Berakhi Ghebreselassie, Eritrea's Minister of Information.

We are greatly indebted to John Young, Sara Vaughan, Fisseha-Tsion Menghistu, Worku Getu, Yussuf Yassin and our publisher's anonymous reader, for invaluable comments on an early draft version of our manuscript.

This study was conducted under the Horn of Africa Research Programme at the Norwegian Institute of Human Rights, University of Oslo. Kjetil Tronvoll heads the research programme, while Tekeste Negash was employed by the Institute as a visiting scholar under the programme during the time of the project.[1] Their joint authorship extends to all parts of the book. The authors are responsible for all the information presented and conclusions reached; the opinions expressed are theirs alone and do not necessarily reflect the opinions of the Institute. We remain solely responsible for any errors of fact and judgement.

Tekeste Negash and Kjetil Tronvoll
Oslo, December 1999

[1] The work conducted by Kjetil Tronvoll on this project was partly sponsored by the DPSIR-NIHR Cooperation Programme at Addis Ababa University. The cooperation programme is financed by the Norwegian Development Agency (NORAD).

Notes on Authors

Tekeste Negash is Associate Professor in Modern History at Dalarna University, Sweden. He has lived and worked in Eritrea, Ethiopia, Italy, Great Britain, Norway and Sweden. He has written numerous articles and several books on Italian colonialism, Eritrean and Ethiopian modern history, and African educational policies. He is the author of *Italian Colonialism in Eritrea* (1987 and 1997); *Eritrea and Ethiopia: the Federal Experience* (1997); *The Crisis of Ethiopian Education* (1990); and *Rethinking Education in Ethiopia* (1996).

Kjetil Tronvoll (a social anthropologist) is Research Fellow and Horn of Africa Programme Director at the Norwegian Institute of Human Rights, University of Oslo. He has conducted anthropological field work in the Eritrean highlands (1991–3, 1997) and in Tigray (1998, 1999). Kjetil Tronvoll served as a UN observer of the Eritrean referendum in 1993 and as an international election observer of the regional election in 1997. He has also been an international observer of the Ethiopian elections for the Constituent Assembly in 1994 and has observed and done research on the elections for Federal and Regional Assemblies in 1995 and 2000. He has published numerous articles and reports on political development, ethnicity and conflict in Eritrea and Ethiopia, and the ethnographic monograph *Mai Weini: A Highland Village in Eritrea* (1998).

Abbreviations

ANDM	Amhara National Democratic Movement
EFFORT	Endowment Fund for the Rehabilitation of Tigray
ELF	Eritrean Liberation Front
EPLF	Eritrean People's Liberation Front
EPRDF	Ethiopian People's Revolutionary Democratic Front
EPRP	Ethiopian People's Revolutionary Party
FDRE	Federal Democratic Republic of Ethiopia
JHMC	Joint High Ministerial Commission
JMC	Joint Ministerial Commission
OAU	Organisation of African Unity
OLF	Oromo Liberation Front
OPDM	Oromo People's Democratic Organization
PFDJ	People's Front for Democracy and Justice (new name of EPLF)
REST	Relief Society of Tigray (TPLF's 'humanitarian wing')
TGE	Transitional Government of Ethiopia (1991–4)
TLF	Tigrean Liberation Front
TPLF	Tigrayan People's Liberation Front
UN	United Nations
UNDP	UN Development Programme
UNSC	UN Security Council

MAP 1 *Eritrea & Ethiopia*

1 Brothers at War

On 6 May 1998 a small group of Eritrean soldiers entered a disputed territorial zone on the Badme plains along the western borders of Eritrea and Tigray, the northernmost regional state in the Ethiopian federation. The move was intended to mark Eritrean presence and interests in these areas, and to substantiate the Eritrean position in already ongoing border negotiations between the two governments. The handful of Eritrean soldiers were confronted by Tigrean militia and security police and asked to put down their arms and return to undisputed territories. A shoot-out between the Eritrean unit and the local militia followed, resulting in a few casualties on both sides. Among the dead Eritreans were the commander of the group, a high-ranking officer and a veteran liberation fighter.

The aftermath suggests that the Eritrean government had expected such a reaction to the movements of its border patrol, and had made military preparations accordingly. Immediately after the skirmish, large contingents of the Eritrean military launched an offensive on several fronts in order to retake what they claimed to be Eritrean territories controlled by Ethiopia. The major Eritrean offensive came as a surprise to Ethiopian authorities in both Mekelle and Addis Ababa. They had viewed the border clash on 6 May as a 'routine' incident, similar to several others during the previous two years which had passed without igniting a larger conflict. Now, to their surprise, Eritrean forces advanced deep within Tigrean-held territories without any notable opposition. The conflict escalated rapidly as both sides mobilised their full armed forces, including air strike support. At the beginning of June the Ethiopian air force bombed Asmara, the Eritrean capital. An hour later, Eritrea retaliated by dispatching its small new air force against Mekelle, the regional capital in Tigray. In four weeks, what had started as a minor border skirmish had escalated into a full-scale bilateral war – the first such war on the continent in decades.

After the first rush of fighting in May–June 1998, active warfare ceased until February 1999. The two parties used the lull in fighting to restock arms supplies left over from the Derg period. Both Eritrea and Ethiopia succumbed to an arms-shopping frenzy, purchasing everything from hand weapons and landmines to tanks and super-modern MIG 29 and Sukhoy 27 jet fighters. Several hundred million US dollars were spent on arms by two of the poorest countries in the world. During the break in fighting, the two biggest armies in Africa were once again mobilised: it is estimated that Ethiopia currently has about 450,000 men under arms, while Eritrea has mobilised 350,000 men and women. The mobilisation of the armies has had a much more radical social impact on Eritrea than on Ethiopia. The Ethiopian government can draw recruits from 60 million inhabitants, whereas Eritrea's population is only 3.2 million. If we estimate that 70 per cent of Eritrea's people are under 18 or above 55 years of age, this indicates that more than 35 per cent of Eritrea's able-bodied men and women are under arms at the front lines! Consequently, the war has a huge impact on the Eritrean economy and society, draining the newly independent state of scarce resources.

In addition to coping with war and mobilisation, both Eritrea and Ethiopia must accommodate a huge number of displaced civilians as a consequence of the war. About 350,000 Ethiopians and some 250,000 Eritreans have been forced to flee their homes and belongings by the militarisation of the 1,000-km border between the two countries. An extra burden on Ethiopia is the threat of large-scale famine in the south, where some 5–7 million people in Konso, Borana and Ogaden are on the brink of starvation. Thus we see history repeat itself in the Horn of Africa: while governments give priority to war ahead of development and drought/famine prevention, people are exposed to the unpredictable whims of nature and marginal food production in the area.

After eight months of *de facto* ceasefire the war flared up again in February 1999 with even greater intensity. A major Ethiopian offensive from mid-February managed to push the dug-in Eritrean forces out of Badme. The Badme battle, or 'Operation Sunset' as the Ethiopian military termed it, was probably the biggest military engagement in Africa since the Second World War. Over 40,000 Eritrean troops stationed along the Badme front had used the eight-month ceasefire to build well-protected defensive positions and trenches, supported by artillery, tanks and a wide zone of landmines. The Ethiopian military command sent about 80,000 troops to make a frontal attack against the Eritrean positions along the Badme front. Wave upon wave of Ethiopian soldiers had to cross zones of landmines and open terrain under heavy enemy fire before they could reach the Eritrean trenches. After several days of intensive ground attacks, backed by bombing sorties by the Ethiopian air force, the

Ethiopian army managed to break through the trenches, and the Eritrean control of Badme collapsed. By 1 March 1999, Badme village and its surrounding areas were once again under Ethiopian control, and as a consequence Eritrea accepted the Organisation of African Unity's Framework Agreement for peace. Many believed that this would put an end to the war, but the fighting continued. A new offensive began on the Tsorona front, followed by clashes on the Bure front at Assab, and at several other places. Since the war is fought with high-tech weapons, but with military strategies reminiscent of the First World War, casualties are extremely high. Neither party confirms its own casualties, however, and both tend to exaggerate enemy losses. Conservative estimates suggest total casualties for both armies so far are between 50,000 and 75,000 troops.

How is it possible for two formerly friendly governments to turn into deadly adversaries in a matter of weeks, willing to sacrifice tens of thousands of their people on the battlefields? Why mobilise people and resources on such a scale, if the reason for the war is – as it is officially stated – some relatively marginal square kilometres of agricultural land? It is truly a senseless war if we rely on such official reasoning – but may there be some hidden motives for the war that explain the intense ferocity demonstrated by the two warring parties? This is the question our book attempts to answer.

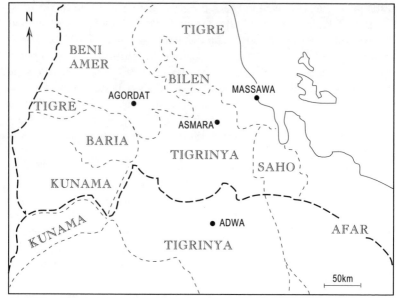

Source: Tekeste Negash, *Italian Colonialism in Eritrea*, 1987, p. 5.

MAP 2 *Ethnic Map of Eritrea*

2 Historical Relations

The modern history of Eritrea begins in 1882 with the Italian occupation of Assab. On the eve of 1890, Italy had three distinct possessions along the African Red Sea coast. The first was the Afar coastline, stretching from the southern part of Massawa up to the Djibouti border. The second took in the vast rugged hills north of Massawa and the western lowlands stretching up to Kassala in the Sudan. The third and most important possession was a small part of the Ethiopian/Abyssinian highlands ceded by the Ethiopian Emperor in May 1889. On the first of January 1890 these three possessions were consolidated into a single entity and given the name of Eritrea.

The colony that Italy created was inhabited by no fewer than nine different ethnic groups and had a population of around 300,000. The Eritrean (Abyssinian) highlanders who were known as the Tigreans (Tigrayans, the Tingrinya)[1] made up 40 per cent of the population and occupied about 20 per cent of the entire territory. In terms of religion, whereas most of the other ethnic groups were predominantly Muslim, the Tigrinyans were adherents of the Ethiopian Orthodox Church.

The Ethiopian state of the period maintained relations of varying intimacy with the different ethnic groups in the region that came to be called Eritrea. The Afar coastline was virtually outside the reach of Ethiopia. Massawa, Zeila and the overland long-distance trade route via

[1] There is no standard term to describe the Tigrinya-speaking population of Eritrea and Ethiopia. In the Amharic language a Tigrinya speaker is identified as Tigre. In the Tigray region he/she is identified as Tigraway (male) and Tigrawit (female). In Eritrea the Tigrinya population inside Eritrea is identified as Tigrinya. Thus, we have chosen to use the term Tigrean to describe the Tigrinya-speaking population in Tigray, and the term Tigrinya to describe the Tigrinya-speaking population in Eritrea. Where we refer to the Tigrinya speakers of both Tigray and Eritrea, this will be specified in the text. Cf. Negash 1987; 1997 and Tronvoll 1998b on the use of Tigrinya and Tigrean to describe the Tigrinya-speaking population both in Eritrea and Ethiopia.

Sudan were its main outlets, and Assab and Djibouti did not figure very prominently until the opening of the Suez Canal in the second part of the nineteenth century. It can thus be argued that the Afar coastline was by and large independent, although the Ottoman Empire and later the Egyptian state claimed they exercised sovereignty over that part of the Red Sea.

The vast region north of Massawa is made up partly of the continuation of the Ethiopian highlands and partly of lowland plains fusing into the Sudanese landscape. Massawa was an ancient port and formed part of the Ethiopian medieval state until the Ottoman Turks occupied it in the latter part of the sixteenth century. The Ethiopian state, primarily a highland state, did indeed extend its control up to Keren. Ethiopian/Abyssinian war chiefs in search of cattle, food crops and slaves frequently raided the vast area of the lowland areas on both sides of Keren.

The Ethiopian/Abyssinian highland region of Eritrea had formed part of the Ethiopian state at least since the early years of the fourteenth century. For most of its history Ethiopia was made up essentially of two closely related ethnic groups, the Tigreans/Tigrinya and the Amhara. The Amhara were more numerous and appear to have had the capacity to assimilate neighbouring peoples, whereas the Tigreans/Tigrinya remained rather confined by the Amhara to the south and the adjoining lowlands to the north and east. Furthermore, the resource base of the Amhara regions was more plentiful than that of the Tigrean/Tigrinya areas. The Ethiopian state was highly decentralised, with the king of kings at the top. Though the Amhara had produced most of the kings, the Tigreans/Tigrinya remained powerful contenders and their sacred city of Aksum was recognised as the ancient seat of the Ethiopian kingdom. Towards the close of the nineteenth century a Tigrean, Emperor Yohannes IV, ruled Ethiopia for eighteen years (1872–9).

Once in Eritrea, it did not take the Italians long to figure out the multiple links binding the Tigrinya to their Tigrean brothers across the border and to their cousins the Amhara further south. Italy felt safe as regards its relations with the rest of the Eritrean population, partly because these were Muslims with bitter memories of Abyssinan/Ethiopian misrule, and partly because Italy had protected and supported the Muslim faith. As regards the Tigrinya, however, the Italians became convinced, as early as 1900, that they could not rely on them because of their cultural, historical and political links with the Tigrean and Amhara peoples in Ethiopia.

Colonialism was an adventure consistently opposed by the Italian taxpayer. It has to be recalled that Italy lost heavily against Ethiopia at the battle of Adwa in March 1896. Italian rule in Eritrea was therefore based on two fundamental principles, the first of which was to contain any form of resistance that might emerge from the Tigrinya of Eritrea. Italy feared that Tigrinya resistance to colonial rule might spill over the border and gain support from the Tigreans and Amhara in Ethiopia. The second principle was to maintain strict good neighbourliness with its Ethiopian neighbour. Italy adhered to its principles for the most part of the colonial period up to the invasion of Ethiopia in 1935.

The nature of Italian colonialism and its impact on Eritrea are not academic subjects only. They are also the main basis for the legitimacy of the Eritrean government of today. There is always, however, a discrepancy between an academic/scientific assessment of the impact of colonialism and the political perception of this impact as acted upon by political organisations. Nowhere is this more clearly demonstrated than in the Eritrean case, both during the 30-year war of independence and under the independent Eritrean government. In the following paragraphs we shall sketch the main features of Italian colonialism and how these have impinged on relations between the Tigrinya of Eritrea and their brothers across the border.

Impact of Italian Colonialism

In the Italian colonial framework, Eritrea was useful to Italy for three reasons. Its first importance was as a conduit for the export and import trade with northern Ethiopia. Throughout the colonial period, Eritrea remained a resource-poor country and did not, therefore, attract Italian or foreign capital investment. By operating the port of Massawa and the trade routes within Eritrea, however, Italy managed to siphon off 25 per cent of the Ethiopian import/export trade. Its presence in Eritrea enabled Italy to include some parts of Ethiopia in its sphere of influence and even eventually to launch its invasion of Ethiopia in 1935.

The second value of Eritrea for Italy was as a source of soldiers for Italian colonial adventures elsewhere. The 'pacification' of Somalia was to a great extent facilitated by the use of Eritrean soldiers. It was, however, especially during the Italian invasion and occupation of Libya that Eritrea and its soldiers proved their usefulness to Italy. Between 1912 and 1932, a permanent force of up 6,000 Eritrean soldiers was deployed in Libya on behalf of the Italian colonial administration. Eritrean soldiers could be put in the field at a fraction of the cost of their Italian counterparts and were better adapted to mobile dryland warfare. It has been argued that the active participation of Eritrean soldiers in Libya enabled Italian statesmen to fund the Libyan adventure without burdening the Italian taxpayer.

The third advantage of Eritrea was its strategic location as a command post for the invasion of Ethiopia and, later, as the main economic and communications centre for the running of Italy's East African empire,

1936–41. Ethiopia was colonised from Eritrea, and the Italians, building on their earlier appreciation of the value of Eritrean soldiers, managed to turn the colony into a reservoir for its colonial army. Between 1936 and 1941, about 60,000 Eritrean soldiers, about 40 per cent of the male adult population, served in Italy's armed forces.

Though the Italians did not encounter serious resistance to colonial rule, they did not cease to suspect their Tigrinya/Tigrean subjects. Developments in Ethiopia were carefully monitored and a series of measures were taken to create borders between the Tigrinya in Eritrea and the Tigrean/Amhara people (who are predominatly Christians) in Ethiopia. They attempted to Catholicise the Tigrinya Orthodox, but without success. They succeeded for a short period of time in creating a separate Orthodox Church for the Tigrinya in Eritrea, although they abandoned this initiative soon after the creation of their African empire.

One of the numerous contradictory measures that the Italians took after the establishment of their East African empire was the creation of a province encompassing all the Tigreans/Tigrinya in the empire, ironically called both Great Eritrea and New Eritrea. Asmara was the capital city of Great Eritrea. The defeat of Italy in 1941 led to the dismantling of the East African empire. Ethiopia regained its independence under the sovereign emperor Haile Selassie, while Eritrea was kept by the British as enemy territory. The Tigrean/Tigrinya people were once again divided into Ethiopia and Eritrea, under the British Military Administration.

Pax Italica was not a zero-sum game, as the Eritrean liberation fronts and the present Eritrean government also acknowledge. The economy was monetised; a small working class had emerged; law and order was established; and there was a marked distinction in material well-being between the Tigrinya in Eritrea and the Tigreans in Ethiopia. Fifty years of uninterrupted colonial rule and the role that Eritrea was made to play during this period left profound traces on a considerable section of the Eritrean population.

One of the most important impacts of Italian colonialism was the demographic growth of the Tigrinya group in Eritrea. By 1940 the Tigrinya-speaking element had grown from 40 per cent to 54 per cent of the population as a whole. Our guess is that this demographic growth has continued and that at present the Tigrinya of Eritrea may constitute up to 60 per cent of the population. The power of the Tigrinya in relation to the other eight ethnic groups, who even together do not reach 50 per cent, is not difficult to appreciate.

Another colonial impact was the evolution of a distinct identity on the basis of the growing gap between the socio-economic realities of Eritrea and Ethiopia. In the 1930s the Italians had propagated the view that Italian rule had 'civilised the Eritreans', while Ethiopia and the Ethiopians were described as backward and thus in need of the 'Italian civilising mission' (Negash 1987: 154–7). The Italians contributed further to the growth of distinct identity by coopting the Eritreans in the pacification of the Ethiopian Empire. This identity was based less on territorial exclusiveness than on the economic advancement which the Eritreans as individuals had achieved, and the privileges awarded by the colonial power in its attempts to coopt them into an enlarged colonial system

Post-Italian Period

The period between 1947 and 1950 is important in gauging the impact of Italian colonialism on Eritrean society. The British, who administered Eritrea on behalf of the Allies, were mandated to prepare the ground for the visit of a Commission of Enquiry made up of the big powers (France, the United States, Great Britain and the Soviet Union). The wind of change had begun to blow and the days of European colonialism in Africa were numbered. The big powers had to dispose of Eritrea after taking into account the wishes of the Eritrean people. The Commission of Enquiry found that 44 per cent of the population (virtually the entire Tigrinya community) preferred unconditional union with Ethiopia. As the big powers could not agree on the disposal of Eritrea, the question was passed on to the United Nations General Assembly in 1948. Slightly more than a year later, the United Nations sent its own Commission of Enquiry to better assess the wishes of the Eritrean population. This Commission presented a majority report in which it recommended the union of Eritrea with Ethiopia. The minority report, on the other hand, urged the granting of independence after a number of years of trusteeship. After numerous diplomatic negotiations, the UN resolved in 1950 that Eritrea be federated with Ethiopia as an autonomous entity under the sovereignty of the Ethiopian Emperor.[2] The act of attaching Eritrea to Ethiopia was known as the Federal Act, but this was partly a misnomer as little federal structure was envisaged in the Act itself.

Why did Eritrea not achieve its independence right after the end of the Second World War? What was the basis of the UN resolution of 1950 uniting Eritrea to Ethiopia? What role did the big powers in general and the United States in particular play in the UN resolution of 1950? What was the political climate of Eritrea in the late 1940s? How effective were Ethiopian strategies as regards Eritrea? These and several more questions were widely studied and debated during the 30-year war of independence. As might be expected, there exist two diametrically opposed interpreta-

---

[2] The best study on this so far is that by Amare Tekle (1964).

tions of these issues. The Eritrean liberation movements and their sympathisers stressed the unifying impact of Italian colonialism on Eritrean society.

It is possible, albeit difficult, to analyse relations between Eritrea and Ethiopia without subscribing to or excluding either of the opposed interpretations. Various authors have been able to look into parts of this topic with varying degrees of success. The most notable of these authors are John Markakis (1990), Lloyd Ellingson (1986), Thomas Killion (1985), Amare Tekle (1964), Eyassu Gayim (1992), Tekeste Negash (1987; 1997) and Kjetil Tronvoll (1998b).

In so far as a common language and a common faith coexisting over a contiguously connected space are the basis for the definition of a 'nationality', as many scholars define it, the Tigrinya in Eritrea and the Tigreans in Ethiopia belong to the same 'nationality'. The Italians who ruled Eritrea until 1941 and the British who administered the area until 1952 believed and acted on the assumption that the Tigrinya-speaking population (who straddle both Eritrea and Ethiopia) are one and the same people. The Ethiopian state and people also maintained the view that all or most of Eritrea had always been part of Ethiopia, and that the impact of Italian colonialism was minimal. Moreover, the area where Tigrinya is spoken formed, according to Ethiopians, the cradle of Ethiopian Christian civilisation stretching back to the early years of the first millennium. Although the Tigrayan Peoples Liberation Front (TPLF) which emerged victorious over the Derg in 1991 supported the Eritrean struggle for independence, it did not put into doubt the unity of the Tigrinya-speaking peoples of Eritrea and Ethiopia.

Such a view was contested by the Eritrean liberation movements during the 1960s, however, and since 1991 by the present Eritrean government. The main argument of the Eritrean government can be summarised as follows: indeed there is a major Tigrinya ethnic group in Eritrea, but the ethnic identity of this group is superseded by a new and more inclusive Eritrean identity. The Eritrean government believes that Italian colonialism laid the grounds for the emergence of a pan-ethnic identity (Eritrean identity as opposed to Tigrinya identity) in the country. In other words, the Tigrinya in Eritrea may speak the same language as the Tigreans in Ethiopia, but they do not share the same political views and objectives (see, for instance, Ruth Iyob 1995).

The views of the Eritrean liberation fronts have been challenged and continue to be challenged (cf. Negash 1997). A recent study on the divergent Eritrean and Tigrean nationalist paths affirmed clearly that the Tigrinya in Eritrea and the Tigreans in Ethiopia still share a common sense of identity (Abbay 1996: 251). It is worth mentioning, however, that the research, essentially based on structured and deep interviews, was conducted in 1994. Another important insight of the recent research is that the government of Eritrea has yet to succeed in creating a new basis of identity to supplant that which already exists among the Tigrinya/Tigreans who straddle Eritrea and Ethiopia. Even more recently, ongoing research being conducted by Tronvoll strongly suggests the existence of multiple layers of identities that are both contextual and fluid.[3]

[3] Tronvoll 1998a, 1999.

3 The Origin of Today's Differences: EPLF–TPLF, 1975–91

The outbreak of violence between Eritrea and Ethiopia was puzzling, considering that TPLF has been portrayed by the international community as the 'little brother' of EPLF, and that they were dependent upon EPLF during the struggle. This understanding of TPLF has also been favoured by EPLF, which frequently portrayed itself as the dominant and leading political movement in the region. Whether this reflected the political and military realities, however, is another question. If one had paid attention to this earlier, the international community might have been in a position to make a modest contribution to improving the tense relations between the two major organisations of the region.

A scholar who has been analysing the TPLF revolution has described relations between TPLF and EPLF as containing 'tensions and pragmatism' (Young 1996). John Young has shed some important light upon how TPLF conceived its relations with EPLF, information hitherto very difficult to access. In the post-Derg period, the two governments have tried to conceal these tensions, while international observers, including diplomats and NGO workers, have tended to overlook, deliberately or out of ignorance, the different political and cultural outlooks of the two regimes. The important fact that the two fronts have not been ideologically reconciled after their conflicting years in the mid-1980s has also slipped the attention of the international community, and likewise been hidden by the fronts themselves. Instead, the relationship between the two governments formed by the old rebel fronts has been portrayed as a 'love marriage'. The two organisations have been described as political movements with a similar ideology and common objectives, led by a group of idealistic men with the same roots who cooperated in the 'downfall of one of Africa's most brutal dictators, Mengistu Haile-Mairam'.

We shall investigate the historical relationship between the two fronts, and try to identify some of the core differences that led to a breach in relations in 1985, and which today constitute important aspects of the current conflict. And we begin by noting that at the very outset of their relationship in 1975 tensions arose owing to differences in ideology and over pragmatic decisions of alliance building.

The EPLF Role in the Establishment of TPLF

When TPLF was established in 1975 in the aftermath of the fall of Emperor Haile Selassie (1916–1974), the Eritrean liberation fronts (ELF and EPLF) had been operating for many years and had gained valuable political and military experience. It was therefore natural that the Tigreans should seek advice and assistance from the Eritrean movements across the border. There were also common linguistic and kinship links between people in the Eritrean highlands (*kebessa*) and Tigray. But because ELF and EPLF were competing movements in Eritrea, and TPLF was only one of many resistance movements in Tigray at that time, the initial alliance between TPLF and EPLF came under pressure.

Before they began armed struggle and established TPLF, representatives of the Tigrean group (at that time called the Tigray National Organisation) had been in contact with the Eritrean fronts, and with EPLF in particular. The first group of TPLF fighters, led by the current foreign minister Seyoum Mesfin, was sent to EPLF for military training and supplies as early as 1975. Soon, however, the growing cooperation between the two fronts was strained by EPLF's relationship with the Ethiopian People's Revolutionary Party (EPRP). EPLF was training EPRP troops in Sahel at a time when TPLF and EPRP had turned against each other in Tigray.[1] This in itself was one of the many paradoxes of the Ethiopian resistance, since EPLF assisted EPRP although EPRP did not unambiguously support EPLF's claim to independence in Eritrea.

The tensions between TPLF and EPRP in this early period of TPLF's existence put EPLF in a dilemma, since they wanted to continue their alliances with both fronts. According to Sebhat Nega, former TPLF leader, the EPLF put pressure on the young TPLF movement and demanded that: 'Unless you are on good terms with EPRP, we cannot support you. We know that the Eritrean struggle is suffering because of the ELF [meaning competing liberation movements], and we don't want to see another "ELF" in Ethiopia.'[2] Yemane Ghebreab, a senior EPLF cadre, explained in this

---

[1] EPRP based their resistance ideology on the principle that the class contradictions within Ethiopia was the crucial contradiction, whereas TPLF defined the struggle according to the contradiction of nationalities (elaborated below).

[2] Interviewed by K. Tronvoll, 19 November 1998 in Addis Ababa. As regards the extensive

regard that EPLF foresaw some of the internal Ethiopian problems with a multitude of competing resistance movements, and thus wanted to reconcile the fragmented political opposition: 'TPLF was insisting that EPRP should not operate inside Tigray. It could operate in other parts of Ethiopia but not inside Tigray. We said that we all worked for the same goal and should operate together.'[3] Such interference by EPLF into non-Eritrean affairs was not well taken by TPLF, who accused EPLF of simplifying the ideological question of Ethiopian resistance. Sebhat Nega explained the difficulties TPLF had with accepting EPRP as an ally, since they did not have the same ideological outlook on the liberation of Ethiopia. Sebhat accused EPLF of pragmatism and opportunism, since they did not challenge EPRP. Instead EPLF put pressure on the small and inexperienced TPLF: 'But because of its size, the EPLF did not want to openly denounce EPRP. It was an opportunistic line, it was not a principle line,' he explains.

As the new relationship with EPLF was put under pressure, TPLF's relations with ELF seemed to improve. ELF was operating in the Badme area (the core zone of conflict today) and had several military operations against Derg positions inside Tigray (Young 1996: 106; 1997: 112–13). TPLF saw these attacks as furthering its own interests, and thus established closer cooperation with ELF. But this relationship soon ceased, as ELF began to assist a competing Tigrean movement, the Tigrean Liberation Front (TLF). TPLF found itself at loggerheads with TLF, which eventually led to strained relations with ELF. Sebhat explained the difficult choices of TPLF:

> We were trying to balance the relations between ELF and EPLF, in particular when the situation with ELF was aggravated. And when we were quarrelling with EPRP, EPLF was not happy. Anyway, we were in a dilemma. But we could not give in on our principles. We could not give up that the national struggle is the primary struggle, or the primary contradiction. And as time passed ELF and EPRP came closer. They became on good terms and formed alliances. Then we clashed with EPRP and drove it out from Tigray. Finally, we were also in contradiction with ELF. In 1981 we and EPLF jointly evicted ELF out of Eritrea.

The confusing period of 1975–6, which showed overlapping and contradictory alliances between the competing fronts in both Eritrea and Tigray, illustrates the pragmatic and somewhat random alignments which were made between the different movements.[4] It seems clear that there

---

[2] (cont.) quotations used in this chapter we wish to enter a caveat. The best way to ascertain the veracity of the narratives was to ask the EPLF and TPLF leaders to corroborate each other's narration. Owing to time pressures and other practical exigencies we were not able to do so. While we believe that the extensive quotations reveal a great deal, we can hardly validate them as reliable historical documents.

[3] Interviewed by K. Tronvoll, 10 October 1998 in Asmara.

[4] According to written information from Dr. Fisseha-Tsion Menghistu and Mr. Worku Geta (both researchers and political activists who live in The Netherlands), the cause of the

was no well-prepared and mutually accepted strategy of joint EPLF/TPLF operations in the first phase after the establishment of TPLF. Likewise, it appears obvious that TPLF was not 'created' or 'initiated' by EPLF, as many have suggested in the past. This idea will be more emphatically dismissed below; for the moment we can let Yemane 'Jamaica' Kidane, an EPLF fighter turned TPLF fighter in 1975 and a current senior cadre, explain this aspect:

> Neither of the Eritrean fronts controlled TPLF. *Nobody* ever controlled us. But in the outside world the assumption was always there. First, because they did not know, and secondly because EPLF always pretended to be in control. But in our history there have been a lot of upheavals between us and EPLF.[5]

Ideological and Political Differences between TPLF AND EPLF

Even at the very start of the contacts between TPLF and EPLF, they disagreed on ideological principles. The ideological reasoning for a Tigrean revolution grew out of the student movement. In their analysis of the Ethiopian society TPLF interpreted the revolution within a Marxist-Leninist framework, blaming the economic, social and political problems of Ethiopia on the suppression of 'nationalities'. The main 'contradiction' they identified was thus not class-based (as other movements, such as EPRP, were quick to point out), but the ethnic domination of the Amhara ruling élite, which suppressed and exploited Ethiopia's other 'nationalities'. The TPLF programme (1976) therefore called for the establishment of an independent republic of Tigray, and defined its struggle as a war of independence. EPLF reacted negatively to this position, maintaining that only Eritrea had the historical and political legitimacy to fight for independence. The EPLF view was that the TPLF should define its struggle as the establishment of a democratic Ethiopia, without developing its ideology to justify an independent Tigray, or the independence of other 'nationalities' for that matter.

The EPLF critique of the 1976 TPLF manifesto's call for the 'liberation of nationalities' remains relevant today, since the Eritrean government is highly critical of the new ethnic federal system in Ethiopia with its *kilil* structure of ethnic states. In the words of Yemane Ghebreab, an EPLF ideologist and senior politician:

> For us the ethnification of politics, creating regions on an ethnic basis, is wrong, and it is going to create problems tomorrow. It is not just going to create problems for Ethiopia, it is also going to create problems for TPLF, because

---

[4] (cont.) TPLF/EPRP conflict was TPLF's refusal to allow the EPRP to operate inside Tigray.

[5] Interviewed by K. Tronvoll, 19 November 1998 in Addis Ababa.

now these [ethnic states] may be junior allies because you are stronger, you have more resources. But tomorrow, when these people become stronger they will think about themselves not as Ethiopians but say Oromos or whatever, and they will say why are we being dominated by TPLF and the Tigreans? So that approach is wrong and counterproductive. They would not accept that argument. We also talked about the Ethiopian constitution and its idea of secession and its ethnic-based participation. We told them [TPLF] you are doing a disservice to Ethiopia just because you want to have an independent Tigray as a fall-back position if your agenda in Ethiopia does not work. You shouldn't impose that agenda on Ethiopia and it's wrong. They wouldn't listen to that either.[6]

EPLF was and of course still is worried about the possible spill-over effect of the ethnic federal system in Ethiopia. The Eritrean governance structure is a unitary, centralised state, where ethnic or regional identities have no place in the political space. Indeed, EPLF is trying by all means and policies to subdue and neutralise ethnicity in Eritrea. It places great emphasis upon creating a national, homogeneous and all-embracing nation with an 'Eritrean' identity (see Tronvoll 1998a, 1999). But, since many of the ethnic groups in Eritrea are represented on both sides of the Eritrean/Ethiopian border (Afar, Saho, Tigrinya and Kunama), the Ethiopian policy of ethnification may directly jeopardise the Eritrean nation-building process. This is extremely worrying for EPLF, and it is an issue they have been addressing since the liberation of Eritrea. It should also be noted that the first statement from the Eritrean Cabinet of Ministers after the violence erupted in May 1998 explained that 'the recurrent border incursions that continue to be perpetrated by Ethiopian forces basically emanate from the narrow perspectives of the Administrative Zones'. The Eritrean government thus perceives a direct link between border skirmishes, culminating in today's conflict, and the ongoing process of ethnogenesis in Ethiopia. One should not underestimate this aspect of the EPLF–TPLF relationship, and how it has impinged upon the bilateral relations between the two countries.

Another area of ideological dispute between the two fronts which came to the fore in the late 1970s, although not as important as the question of nationalities, was a difference in interpretation of the status of the Soviet Union as the vanguard of communism. This was at the time a much-debated ideological issue in Marxist-Leninist resistance movements around the world, but particularly so in the Horn of Africa where the Soviet Union was the main ally of, and provider of arms to, the Derg regime. TPLF decided in 1977 that the 'communist party of Russia is a revisionist party, and the system is a social-imperialist system',[7] thus dismissing the Soviet Union's claim to be a vanguard state. TPLF instead sought support

[6] Interviewed by K. Tronvoll, 10 October 1998 in Asmara.
[7] Cf. Sebhat Nega, interviewed 19 November 1998 in Addis Ababa.

in the Albanian model of communism and was in particular inspired by their self-reliance ideology. EPLF, on the other hand, viewed the Soviet Union as a socialist system run by a Leninist-style communist party. They defended both the party and the state system of the Soviet Union, and explained away Soviet support for the Derg by saying that they had misunderstood the political context in the Horn, thus opting for an incorrect foreign policy.

Differences of Military Doctrine

Among many facets of difference between the two fronts, military strategy was another source of tension and trouble. EPLF was already a viable military front at the time when TPLF commenced its military activity. Some of the EPLF leaders – notably Romedan Mohammed Nur, EPLF's first leader, and Issaias Afwerki, the leader since 1987 – had received their military (and political) training in China, while others had learnt their trade in Cuba. Additionally, when Haile Selassie's regime fell in 1974 and the military came to power, many Eritrean army officers were uncertain about the new rulers and over time defected to EPLF. Some observers believe that these army officers brought with them the concept of conventional warfare into EPLF ranks, which led to the development of the idea of establishing and defending a liberated base area behind fixed positions. At the first EPLF Congress in 1977 a three-point military strategy was adopted. First, they should conduct positional or fixed warfare, defending the liberated areas from enemy attack, and from these positions proceed to liberate the country step by step. Second, in the contested areas they should wage mobile warfare; and thirdly in Derg-controlled territory they should depend upon a strategy of guerilla warfare (cf. Pateman 1990: 122). Consequently, the EPLF defended their Sahel base area fiercely, and kept the main bulk of their army behind the trenches. From these fixed positions they launched attacks and raids into Derg-held territory and the contested areas.

As mentioned above, at the start of their relationship TPLF sought training with EPLF for their inexperienced fighters, an arrangement that benefited both sides. The TPLF fighters gained skills and were also provided with arms and ammunition, while EPLF in return received substantial and vital military support to defend their base areas against Derg attacks. This was particularly important during the Red Star offensive (1982), and again in the 'creeping offensive', as it was termed, in 1983. During the Red Star campaign there were as many as 5,000 TPLF troops helping to defend the EPLF-controlled areas. But for their presence, it is quite possible that the Derg forces would have managed to

17

penetrate the EPLF trenches, with severe consequences for Eritrean resistance.

TPLF's assistance to EPLF during the Red Star campaign and after was not uncontroversial among its leaders. By sending their troops to Eritrea, their own military activity in Tigray was weakened, or 'paralysed' as Sebhat Nega termed it. TPLF was also opposed in principle to a conventional type of warfare, since this alienated the liberation movement from the masses they were supposed to liberate. In the words of Sebhat Nega:

> We had been raising it earlier [with EPLF], that the military strategy of EPLF was wrong, holding fixed positions, because they stayed for years in the trenches. Therefore the liberation of the people was not there. If you liberate the people physically, the liberation of outlook doesn't exist, they can increase their forces and weaken the Derg. If you are mobile, they can operate over a three–four times bigger area to weaken the Derg. Therefore, we had been indicating to them that this fixed, or conventional, type of war cannot weaken the Derg. On the opposite, it would weaken themselves, because they cannot multiply their forces, they cannot replace their forces. They cannot weaken the Derg. Therefore we were advising them that they should quit these fixed-trench defence lines.[8]

For TPLF, this strategy was questionable not only on military grounds, but also in the sense that it hindered a broad-based peasant participation. TPLF argued that EPLF's devotion to conventional warfare was an indication of the development of a professionalised military leadership which could undermine the 'democratic' character of the war (cf. Young 1996: 114). When TPLF addressed this issue with EPLF, according to Sebhat, the latter became 'furious' and failed to see the advantages of a general strategy of mobile and guerilla warfare. Then, in 1983, TPLF withdrew their troops from Sahel, partly in order to regain control over areas in Tigray occupied by ELF during the Red Star campaign.[9] This action compelled the EPLF to change their strategy towards the TPLF. According to Yemane Kidane, this was one of the main reasons for EPLF's decision to close the Barka route for emergency relief aid into Tigray in 1985 (see below).

We believe that these different experiences have had some impact on the current crisis. Experienced in conventional war, the Eritrean side has much more skilled and better-equipped artillery and tank forces than the TPLF/EPRDF. They are also probably better trained in defending fixed positions and in trench warfare.[10] This almost certainly gave the Eritrean

---

[8] *Ibid.*

[9] Interview, Yemane Kidane, 10 October 1998 in Addis Ababa.

[10] On this point, it is interesting to note that EPRDF released in September 1998 five Derg generals and two colonels who had been accused of war crimes, on the grounds that they lacked sufficient evidence. These generals were notably responsible for the ground forces logistics and supply departments, and for the logistics department in the air force – expertise much needed in today's TPLF-controlled Ethiopian army.

forces the upper hand in the current conflict, during the time they held areas that Ethiopia wanted to reclaim. Since June 1998, Eritrean forces have dug themselves in, building trenches and fortifications which will make it difficult for Ethiopia to impose a military solution on the current *status quo* without considerable human sacrifices. Eritrean commanding officers explain that the two parties know each other's military capabilities and strategies intimately, and that this is the best insurance they have against a TPLF attack: the TPLF military commanders would not (according to EPLF officers), as the situation stands today, dare to challenge the EPLF positions. To break through, they need a ratio of at least 3:1 and preferably 5:1 in military troops, according to EPLF military officers. Some few weeks after this information was gathered among military representatives in Badme by K. Tronvoll, however, Ethiopian forces attacked Eritrean positions in a major offensive. After two weeks of intense fighting, the Eritrean positions were forced to withdraw and surrender Badme to Ethiopia (see below).

Breach of Relations 1985–8

These differences in ideology, politics and military strategy led to a total breach of relations between the two fronts in 1985. For three years, until 1988, the two movements had no cooperation or military coordination. It is difficult to identify the factor which triggered the breach. Meles Zenawi has offered the view that the most important difference between EPLF and TPLF was the issue of the Soviet Union (Young 1996: 115). Today, however, both Sebhat Nega and Yemane Kidane emphasise EPLF"s closure of the Barka route – from the Sudan through western Eritrea and into Tigray – as crucial to the breach in relations. The Barka route was the logistical route on which TPLF and its humanitarian wing the Relief Society of Tigray (REST) were dependent for channelling in provisions and relief aid to the famine-hit population of Tigray. While preparing to attack Barentu in the western lowlands of Eritrea, EPLF denied international NGOs and TPLF/REST use of the supply line through EPLF-controlled territory. Since this was at the height of the 1984/5 famine, the closure could have had disastrous consequences in Tigray. But TPLF managed, in a matter of a few months, to build a new supply route from western Tigray directly into Sudan, thus avoiding a high toll of deaths from starvation. Sebhat believes that EPLF did this to 'kneel them down' since it did not accept TPLF"s analysis of the nationalities contradiction in Ethiopia.

EPLF, on the other hand, has a different view on the breach of relations, and emphasises the politico-ideological aspects. Yemane Ghebreab has explained that:

[TPLF] came out and said that its relations with the EPLF were only tactical, because it was not a democratic organisation, it was not opposed to Soviet social-imperialism, it was not led by a proper worker's party, its military strategy is wrong, it was militaristic, and it did not believe in a real war based on its population.[11]

Of relevance here is the distinction made between strategic and tactical relationships within Marxist-Leninist movements. A strategic relationship implies that the cooperating movements have the same objectives of struggle, resting on the same interpretation of the ideological rationale behind their struggles. A tactical relationship, on the other hand, only involves a common objective – in this case the defeat of the Derg – whereas the ideology of resistance differs. Thus, when TPLF stated that their relation with EPLF was purely tactical, this was an explicit attack on EPLF's justification of their liberation struggle. Yemane Ghebreab elaborates:

So they [TPLF] said that EPLF was a nationalist organisation engaged in bourgeois revolution. And therefore, the TPLF could only have a tactical relationship with the EPLF. And we [EPLF] told them that that was no problem and they can consider us whatever they want but we have an enemy, and we should cooperate in fighting that enemy. They [TPLF] said 'No, we have to explain this to the Eritrean population. The Eritrean population is being misled. If the Eritrean population is led by the EPLF, then tomorrow there will be problems in Eritrea.' So then they started trying to create organisations in Eritrea that fit their image of a progressive organisation. So the problems continued.

In 1985 TPLF began, as a tactical move, to support the Eritrean opposition movements in their fight against EPLF hegemony. TPLF support of the Eritrean movements (the Eritrean Democratic Movement and the Eritrean Liberation Front Central Command, called *Saghim*, a splinter group of the original ELF-CC) continued after the liberation of Eritrea until 1994, when EPLF assassination squads wiped out central Eritrean opposition leaders in Tigray.

The two fronts resumed cooperation in 1988, but not on such close terms as before the breach of relations in 1985. The cooperation was basically of a military nature, a point stressed by Yemane Kidane who confirmed that the two fronts were not reconciled ideologically and politically:

Never, never. Only a military relationship. Ideologically never, politically never. We maintained our differences. So we always say it is a tactical relationship, not a strategical relationship. If they call it strategic, it is up to them.[12]

---

[11] Interviewed by K. Tronvoll, 10 October 1998, in Asmara.
[12] Interview, Yemane Kidane, 10 October 1998 in Addis Ababa.

Conclusion

In this chapter we have identified some differences and tensions between EPLF and TPLF which had their origin during the struggle against the Derg.[13] It has been very difficult to get statements from senior cadres of the two fronts on these issues prior to May 1998, since both sides tried to portray their post-Derg relationship in an amicable manner, probably for tactical reasons. EPLF needed support from TPLF in its claim for national independence, while TPLF depended on EPLF's support against the other Ethiopian resistance movements to stabilise the situation in Ethiopia and to gain and remain in control of the whole country. The EPLF–TPLF relationship is, therefore, better described as a marriage of necessity than a marriage of love.

It is difficult to assess how important these differences are in explaining the current outbreak of violence and the escalation of the conflict. It seems obvious, however, that today both parties make these historical differences relevant and applicable in explaining and delegitimising each other's positions. It is, therefore, of crucial relevance to maintain awareness about these factors. One should also be aware that both EPLF (or rather PFDJ) in Eritrea and TPLF in Ethiopia remain ideologically anchored movements; they define and assess current policies and situations on the basis of long-cherished principles. Many international observers and the diplomatic community were misled by the rhetoric of democratisation and market liberalism in the two countries. A closer look at the organisational structures of the two movements, however, and at the ideological justifications offered for some of their policies, reveals the resilence of strong ideological thinking combined with cultural, social and historical variables which are difficult for outsiders to identify and interpret.

[13] See also Ghidey Zeratsion, 'The Ideological and Political Causes of the Ethio-Eritrean War: an Insider's View', paper presented at the International Conference on the Ethio-Eritrean Crisis, Amsterdam, 24 July 1999. Ghidey Zeratsion was one of the founding members of TPLF and served in its top leadership before he left for Europe in 1987. He stresses the same factors as mentioned here to explain the tense EPLF–TPLF relations during the struggle against the Derg.

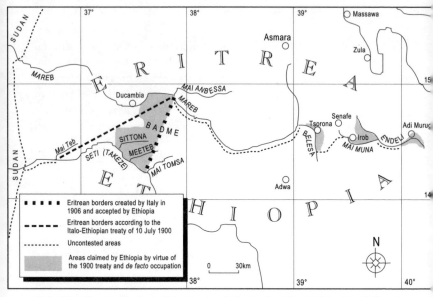

Source: Gabriele Ciampi: 'Componenti cartografiche della controversia di confine Eritreo–Etiopica', *Bollettino della società Geografica Italiana*, Serie III, 12(3) (1998), p. 530.

MAP 3 *Contested Areas Along the Delimited but not Demarcated Border Between Eritrea & Ethiopia*

4 Border Issues

Eritrea's international borders were negotiated and delimited in 1900, 1902 and 1908. The Eritrean government has insistently maintained that these treaties are clear enough. It is uncertain how cognizant Eritrea is of the ambiguity of the treaties, and of the role of the principle of *uti possidetis* or actual possession. Admittedly, there were no armed border clashes between the Italian colony of Eritrea and Ethiopia during the colonial period. The Italian policy of good neighbourliness *vis-à-vis* Ethiopia, the military inability of the Ethiopian state to challenge the Italian colonial army, and the possibility that Italy would have used border incidents as a *casus belli* may have been the main reasons for the apparently peaceful coexistence observed during most of the colonial period.

Recent studies, however, have brought to light aspects of these borders and treaties that could take decades to untangle if rival nationalisms remain intransigent. According to an exhaustive study of the colonial cartography by the geographer Ciampi, none of the border treaties between Eritrea and Ethiopia (1900, 1902 and 1908) were properly delimited or demarcated.[1] Citing the first Italo-Ethiopian treaty of 10 July 1900 (see Map 3) Ciampi noted that the map attached to the treaty was a highly simplified sketch that was entirely unreadable. If one were to go by the letter of the treaty of July 1900, a great part of what is now Eritrea would revert to Ethiopia.[2]

The map that the Eritrean government believes to be the product of the treaty of 10 July 1900 is actually a map produced by Italian cartographers in 1906. The colonial map produced prior to 1906 was different from that produced thereafter. According to Ciampi's reconstruction, Italian cartographers changed the vaguely delimited boundaries, as can be

[1] Ciampi 1998: 529.
[2] *Ibid.*: 533.

seen from Map 3. Thus it is only after 1906 that the present unilaterally delimited but never demarcated boundary, later to be the basis for the position of the Eritrean government, came into effect.[3] There can however be no doubt that the changes introduced by the Italian government were in violation of the treaty of 1900,[4] although one can discuss the motives that inspired the changes.

A similar interpretation was also made by the historian Federica Guazzini in her recent book on the making of Eritrea's borders.[5] According to Guazzini, the Italian colonial authorities deliberately refused to demarcate the borders between Eritrea and Ethiopia agreed in 1900, 1902 and 1908. Instead, Italy chose to manipulate the colonial map so as to include the larger part of the Badme plains under its territory. In pursuing this line of action Italy resorted to what geographers describe as the 'persuasive functions' of maps.[6] In plain language this means that Italy unilaterally interpreted the treaty of 10 July 1900 and proceeded to present a new map as a true interpretation. Both Guazzini and Ciampi express their surprise that the Ethiopian government went along with this map, as is evidenced by the *National Atlas of Ethiopia* of 1985.

One of Ciampi's conclusions is that someone has to be prepared to explain how the border was changed between 1900 and 1906. It is worth mentioning that it was not at all a question of cartographic error. The decision to move the lines of the delimited boundary was deliberate and was taken by high-ranking officers within the Ministry of Foreign Affairs. Neither is there any uncertainty as to when this took place.[7]

In actual fact the Ethiopian government was not altogether unware of the Italian machinations. As late as 1916, according to Guazzini, Ethiopia protested against Italian presence in areas well beyond those delimited by the treaty of 1900, but to no avail.[8] It was only during the governorship of Corrado Zoli (1928–30) that Italy established some sort of control along the Badme border.[9] From the late 1920s, however, Ethiopia was in no position to engage Italy on such trivial issues; in a few years the whole of the country was to fall prey to the revanchist aggression of Italian Fascism.

[3] *Ibid.*: 539. The decision to abandon the Mai Teb–Mai Anbessa boundary line was taken on the specific order of de Chaurand, a miltary officer at the Instituto Geografica Militare who was at the same time a high-ranking employee of the Ministry of Foreign Affairs. Ciampi leaves open the question whether such a deliberate, unilateral change of borders, favouring Eritrea at the expense of Ethiopia, was done in good faith (according to the intent of the treaty), or was part of the expansionist policy of colonial powers.

[4] For a rather naïve and at the same time dogmatic assessment of the evolution of the Eritrean borders, see Asmerom and Asmerom 1999: 43–88.

[5] Guazzini 1999a.

[6] *Ibid.*: 324.

[7] Ciampi 1998: 539

[8] Guazzini 1999a: 325.

[9] *Ibid.*: 330. By this period, however, Italy had almost completed secret plans for a military offensive against Ethiopia, which it carried out successfully in 1935–6.

The other areas of conflict that were supposed to have been dealt with by the treaties of 1902 and 1908 exhibit the same problems of demarcation. Ciampi mentions the peculiar situation of the district of Irob (see Map 3). This region appears to fall within the Eritrean territory, although it had always been administered from the Ethiopian province of Tigray. The Irob region was a veritable Ethiopian enclave inside Eritrea. There are several documents from the colonial period showing clearly that the district of Irob was a contested area and that its inhabitants preferred Ethiopian administration.[10] The Italian occupation of Ethiopia made the Irob issue redundant. As the entire province of Tigray was lumped together with Eritrea, thus creating Great Eritrea (1936–41), it made little difference who administered them.

As far as we know the British, who administered Eritrea between 1941 and 1952, made little effort to change the allegiance of the Irob – something that Italy had failed to achieve during more than three decades of its rule in Eritrea. The subsequent federal structure that linked Eritrea and Ethiopia (1952–62) also helped to sideline the issue of who administered the Irob as an internal matter of minor significance.

The 1908 treaty, designed to delimit the boundary of the southern coastline with the French possessions in Djibouti, was likewise remarkable for its vagueness. The only substantial article of the treaty was a stipulation that the boundary would proceed in a southeasterly direction from the Italian fort of Rendacomo, parallel to and at a distance of 60 kilometres from the coast, until it met the frontiers of the French possessions in Somalia. Like the other two, the treaty of 1908 was never demarcated.

Discussions and disagreements as to the exact borders of Eritrea arose for the first time in 1976. The main contenders in this issues were ELF and the newly established TPLF. According to later accounts put forward by members of TPLF, ELF had expanded its territory to the Badme area. The Kunama minority group together with semi-pastoralist groups from the Eritrean highlands inhabited this area – but on the Ethiopian side of the border. In one view of the matter, ELF was following its own people and trying to exercise authority over them. The TPLF account states that, with the support of the population, TPLF managed to push ELF away from the Badme area. A few years later, TPLF and EPLF jointly defeated ELF, expelling it completely.[11]

In 1984, the border issue surfaced again and was raised by EPLF. In early January of the same year, a meeting was held between the two fronts. TPLF, admitting that there could be disputed areas along the border, pointed out that it had no mandate to delimit and demarcate the

---

[10] Zoli 1931: 715–46. Zoli was the governor of Eritrea in 1928–30.

[11] EPLF continues to maintain its silence on this issue, whereas ELF and TPLF are open about it.

Ethio-Eritrean border. TPLF, therefore, proposed that the borders should remain as they were and that border negotiations could be initiated at the end of the struggle. EPLF accepted TPLF's proposal.[12]

It is most probable that this was how matters stood when Eritrea became formally independent in 1993. But we do not think that there was an agreement. The principles of cooperation between the transitional government of Ethiopia and the provisional government of Eritrea, adopted by the national conference in July 1991, did not mention border issues.[13] As far as we know, neither the Ethiopian nor the Eritrean governments negotiated on borders at any time during the two years that preceded Eritrean independence. As an analysis of the correspondence between the President of Eritrea and the Prime Minister of Ethiopia shows (see Appendix 3), borders and border negotiations were not given priority consideration. Only in the summer of 1997 did border issues capture the attention of the Eritrean government, but by then relations between the two countries had reached a low level due to basic disagreements on economic relations. The unfolding of the border dispute from the summer of 1997 is worth following more closely.

Early Development of the Conflict

On 16 August 1997 the President of Eritrea wrote a letter to the Prime Minster of Ethiopia on the grave situation in the border areas. The previous month, according to the President, Ethiopian forces had forcibly occupied the village of Adi Murug. He deplored this action and urged his Ethiopian counterpart to take measures that would head off unnecessary conflict. The letter of 16 August is quite revealing of Eritrean government policy on border/boundary issues. The President noted that the border area had not been delimited (demarcated) but asserted the existence of traditional knowledge on where the border lay. He further stated that the Eritrean government accorded border demarcation a low priority in view of Eritrea's present and future ties with Ethiopia. Finally, the Eritrean

---

[12] We are grateful to Ghidey Zeratsion, a founding member of TPLF and a participant in the 1984 negotiations, for this information. Ghidey Zeratsion has lived in Norway since 1988.

[13] We have in our possession a three-page unsigned document known as 'Principles of Cooperation between the Transitional Government of Ethiopia and the Provisional Government of Eritrea Adopted by the National Conference for the Establishment of a Transitional Government in Ethiopia', which took place in Addis Ababa from 1 to 5 July 1991. The main points of the document are: the recognition on the part of Ethiopia of the right of the Eritrean people to determine their political future; the corresponding recognition on the part of Eritrea; the importance of the port of Assab to Ethiopia, thus making Assab a free port to Ethiopia; and the establishment of a common defence pact against aggression and destabilisation. Although we consider the document genuine, we wish to stress that we have been unable to ascertain its veracity in a conclusive manner.

President pointed out that there was no justification for Ethiopia's resort to force, as it would not have been difficult to settle the matter amicably.

Ten days later, the Eritrean President wrote yet another letter, stating that Adi Murug was inside Eritrea and that the Ethiopian forces had expelled Eritrean officials and dismantled the existing Eritrean administration. The letter further mentioned that the Ethiopian forces in the Badme area had taken similar action. Stressing the unjustified nature of Ethiopian aggression, the President informed the Ethiopian Prime Minister that the Eritrean government has assigned a committee to look into the matter. The President suggested that the Prime Minister also assign officials so that committees from both sides could meet and look into the issues.

The two letters cited above, together with a reply from the Ethiopian Prime Minister, were made public by the Eritrean government in the course of August 1998. The Ethiopian Prime Minister's letter is not dated, but it appears that it was written in reply to the second letter from the President of Eritrea. The Prime Minister stated that the areas controlled/ occupied by the Ethiopian forces were not within the disputed localities and that his understanding was that prior consultation was required only in disputed localities. He further wrote that both countries needed to follow the agreement reached earlier by both states.[14]

There are at least two conclusions that can be drawn from the exchange of letters. First, it reveals that border negotiations had started earlier than August 1997. This much is revealed by the Ethiopian Prime Minister's letter. Furthermore, there appears to exist a framework of understanding on how to resolve border disputes, as mention is made of the existence of an earlier agreement. It is unfortunate that the letter does not reveal more information. Did the parties reach an agreement after they had come to power, or are they referring to the 1984 agreement? Or was the Ethiopian government referring to an agreement from 1993? The Ethiopian Foreign Minister revealed a week after the outbreak of the conflict (19 May 1998) that an agreement was reached between the two countries on the eve of the Eritrean declaration of independence. According to his account, both countries acknowledged the existence of disputes regarding various localities along their common borders and therefore agreed to resolve these disputes through bilateral negotiations. He further stated that, in the event of failure to resolve such issues bilaterally, the two countries would resort to third-party involvement, up to and including arbitration.

---

[14] Ciampi writes (1998: 549) that Adi Murug was peacefully returned to Eritrea after the Ethiopians had concluded their military operation in July 1997. Unfortunately, the author does not provide sources to back up this statement.

Ethiopian Views

An important outcome of the exchange of letters was the creation of a joint border commission that met for the first time in November 1997. Eritrea took the initiative to the commission. No minutes have been made available, although it is rumoured that high military officials from both countries were present. The joint commission agreed, according to Yemane Ghebreab (Eritrean member of the commission), to meet within two months to settle the dispute, but the Ethiopians repeatedly postponed the meeting.[15] According to both Ethiopian and Eritrean accounts, the second meeting was duly held in Addis Ababa on 8 May 1998. When the joint border commission was in session, the Ethiopian government was informed that a limited number of Eritrean forces had crossed the border and occupied the areas around Badme. The Ethiopian account states that the Ethiopian forces informed the Eritrean forces that they were not allowed to enter Badme armed. The Eritrean forces are alleged to have replied that Badme was theirs and they could enter with arms if they so wished. Ethiopia states that, when opposed, the Eritrean forces opened fire and inflicted some casualties. When Ethiopian forces returned the fire there were casualties on the Eritrean side. Soon after, according to the interview given by the Ethiopian Prime Minister, an Eritrean force led by several commanders encircled Badme. While this was taking place in the Badme area, at Addis Ababa the joint border commission was holding its second meeting. The events taking place at the border area were the subject of discussion and, according to the Prime Minister, an agreement was reached on three points:

- It was agreed that those Eritrean forces inside Ethiopian territory should withdraw until the border was properly demarcated.
- To carry out a joint enquiry to establish who started the border clashes. This was necessitated because of the conflicting evidence: the Eritreans stated that it was the Ethiopian police who first opened fire, and the Ethiopian police said that it was the other way round.
- To hold a meeting after two months to finally demarcate the border between the two countries.

The main sources for the reconstruction of events since the exchange of letters are Ethiopian. These are mainly the interviews given by Ethiopian officials a few days after the outbreak of the conflict. We have no similar accounts from Eritrea, with the exception of a personal interview with Yemane Ghebreab and other informal interviews with Eritrean officials conducted by K. Tronvoll in September/October 1998. Despite this

---

[15] Interview by K. Tronvoll with Yemane Ghebreab, 10 October 1998 in Asmara.

imbalance, it remains interesting to follow to its conclusion the Ethiopian version of the unfolding of events prior to the declaration of war.

The Ethiopian account states that since the Eritrean Minister of Defence was the leader of the Eritrean border commission, the Ethiopians expected that upon his return to Eritrea he would proceed to implement the agreement he reached on 8 May 1998. According to Ethiopian accounts, however, Eritrea began sending more troops to the area instead of withdrawing. The Ethiopian Prime Minister then wrote a letter to the Eritrean government requiring it to abide by the agreement recently reached. The Eritrean reply, according to the Ethiopian Prime Minister, was that the period of two months was too long, that a border commission could not solve the border dispute, and that it preferred to explore the possibility of involving a third party in the border negotiations.

In his reply to the Eritrean government, the Ethiopian Prime Minister stated that he had no objection to the inclusion of a third party and that he would do what he could to find a speedy solution. Meanwhile, the Ethiopian Prime Minister insisted that the Eritrean government forces leave the occupied areas as undertaken in the agreement.

Eritrean Views

If, as the Ethiopians claim, the two sides had agreed to resort to third-party involvement, why did the Eritrean government opt for the occupation of a disputed locality by force? In a statement issued on 14 May, the Eritrean government acknowledged the existence of border disputes and claimed that these disputes were caused by the unlawful practices of the Ethiopian army, which occasionally made incursions into Eritrean territories. Despite these periodic occurrences, Eritrea stated, it endeavoured to resolve these recurrent problems through bilateral negotiations. On Wednesday, 6 May 1998, while the Eritrean delegation was on its way to Addis Ababa for border negotiations, Ethiopian army contingents that had already penetrated Eritrean territory opened fire on an Eritrean unit that approached them for dialogue, causing heavy casualties. This unprovoked attack triggered off a cycle of clashes in the area.

The statement of 14 May further added that the two leaders had agreed to resolve the 6 May events peacefully, and to demilitarise the area until such time as the issue was resolved. According to the Eritrean government statement, the declaration that the Ethiopian parliament passed on 12 May was a breach of agreement on the part of the Prime Minister of Ethiopia, and could only be interpreted as a declaration of war (see Chapter 7 for an elaboration of the Eritrean position).

5 Economic Relations

It is indeed surprising that the Eritrean–Ethiopian border dispute has given rise to the recruitment and deployment of huge forces, quite disproportional to the issues of conflict. The areas that the Eritrean forces are accused of occupying by force amount to a few hundred square kilometres of the most marginal land in the region. Yet the Eritrean government is suspected of having an army of close to 350,000, while the Ethiopian army may have more than 450,000 soldiers along the border. It is deplorable that massive arms purchases and recruitment programmes have once again turned the region into a highly militarised part of the continent. It is estimated that from May 1998 until the end of 1999 the two countries spent several hundred million US dollars on arms. Moreover, the daily cost of maintaining the hundreds of thousands of soldiers along the border is several million US dollars. These are scarce resources siphoned away from development projects.

The temptation to search for domestic or economic motives behind foreign policy initiatives and even military interventions has a long tradition in academic and non-academic analysis of inter-state relations. Most of the time, however, it is difficult to establish a causal link between domestic and economic pressures and the conduct of military interventions. At this stage the Eritrean–Ethiopian border cannot be interpreted in this manner, partly because the outcome of the conflict is yet to be known – and it is bound to shape and reorder the impact that domestic and economic factors may have contributed as motives.

We do not immediately subscribe to the views, mainly originating from Ethiopian quarters, that economic issues are the primary motives for the Eritrean–Ethiopian border dispute. It is very possible that the quest for a final delimitation of borders and hence the strengthening of Eritrean identity might have been a more powerful motive than economic factors.[1] We believe that inter-state conflicts have multiple layers of causes. Concentration on only one cause or motive runs the risk of glossing over other issues which at a later stage may emerge as major motives for intervention. Yet we believe that a comprehensive account of the economic relations of the two countries both before and after independence is important for a fuller understanding of the dimensions of the conflict. We also believe that knowledge of the economic dimensions could become useful in the process of post-conflict normalisation.

Economic Harmonisation and Integration

The victorious entry of the EPLF into Asmara in May 1991 signalled the emergence of a *de facto* independent state of Eritrea. Legally, though, Eritrea was part of Ethiopia until the holding of a referendum in April 1993 and the formal declaration of independence on 24 May 1993. Up to 1993 there were no formal trade regulations between the two countries. Relations were formalised in September 1993 with the signing of what came to be called the Asmara Pact. A joint communiqué issued on 27 September 1993 revealed that the countries had signed 25 protocol agreements aimed at reinforcing and further expanding fields of cooperation. Special mention was made of economic cooperation: the parties undertook to work together and to coordinate their development strategies through harmonisation of economic policies. The 25 protocol agreements signed in Asmara covered all fields of cooperation, including a defence pact and all public affairs from tourism to education. The Asmara Pact of 1993 created a framework for the implementation and follow-up of the protocol agreements. Three joint technical committees in the political, economic and social fields were created. A joint ministerial commission that met once a year was entrusted with monitoring the implementation of the agreements.

The protocol agreements have not been made public. Through the courtesy of the Ethiopian Ministry of Foreign Affairs, however, we have been given access to the agreed minutes of the joint ministerial commission meetings between 1993 and 1997. The most important protocols of the Asmara Pact were undoubtedly those on harmonisation of economic policies and on trade. Although we do not have access to the entire documents, the summary we have seen suits the purposes of this study. The salient points of the harmonisation protocol were:

- To harmonise exchange rates policies and interest rate structures.
- To work out a mechanism for making the growth of the money stock consistent with the inflation objectives of the two countries.

---

[1] This hypothesis is further elaborated by K. Tronvoll (1999).

- To work out a scheme to synchronise policies related to foreign exchange surrender requirements, allocation of foreign exchange to importers, capital flows and external debt management.
- To gradually harmonise policies regarding tariffs, sales tax, excise tax and profit taxes.
- To harmonise investment policies.
- To provide national investors in both countries with the same and equal treatment in both territories.

Between September 1993 and July 1996 three joint ministerial commissions were held, the last of these in Addis Ababa. The most important issues discussed at these meetings related to trade, investment and nationality, but very little progress was made. On the question of trade, Ethiopia argued in 1996 that it had created the institutional infrastructure according to an agreement of the previous year to establish a Free Trade Area as a first step towards harmonisation and economic integration. This agreement was in effect a further elaboration of the protocol on economic harmonisation signed in 1993. Eritrea, on the other hand, proposed a review of free trade in the light of the protectionist trend observable in Ethiopian trade policy.

The minutes of 1996 reveal that the two countries had incompatible views in other areas such as investment and the free movement of people. Eritrea suggested that trade and investment should be open to resident nationals without restriction. It argued that there was a need to reconcile investment laws and practice through bilateral investment promotion and protection, and expressed its dissatisfaction with the separate treatment of the issue of Eritreans residing in Ethiopia. Eritrea pointed out that the main demand for investment licensing in Ethiopia was coming from non-resident Eritreans. Eritrean interest in developing banking and transport businesses lacked the positive encouragement of an investment agreement. In any case, determining the residence of a national required an agreed definition of residence to ensure fair and reciprocal treatment. As Eritrea saw it, the best way to deal with the issue of investment was through a comprehensive bilateral promotion and protection agreement which would delineate the areas of investment open to the nationals of both countries, irrespective of whether they were residents or non-residents.

Ethiopia, on the other hand, maintained that it would have to restrict the participation of resident and non-resident nationals from Eritrea, particularly in the spheres of banking, insurance, electricity and power supply, and air transport services. On the question of nationality, both sides agreed that Eritreans who had been enjoying Ethiopian citizenship should be made to abide by their choice. It was decided, however, that the implementation of this agreement should await the decision granting freedom of trade and investment in either country to nationals of both Ethiopia and Eritrea.

By 1996 the implementation of most of the 25 protocols signed between the two countries was greatly hampered by the lack of progress in substantial agreements on trade and investment. Eritrea felt that it was effectively shut out of the Ethiopian economy. Eritrea could neither import Ethiopia's exportable goods nor re-export to Ethiopia goods imported from a third country. Eritrean enterprises were not allowed to invest in certain sectors of the Ethiopian economy and, furthermore, the Ethiopian government was setting investment restrictions on Eritrean resident nationals. Eritrea thus argued that Ethiopia was implementing a protectionist policy, and therefore proposed that the entire agreement of 1993 be reviewed to seek solutions to the operational difficulties encountered in the process of implementation. The parties agreed to set up a joint review committee – which, it appears, was immediately established – to resolve this and related issues. The committee's mandate was described in the minutes:

- To review the implementation of the agreement.
- To identify major constraints.
- To propose measures to facilitate implementation.
- To submit a report within three months (that is, before the end of 1996).

When the joint review committee duly submitted its report on 1 January 1997, its conclusions were clear. The report stated that, despite the agreement, few practical measures had been taken to harmonise economic policies owing to the absence of developed banking, transport and communication systems and other institutional mechanisms required for coordination within the framework. The report further noted that separate new investment codes, tariff regimes, and exchange and interest rates had been introduced by the two countries since the signing of the agreement.

The implementation problems that the protocol agreements on economic relations encountered reflected a lack of political will as well as inability or incapacity to act in the best interests of the two countries. We believe that the problems identified by the joint review committee make this point:

- Restrictions had been imposed on Eritrea's import of Ethiopia's exportable products.
- Eritrean customs personnel had demanded overtime payment from Ethiopian traders.
- There was a serious lack of adequate institutional mechanisms.
- No action had been taken to combat illegal trade.
- There were several types of local charges and intermediate payments.
- Licensing systems were different and discriminatory.

The review committee report struck an optimistic note when it judged the divergence between the investment policies and tariff regimes of the two countries to be narrower in 1996 than it had been in 1993. At the same time, the report proposed that harmonisation of macroeconomic policies be addressed pragmatically at the proper time. Before that, the two countries had to reach a high level of cooperation in the less demanding integration of free trade and the achievement of a customs union. As a point of departure the joint review committee recommended a thorough revision of the existing agreements in areas of trade, customs, transport, port and transit services and macroeconomic harmonisation, and the conclusion of new agreements in the areas of banking, investment promotion and protection, and institutional cooperation. Finally, the joint review committee concluded that

> Given the common currency (though the introduction of a new currency in Eritrea is imminent), the relatively high level of cross-border trade, the use of common ports, to mention but a few [advantages], Ethiopia and Eritrea are in a better position than most African countries to move into economic integration in a relatively short time.

In spite of the optimism of the joint review committee, however, its report could hardly hide the fact that the two countries had widely different perceptions and practices as regards economic cooperation. Thus Eritrea sought to create conditions where its resident nationals and other Eritreans could invest freely in Ethiopia, arguing that the solution to the problem of illegal trade (smuggled goods to and from Eritrea) – which was of great concern for Ethiopia – could only be solved through a comprehensive investment promotion and protection agreement. For the Ethiopian government, the major issues, in addition to smuggling, were foreign exchange discrepancies and the protection of certain sectors of the economy in the interest of its nationals.

The report of the joint review committee was completed on 1 January 1997; it is most unlikely that its major recommendation was followed.[2] According to the Ethiopian Ministry of Foreign Affairs, no joint ministerial commission meeting was held in 1997.

New Currencies and the Search for a New Economic Relationship, 1997

The introduction of a new Eritrean currency (the nakfa) and Ethiopia's response in terms of its trade policy were the main events of 1997. In the aftermath of the defeat of the Derg in May 1991, the victorious fronts (EPLF and EPRDF/TPLF) had reached an agreement on three essential

---

[2] Interview with Yemane Ghebreab, 10 October 1998 in Asmara.

points. These were: (1) the application of a common currency until such time as Eritrea issued its own currency; (2) that Assab and Massawa would be free ports for Ethiopia; and (3) that Ethiopia would run and maintain the Assab oil refinery.

The nakfa was launched in November 1997, at a time when the so-called economic harmonisation agreement had ceased to function. Indeed, by the beginning of 1997 there was virtually nothing of substance left of the Asmara Pact of 1993. The only part that may have functioned during most of 1997 is the defence pact, on which little information is available. The knowledge that the two countries have failed to make progress in harmonising their macroeconomic policies is not based on hindsight. The joint ministerial commission of July 1996 and the joint review committee report of January 1997 clearly pointed to a series of implementation problems.

According to information revealed by the director of the Bank of Eritrea in November 1997, Eritrea informed Ethiopia in writing of the procedures for the introduction of the nakfa, as well as its strength in relation to the Ethiopian birr.[3] It appears that there were no formal negotiations between the two countries on the issue of the new Eritrean currency throughout 1997. The director of the Bank of Eritrea seemed to support such a conclusion when he further stated that Ethiopia did not comment on Eritrea's currency document until the beginning of October. And, when the reply came, Ethiopia simply informed Eritrea that it would trade with its neighbour through the Letter of Credit, as it did with other countries.[4]

The answer given by the director of the Bank of Eritrea is not entirely correct. The Ethiopian Prime Minister had informed the President of Eritrea as early as August 1997 about Ethiopia's preference for the Letter of Credit system.[5] This information might not have been made available to the director of the Eritrean Bank. Eritrea proposed that the currencies of the two countries would bear the same value (at a rate of one to one) and that the two currencies should be freely serviceable in both countries.[6] Ethiopia's response was negative on both counts. Ethiopia stated that it would not accept parity of the two currencies, owing to the different exchange policy regimes prevailing in the two countries. It argued that the Eritrean policy of the primacy of market forces over exchange and interest rates could not be reconciled with Ethiopia's monetary policies, in which a certain amount of control was exercised over exchange and interest rates. Initially, therefore, Ethiopia proposed that all trade with Eritrea be

---

[3] *The Reporter*, November 1997 (dated as Hedar 1990, Ethiopian calander).

[4] *Ibid.*

[5] Exchange of letters between President Issaias Afwerki and Prime Minister Meles Zenawi, made public by the Eritrean government in August 1998.

[6] *The Reporter*, November 1997 and interview with Yemane Ghebreab.

conducted through the Letter of Credit system: that is, in hard currency. Later on, however, it revised its position and proposed that cross-border trade up to 2,000 birr be exempted from the Letter of Credit regime.[7]

The Ethiopian position was communicated to the Eritrean government no later than the end of July 1997. By mid-August 1997, there was deadlock on most of the issues. There was no agreement on free circulation of currencies. Eritrea rejected Ethiopia's proposal of limited cross-border trade. It argued that according to its open-door policy it could not establish mechanisms to implement the Ethiopian procedures of limited cross-border trade. In the words of the director of the Eritrean Bank, Eritrea warned Ethiopia of the problems that would arise. These problems were, first, the definition of petty and big trade, and, second, that the policy of conducting trade in US dollars would encourage smuggling. Eritrea argued that there was no problem as far as it was concerned, since the country did not have currency restrictions, but that goods bought in Eritrea would be considered smuggled goods in Ethiopia.[8] These were the main issues raised in correspondence between the leaders of the two countries.

In a letter to the President of Eritrea, Prime Minster Meles Zenawi wrote that Ethiopia would implement the Letter of Credit system and that it would also attempt to control the cross-border trade, even though such unilateral control would create unnecessary problems. The Ethiopian Prime Minister further wrote that the Eritrean government could not simply say that the control of cross-border trade was only Ethiopia's problem, and that it was appropriate that Eritrea should support Ethiopia's implementation policy. If there were changes that Eritrea would like to propose, then the two countries could look for better ways of implementation through negotiation and dialogue.[9]

As far as we know, there were no further negotiations between the two countries on the issue of cross-border trade, on the modalities of introducing new currencies, and on the settlement of trade accounts. The Eritrean government introduced the nakfa, while at the same time the Ethiopian government replaced its old notes with new ones in order to offset the uncontrolled flow of old birr from Eritrea.

On 1 January 1998, the Ethiopian government issued rules designed to regulate trade between the two countries. A Letter of Credit was required for merchandise and services exceeding 2,000 birr. The central government in Addis Ababa and the regional authorities in Tigray were entrusted with implementing the new trade regime, which had an immediate impact. The price of salt, the most important item exported from Eritrea, went up,

---

[7] *Effoita*, 4 (1998) (dated as Tahsas 1990, Ethiopian calendar).

[8] *The Reporter*, November 1997; exchange of letters between Issaias Afwerki and Meles Zenawi.

[9] Exchange of letters (see Appendix 3).

while in Eritrea the price of teff (a food crop in high demand) was three times as high. As regards other items, however, the new trade policy created a barrier between the two countries that had never existed before. In an interview released towards the beginning of February 1998, Prime Minister Meles Zenawi admitted that the Eritrean government had not yet introduced the Letter of Credit system and that there were some implementation problems on the Ethiopian side as well.

A couple of months later, the President of Eritrea gave a long explanation of why his country rejected the Letter of Credit system. In particular he raised the following issues:

- Eritrea had no intention of creating a new wall between the Eritrean and north Ethiopian people, who had a long common history. Transaction costs of implementation were bound to be very high and many mistakes were bound to be committed in attempts to implement inherently unfeasible policies. Such mistakes could have adverse effects on the relations between the two peoples. Other alternatives ought to have been identified.
- Ethiopia's policy discriminated against Eritrea. Ethiopia did not implement a similar system on its borders with Djibouti, Somalia and Kenya.
- The aim of Ethiopia's new policy was to prevent Eritrea from participating in the Ethiopian economy – for example, in the agro-industry, transport and finance sectors.
- Ethiopia was creating manufacturing establishments as import substitutes. The Letter of Credit system was devised in order to prevent competition from Eritrean establishments. Ethiopia's policy was purely protectionist.
- The protocol agreements on economic harmonisation and trade had reached a dead end. The two countries failed to agree on common investment policies.[10]

Eritrea, while respecting Ethiopia's policies, would continue to look for better alternatives, although 'the present situation', in the words of President Issaias, 'should not continue for an indefinite period of time'.[11] The Eritrean and Ethiopian people are bound to live together and 'we cannot change the geographical and historical links that bind the peoples of the two countries'.

Economic Competition Between Eritrea and Tigray

As far as the Tigray region is concerned the Eritrean–Ethiopian conflict has a deeper meaning than a mere border dispute. According to Gebru

[10] *Aser* 3: 10 (April–May 1998) (dated as Megabit-Ginbot 1990, Ethiopian calendar).
[11] *Ibid.*

Asrat, the governor (or president) of Tigray, Eritrea provoked the war because its hegemonic position in Ethiopia was threatened by the economic development of Tigray.[12] Such a view, widely publicised since the outbreak of the conflict, may not fully explain the causes of the dispute, but there can be no doubt that is solidly supported by the TPLF leadership in Tigray. It is indeed worthwhile to attempt to explain the thinking of TPLF and the people of Tigray, for several reasons. First, we believe that the Eritrean–Ethiopian border dispute cannot be explained without taking into account the role of TPLF and the people of Tigray. Second, we believe that the normalisation of Eritrean–Ethiopian relations will be difficult, if not impossible, if it does not take into account the perceptions of TPLF and the people of Tigray.

On the eve of the Italian colonisation of Eritrea, the Tigray region was the centre of political power in the Abyssinian landscape. Tigray had access to the Red Sea trade through the port of Massawa that it indirectly controlled. The Tigrean leaders of the late nineteenth century were able to make use of freely imported firearms to impose their rule over the central parts of Ethiopia, including, of course, most parts of present-day Eritrea. Prior to Italian colonialism the Tigray region was geographically and ethnically a well-demarcated landscape. At present the Tigreans straddle the Eritrean–Ethiopian border.

While the majority of the Tigreans live in Ethiopia, the Tigrinya of Eritrea constitute about 60 per cent of that country's population and its major political power base. Like most of Eritrea the Tigray region is severely degraded owing to uninterrupted settlement stretching over several thousands of years. According to a study conducted in 1994, the Tigrinya of Eritrea and the Tigreans in Tigray share the same primordial affinity (or 'deep-rooted historical identity') after more than half a century of European colonialism and thirty years of 'Ethiopian colonialism' (Abbay 1998: 332).

Towards the end of the last century two events signalled the decline of Tigray. The first was the Italian colonisation of the Red Sea coastline and the eventual establishment of the colony of Eritrea. Not only was the Tigray region divided into two (between the Italian colony of Eritrea and Ethiopia), but Tigray was denied direct access to the Red Sea trade. The major implication of Italian colonialism was the weakened position of Tigray in Ethiopia.

The second event was the shifting of power from Tigray to Addis Ababa. Located at the northern fringes of hitherto virgin lands (in terms of agriculture), Addis Ababa and the new political dynasty became more interested in the southern regions. Most of the cash crops for export were located in the south and southwest of the country. The establishment of

[12] *The Reporter*, 1: 9 (May–June 1998) (dated as Sene 1990, Ethiopian calendar).

Addis Ababa and the acquisition of new territories (Ethiopia expanded to three times its former size between 1865 and 1890) meant that Tigray lost whatever economic and strategic significance it might have had in the past. Thus neglected by Addis Ababa, and effectively isolated by the Italian occupation of Eritrea, Tigray became a marginalised province for most of the twentieth century. Yet the memory of a golden age with Aksum as the cradle of civilisation and the brief but eventful reign of Yohannes IV (1872–89) remained alive (Abbay 1997).

Between 1975 and the downfall of the Derg in 1991, TPLF fought for the right of the people of Tigray to self-determination. TPLF argued that their region was neglected and oppressed by successive Ethiopian regimes. The Tigray people, TPLF argued, deserved a better future and above all the political power to determine their economic and social development. At an early stage of the armed struggle against the Ethiopian military government, TPLF entertained, although briefly, the idea of establishing an independent republic of Tigray. The possibility of breaking away from Ethiopia was later rejected, but remained alive as an article of faith: the right of nations and nationalities within Ethiopia to secede if and when two-thirds of the majority of a given nation or nationality so demanded.

It is possible to argue that this long period of isolation and marginalisation ended with the coming to power of EPRDF in 1991. The Tigrayan Peoples Liberation Front, established in 1975, was the liberation movement mainly responsible for fighting and defeating the military regime in Ethiopia, in parallel with EPLF's struggle in Eritrea. In 1989, TPLF created EPRDF to accommodate the Amhara and Oromo peoples in the struggle against the Derg, establishing the Amhara National Democratic Movement (ANDM) and the Oromo Peoples Democratic Organisation (OPDO). Since 1991 Ethiopia has thus been ruled by EPRDF, with TPLF as the largest and best organised movement in the coalition. One of the most radical measures taken by EPRDF since it came to power has been the reconstitution of the country into regions along ethnic lines. Since 1991 Ethiopia has been divided into nine national regional states, one of which is Tigray, the home base of TPLF. In 1995 Ethiopia became a federal state in which considerable local power was given to the national regional states.

While the EPRDF coalition rules in Addis Ababa, the only political power with a grip on the fate of the people of Tigray is TPLF. It can be argued that the reconfiguration of the country into federal states and the establishment of TPLF-dominated central power at Addis Ababa has infused new life into the Tigray national regional state. For the first time in the twentieth century, the people from Tigray rule Tigray – and, moreover, Tigray has a government at Addis Ababa that is favourably disposed to the development of the region.

Although we do not intend to review the discussion, we find it relevant to note the lack of objectivity of the charges made against the central government as regards its policy on Tigray (cf. Assefa Negash 1996). It is indeed true that the relative success of the Tigray region is to a large extent based on the existence of a sympathetic government at Addis Ababa. This has meant that Tigray can now depend on getting its share of donor funds and that the central government can easily draw the attention of donor organisations to the needs of Tigray.[13] Earlier governments, as we have seen, had virtually ignored what was deemed to be a resource-poor region lacking exportable products. What has so far been decisive in the development of Tigray, in contrast to other regions, is the effective presence of the TPLF government. At the time when the country was reconfigured into ethnic-based boundaries, Tigray was the only region that had a system of government in place.

The Tigrean development strategy is very similar to that carried out by the Eritrean government. The TPLF government in Tigray puts a great emphasis on the development of agriculture and some basic manufacturing plants. Between 1993 and 1996 the regional government in Tigray established a pharmaceutical factory, a couple of textile plants, a tannery and a cement factory. These small and barely efficient establishments, though essentially designed to meet local needs, could also potentially sell their surplus to the rest of the country.

The organisational approach to capital accumulation and business management is also similar to that pursued in Eritrea. In Tigray, the Relief Society of Tigray (REST), established in 1978, was engaged not only in providing badly needed relief to the war- and drought-affected civilian population, but also as an economic enterprise in the bulk transport sector.[14] The Tigray Development Association is another organisation which since the early 1990s has been ploughing funds collected from Tigreans in the diaspora and in other parts of Ethiopia into development projects. Both these organisations are firmly controlled by TPLF, an increasingly active economic actor in the period since 1993 when many ostensibly private companies have been established. Some of these 'para-partatal' companies (economic firms owned by political parties) now have a dominant position in such areas as information (MEGA), transport (GUNA) and insurance. There is a well-warranted fear that business enterprises owned or controlled by political parties in power can seriously undermine the chances of private Ethiopian business interests.[15] Tigray's development strategy entered a new phase with the establishment of the

---

[13] For budget allocation to the regions, see Hansson 1996.

[14] *Ethiopian Non-Governmental Business: Companies Controlled by or Associated with EPRDF-Member Organisations*, a confidential consultancy report, Addis Ababa, September 1997.

[15] *Ibid.*

Endowment Fund for the Rehabilitation of Tigray (EFFORT) in 1995. EFFORT is strictly controlled by TPLF, with a mandate to build up the industrial and economic structure of Tigray. By 1996 EFFORT had taken over at least 13 of the companies set up by TPLF and restructured them. The total investment volume was estimated in 1996 to be 2.7 billion birr.[16]

Eritrea and Ethiopia: the Web of Economic Links

Up to 70 per cent of Eritrean exports are destined for Ethiopia, while only 9 per cent of Eritrean imports are from Ethiopia. As well as salt, Eritrea exports a high proportion of manufactured goods. In 1996 it exported goods and services to the value of 525 million birr (US$85 million). A brief history of Eritrea's modern economy will explain the nature of the economic links that, we believe, will continue to bind the two countries.

Between 1935 and 1941, Eritrea was the main military depot as well as the communication and financial centre of the Italian East African empire. During this period there were more Italians than Eritreans in Asmara (Tekeste Negash 1987: 53). The invasion of Ethiopia and the pacification of the newly created empire transformed Eritrea into a colony of settlement. About 15 per cent of the population of Eritrea were Italians. Massawa and to some extent Assab became the main ports of the empire for goods and services from Italy. Although Addis Ababa was the capital of the East African empire, the commercial and economic centre was destined to be Eritrea. Italy's first colony was close to Italy and the Italians felt more at home in Asmara than anywhere in the newly conquered empire. There were more commercial and industrial firms in Eritrea than in all the other provinces of the empire put together. Table 5.1 shows Eritrea's role.

Table 5.1
Industrial & Commercial Firms in the Italian East African Empire, 1940

Province	Number of industrial firms	Number of commercial firms
Eritrea	2,198	2,690
Somalia	584	659
Shewa	561	634
Harar	223	166
Amara	163	510
Oromo and Sidama	278	126

Source: Tekeste Negash 1987: 52.

[16] *Ibid.*

Italy's defeat in 1941 did not lead to the immediate or drastic withdrawal of Italian capital and expertise. The British Military Administration that took over Eritrea in 1941 assisted the Italian industrial and commercial community to restructure the economy. The British motive was clear; they wanted the Italian community to contribute to the war effort. Many firms went bankrupt soon after the end of the Second World War, as they could not compete with European firms in the Middle East. But most of the manufacturing plants which were to remain in Eritrea after the Second World War were in fact those which were established during the British Military Administration (1941–52). A main reason for their survival was their easy access to the Ethiopian market. The union of Eritrea to Ethiopia, first in the form of a federation and later as an integral part of the country, further consolidated the orientation of Eritrean manufacturing sectors towards Ethiopia.

Eritrea's dominant position in Ethiopia remained strong despite the vigorous industrialisation policy of the Ethiopian imperial government around the Addis Ababa–Debre Zeit line. Eritrea maintained its competitive advantage due to its proximity to the outside world and the presence of its 10,000-strong Italian community. The Eritrean economy was entirely dominated by Italians well into the early 1970s. It was estimated in 1975 that up to 35 per cent of all the industrial and manufacturing establishments of the Ethiopian Empire were located in Eritrea (Sherman 1980).

Eritrea may have lost ground industrially as the war for independence grew in intensity after 1975. The nationalisation of manufacturing plants carried out by the military regime that replaced Emperor Haile Selassie had driven the Italian community out of Eritrea. The nationalised establishments continued to function but, as the President of Eritrea remarked, they were old and run-down. The negative impact of the nationalisation of manufacturing enterprises notwithstanding, the Eritrean plants were back in business soon after independence. Table 5.2 shows the growth of Eritrean exports to Ethiopia.

Table 5.2
Eritrean Exports, 1993–6 (Million Birr)

Year	1993	1994	1995	1996
Eritrean exports	209	397	528	526
Exported to Ethiopia	130	207	354	342
Exported to Sudan	47	58	76	51

Source: The Reporter, 1: 9 (May–June 1998) (US$1 = 7 birr).

Unfortunately, we do not have adequate knowledge of who owns what in Eritrea. It is most plausible, however, that the Eritrean government inherited the nationalised plants. The little information that is available indicates that privatisation has only just begun. As in Ethiopia, the dominant political organisation (in this case EPLF/PFDJ) is a major owner of economic enterprises.[17] In addition to the considerable trade surplus, the Eritrean government earned about 150 million birr annually from various fees and dues payable at its ports of Massawa and Assab.

Throughout the last five years a major issue of contention between the Eritrean and the Ethiopian governments has been the disposal of the Eritrean trade surplus. As long as the two countries had the same currency, the Eritrean government could recycle its surplus fund inside Eritrea. But the Eritrean government preferred to invest in Ethiopia both its trade surplus and the funds it could collect from the Eritrean population in the diaspora.[18]

The importance of the Ethiopian market to Eritrea can hardly be exaggerated, which is why the Eritreans tried to safeguard the country's long-term interests through an investment promotion and protection agreement with Ethiopia. Eritrea failed to persuade Ethiopia of the joint benefits of such an agreement, partly because its market-driven foreign exchange and interest rate policies remained unacceptable to its neighbour. But we believe that there could be other reasons as well. Both the Ethiopian government and the Tigray region may have felt that the combined forces of the Eritrean government and the Eritrean community in Ethiopia would have undue influence on the direction and orientation of the Ethiopian economy.

From the minutes of the joint ministerial commission meetings we learn that the Eritrean government did not shy away from expressing their position, as well as their vision of the nature of economic relations. They rejected outright the Ethiopian trade proposal on hard currency and warned the Ethiopian government that such an arrangement would not work. The Eritrean government argued that Ethiopia's policy would encourage smuggling in the cross-border trade and that they would not be able to do anything about it. One can argue, indeed, that when the Ethiopian government proceeded to implement its new trade policy, the Eritrean government considered this to be a declaration of economic war.[19]

[17] *Aser*, 3: 10 (April–May 1998).
[18] Both TPLF and EPLF have a long tradition of levying taxes on Eritreans/Tigreans in the diaspora.
[19] Kiflu Taddesse, *Tobia*, 5: 11 (September 1998).

Conclusion

In the mid-1990s it was widely rumoured that the Eritrean government had complained to the government in Addis Ababa that the factories in Tigray would compete with Eritrean export products. It was only after the collapse of the protocol agreements on economic harmonisation and trade, however, that official statements were made on the nature of the competition. In April–May 1998, the President of Eritrea explained that Ethiopian trade policy was designed to protect the market for Ethiopian (and Tigrean) manufactured products by creating barriers for similar Eritrean products. The new trade policy made it impossible for Eritrean products to compete in the Ethiopian market on equal terms with goods produced inside Ethiopia.[20]

It is possible to argue that the leaders of Tigray built their economic strategy on the eventual exclusion of Eritrean goods from the Ethiopian market. The TPLF leaders were fully aware that many Ethiopians and especially the people of Addis Ababa and the free press were campaigning for the regulation of trade between Eritrea and Ethiopia. At the bottom of all the founded and unfounded anti-Eritrean rumours lay the manner in which Eritrea gained independence. There was a widespread feeling that the Eritrean conflict, involving the entire Ethiopian population, had been decided by TPLF and EPLF. And there was a widespread accusation that, on the eve of the referendum for the independence of Eritrea, the Ethiopian government had failed to defend Ethiopia's interests. The Ethiopian people were not involved, nor were they encouraged to express their views. Criticism continued unabated as Eritrean merchants in Ethiopia were seen to gain from double citizenship (Abbink 1998).

It is, therefore, possible that the leaders of Tigray came to believe that sooner rather than later Tigray would supply the products which otherwise would have come from Eritrea. This line of speculative argument, although it borders on conspiracy theory, appears plausible – but we do not believe that is the only cause of the conflict.[21] Whatever the ulterior motives pursued by the leaders of Tigray, a competitive situation existed between Eritrea and Tigray. The Eritreans may have believed that what was going on in Tigray was part of a long-term strategy for ousting Eritrea from the Ethiopian economic landscape. The Tigreans, for their part, may have regretted such an attitude. After the abortive attempt to bomb the pharmaceutical plant in Tigray in June 1998, the Tigrean leaders accused Eritrea of pursuing a deliberate policy of impoverishing Tigray.

[20] *Aser*, 3: 10 (April–May 1998).
[21] Ethiopia's Prime Minister told a group of American professionals in 1993 that he would be satisfied if within 25 years every Ethiopian would have three meals a day, some decent clothing and a roof over his head.

We do not believe that the state of competition between Eritrea and Ethiopia should have led to war. With political stability in both countries, and modest economic growth, the nascent Eritrean and Ethiopian manufacturing plants could have coexisted and shared the Ethiopian market. We believe that it was the trade regime adopted by Ethiopia that gave a push to the conspiracy theories developed by both sides.

6 Side Effects of the War

The Eritrean–Ethiopian border conflict has had an immense impact on both countries in terms of military mobilisation and refocusing government policies in a latent state of war. In addition to these immediate and obvious consequences, the conflict also has a broader sphere of influence on social, economic and political aspects of the two societies.

Ethnic Deportations

The history of deportations and the underlying currents that drive them stretch beyond the present conflict and involve the political orientations of the ruling parties of both countries. Between 1991 and 1993 the EPLF government in Eritrea expelled at least 125,000 Ethiopians, most of whom were Tigrean civilians, on the pretext that they were related to the Ethiopian army and the former Derg regime. Thousands of them found their way to Addis Ababa and are to this day to be seen in their temporary shelters around the public buildings of the capital. The story of the deportations did not hit the international headlines because EPRDF then, in sharp contrast to the present, understood and supported the action of the Eritrean government. The Ethiopian government neither protested against the deportations nor extended any assistance to the deportees once they arrived in Ethiopia. It is claimed that the harassment of Ethiopian residents in Eritrea, the great majority of whom were from the Tigray regional national state, continued well into 1995.[1] Yet among many Ethiopians of all walks of life, and in particular among the people of Tigray, the action taken by Eritrea left behind it a negative attitude towards Eritrea and Eritreans.

---

[1] Personal communication with Dr Fasil Nahum, adviser at the Prime Minister's Office, Addis Ababa.

In Ethiopia too, the politicisation of ethnicity can be described as the precursor of the eventual launching of the politics of ethnic cleansing. Soon after the configuration of the country into ethnic boundaries, thousands of people were forced to go back to their ethnic regions. In certain parts of the country hundreds of innocent people were massacred because they, or their forefathers, happened to have settled in areas to which they had no ethnic affiliation. In July 1998, several hundred were killed in the southern region of the country in incidents that arose out of delimitation of ethnic borders. The ethnic policy, described by a historian of modern Ethiopia as a virus worse than HIV/AIDS, continues to be criticised by the private press and most of the political opposition parties.

The effects of the conflict, whether it is seen as a border dispute or as arising from the economic policy changes introduced by Ethiopia, will be of a long-term nature. The war propaganda, with its heroisation of the Kalashnikov, and the media hate machinery have reached such a pitch of intensity that it could take a considerable time to reconcile and normalise relations between the two countries. The process of normalisation would have to be initiated piecemeal and with a full understanding that it would take a considerable time (probably several years). A radical change of government either in Eritrea or in Ethiopia could, of course, have a sharp impact on the normalisation process – as when sweeping changes of policy followed the downfall of the military regime in Ethiopia in 1991.

According to Eritrean government sources, Ethiopia has expelled more than 67,000 Eritreans who up to their expulsion enjoyed Ethiopian citizenship.[2] In the early stages of the conflict the Ethiopian government stated that it was only expelling those Eritreans whom it considered a threat to its security – those with military experience or training, members of EPLF/PFDJ, and economic benefactors of the Eritrean government. Later on, the government attempted to justify its continuing deportation of Ethiopians of Eritrean origin as a response to similar actions taken by the Eritrean government. Growing evidence of the manner and magnitude of deportations has shown, however, that many of those deported did not in any way constitute a threat to Ethiopia. Deportations were accompanied by human rights violations: the deportees were neither given an opportunity to challenge the charges nor adequate time in which to dispose of their properties.[3] Senior Ethiopian officials (Yemane Kidane and spokesperson Selome Tadesse) have admitted in interviews with the authors that deportation procedures have led to mistakes and to the suffering of innocent people.

The Ethiopians, on their side, claim that since the outbreak of the

---

[2] The government weekly newspaper, *Eritrea Profile*, regularly features the deportation of Eritreans from Ethiopia.

[3] Human Rights Watch, *Annual Report*, 1999.

conflict Eritrea has deported about 39,000 Ethiopians,[4] a claim repeatedly denied by Eritrea. As with the Eritrean figures, the alleged number of Ethiopian returnees from Eritrea may be exaggerated. But even if half of the numbers quoted by both governments are true, the human tragedy caused by such deportations is indeed deplorable. For the moment Ethiopia continues to deport Eritreans on the untenable rationale that the deportees are a threat to the country's security, or as a response to Eritrea's 'deportation' of Ethiopian citizens. And Eritrea continues to maintain that it has not deported Ethiopians and that those who continue to leave Eritrea do so willingly. The facts are difficult to establish, and even in the future we may not be able to know for certain the magnitude of the deportations. It should be mentioned, however, that UNDP, Amnesty International and other international observers to Eritrea have stated that, to their knowledge, no official policy of deportation of Ethiopians exists, and that those who are returning to Ethiopia do so willingly. One of the authors of this book, while visiting Eritrea in September–October 1998, talked to several Ethiopians, both in Asmara and in the rural areas, who confirmed that they could continue to live and work in the country if they so wished.

Related to the deportations is the displacement of several hundred thousand people who have lived in and around the disputed areas. Ethiopian sources have insistently stated that Eritrea's occupation of Badme and Zalambessa has resulted in the displacement of thousands of innocent civilians. According to Ethiopian sources, by the end of December 1999 the number of the displaced had reached 350,000. Here again the exact figures may be difficult to establish, but there can be little doubt that a huge displacement of people on both sides of the border has taken place. It is most probable that the high figure of the displaced includes those who had to give way during the deployment of about 400,000 soldiers on both sides of the Eritrean–Ethiopian border.

It is unfortunate that in both countries, but particular in Ethiopia, one can discern a tendency towards ethnic cleansing. A dangerous precedent is being established which in a way empowers those in control of the state to look through the prism of ethnicity and act accordingly. While the policy of ethnic cleansing is carried out, both countries continue to proclaim that Eritreans and Ethiopians are brotherly peoples. So far ethnic deportation and harassment has been the prerogative of the two governments; we have heard of a few cases in Ethiopia, however, where individuals have taken the law on their hands.

---

[4] Statement by the Ethiopian Spokespersons Office, 10 December 1998.

Restructuring Eritrea's Economy

Recently Alemseged Tesfai, an EPLF researcher, concluded in an exemplary analysis of Ethio-Eritrean relations that Ethiopia's protectionist economic policy had forced Eritrea to de-escalate its traditional intensive trade practices with Ethiopia.[5] His conclusion relied heavily on the minutes of the joint ministerial commission meetings, and on import and export trade figures. He noted that Eritrea was effectively prevented from re-exporting goods imported from a third country, which in terms of volume meant an annual loss of trade worth over 100 million birr/nakfa. Alemseged Tesfai also pointed out that Eritrea was prevented from importing items classified either as 'in short supply' or as export items. Because of such restrictions, Eritrea's favourable trade balance with Ethiopia (in the range of 100 million birr per annum) was completely reversed. By 1996, Eritrea's imports from Ethiopia were 60 million birr more than Eritrea's exports to Ethiopia. The trade relations that existed before 1996 were favourable to Ethiopia, even though Eritrea had a favourable trade balance. Ethiopia, according to Alemseged Tesfai, had forced Eritrea to de-escalate its trade and to seek and expand alternative markets.

We concur with this lucid analysis of the economic relations that existed between the two countries. A major area of discrepancy lies, however, in the policy implications of the analysis. The author's aim is to show that the Eritrean–Ethiopian conflict had very little to do with Ethiopia's protectionist policy, and much to do with Ethiopia's desire to reoccupy parts of Eritrea.[6] Alemseged Tesfai appears to argue that Eritrea was taking de-escalation of its trade as a simple matter of changing trade partners and that the goods and services earlier destined for Ethiopia would readily find a market elsewhere.

In another thought-provoking article, Woldai Futur has put forward the opinion that there is no evidence that the cessation of economic and financial ties is hurting Eritrea more than Ethiopia. Woldai Futur, a former employee of the World Bank, is an economic adviser to the state of Eritrea. His main contention is there are no commodities that Eritrea used to import from Ethiopia that it cannot get from other countries. Likewise, the author argues, there are no commodities that Eritrea used to export to Ethiopia which it cannot export to other countries.[7]

Neither the minutes of the joint ministerial commission meetings nor the interview given by the President of Eritrea on the eve of the border

[5] Alemseged Tesfai, 'The Cause of the Eritrean–Ethiopian Border Conflict', *Eritrea Profile*, 5 December 1998.

[6] *Ibid.*

[7] Woldai Futur, *Eritrea Profile*, 12 December 1998.

dispute underestimate the seriousness of trade barriers. While conceding that both the authors reviewed above are engaged in hypothetical scenarios and theoretical possibilities, we are bound to question the wisdom of their advice. If the Eritrean–Ethiopian conflict cannot be linked directly to trade barriers, its direct effect since May 1998 has been the total cessation of trade between the two countries. As long as the conflict remains unresolved, Eritrea can neither export to nor import from Ethiopia. The rerouting of Ethiopia's import and export trade from the Eritrean ports to Djibouti is bound to put additional stress on the Eritrean economy. The restructuring that Eritrea is bound to undertake failing a speedy normalisation of relations will create immense challenges, and only the future will reveal its success and orientation.

A very useful analysis, emerging from a non-official source in Ethiopia and offering another perspective of the challenge of restructuring Eritrea's economy, is that of Kiflu Taddesse.[8] The author argues that Ethiopia's decision to trade in US dollars has created serious economic dislocations in both countries. This new trade policy has forced Eritrea to restructure its economy, and if this policy of restructuring fails, the author predicts that Eritrea will take measures to bring about a change of policy in Ethiopia. Regarding the Ethiopian economy, Kiflu Taddesse sums up common knowledge on the three major competing forces. These are the EPRDF/TPLF-controlled enterprises known as 'para-partatals', the private capitalists and, third, the Eritrean government and its own 'para-partatals'. It was widely known that the Eritrean government and its enterprises were engaged in economic activities. Through the new Ethiopian currency and the new trade policy, Kiflu Taddesse further argues, the Ethiopian government has 'ambushed' the Eritrean government and incapacitated its potentially dominant role in the Ethiopian economy. The Ethiopian government has thus eliminated its main competitor, namely, the Eritrean government. Kiflu Taddesse's conclusion is indeed instructive: that although in the short run the Ethiopian government may appear to have protected the national interest, it has done so at the price of rupturing relations with Eritrea.

Is Eritrea's total restructuring of its economy possible? Is it desirable? What would be the political implications of failed restructuring? It is of course theoretically possible for Eritrea to redirect its export and import trade away from Ethiopia. Such restructuring, however, would require a considerable input of capital and sustained capacity building. A commercially viable discovery of oil may be of crucial importance in providing the capital infrastructure for a radical restructuring of the economy. As things now stand, Eritrea has very few products that it could export to

---

[8] Kiflu Taddesse, *Tobia*, 5: 11 (September 1998), Amharic text.

other countries. In a recent interview given to the government weekly, *Eritrea Profile*, the governor of the Bank of Eritrea admitted candidly that Eritrea had no source of foreign currency other than remittances from its citizens in the diaspora.[9] He added that Eritrea's tourism, fisheries and salt-mining sectors were potential sources of foreign currency.

Decline of Development in Northern Ethiopia

Most of Eritrea's exports were consumed in the northern parts of Ethiopia, mainly in the regions of Tigray and Amhara. Most of Eritrea's imports also originated in northern Ethiopia. The total disruption of trade has thus affected northern Ethiopia as well as Eritrea. Ethiopia's embargo on Eritrean ports may affect Eritrea's revenue in the short run, but in the long run Ethiopia stands to lose. Northern Ethiopia would be affected severely by the cost of rerouting the outlets of its import and export trade away from Massawa and Assab to Djibouti. Foreign goods destined for northern Ethiopia now have to be transported all the way from Djibouti. For the northern regions of Ethiopia, and in particular for the Tigray regional national state, there is really no good alternative to the port of Massawa, with the possible exception of Port Sudan in Sudan. The troubled relationship between Addis Ababa and the Khartoum regime, however, with rebel movements controlling parts of the transit area between Port Sudan and the Ethiopian border, makes it unlikely that this would be a viable port for northern Ethiopia.

Politics of Destabilisation

The most worrying effect of the dispute has been the politics of destabilisation pursued by both governments. At the official level the conflict between the two countries is over the exercise of territorial sovereignty. The Ethiopian government threatened to go to war if the Eritrean government failed to withdraw its troops from the areas it occupied by force on 6 May 1998. The Eritrean government came up with several proposals for peaceful resolution of the dispute short of complying with the Ethiopian government's demands of unconditional withdrawal.

The Eritrean government media (*Eritrea Profile* and *Hadas Eritra*, the Tigrinya paper)[10] have stressed the following three points: first, Ethiopia is ruled by TPLF minority power; second, Eritrea does not believe that it

[9] Tekle Beyene, Governor of the Bank of Eritrea, *Eritrea Profile*, 21 November 1998.

[10] Eritrea beams a daily anti-TPLF radio programme to Ethiopia in Amharic and Tigrinya. We have not analysed the contents of these programmes.

can resolve the conflict as long as TPLF continues to control and dominate Ethiopia; third, the Eritrean government has stated repeatedly that its conflict is mainly with TPLF and not with the rest of Ethiopia.

The Ethiopian government, likewise, has identified EPLF as the main enemy of both the Ethiopian and the Eritrean people. In a well-publicised article by one of the military leaders of the EPRDF/TPLF,[11] the objective of the Ethiopian government is no longer to ascertain territorial sovereignty but to create the conditions for a long-lasting peace by annihilating EPLF once for all. Furthermore, Ethiopia continues to urge the population in Eritrea to change their government and to oppose its anti-Ethiopian policy.

It is very difficult to judge the impact of the politics of destabilisation conducted by both countries. It is also difficult to gauge the type and intensity of the undercover activities supported by each government to arouse internal uprisings in the other's country. The Ethiopian government has accused Eritrea of extending support to the opposition in Ethiopia, in particular to the Oromo and Somali liberation movements. The Eritrean government has accused Ethiopia of attempts to undermine the unity of the Eritrean people.

Prospects for Speedy Normalisation

We suspect that the intensity of mutual hatred and suspicion among the leaders of both governments will have a negative impact on the normalisation process. The border dispute, which could have been resolved peacefully, led to a long-drawn-out conflict in which the politics of destabilisation assumed the upper hand. In the process, the populations of both countries have been drawn into a conflict basically created by a small group of political leaders in the two governments.

[11] *Weyin*, a TPLF weekly paper, 6 September 1998 (Tigrinya text).

7 Conflict & Negotiation

Several third parties offered their services as negotiators when news of the Eritrean–Ethiopian border conflict surfaced in May 1998. In this chapter we unfold the various stages of the conflict and identify the different actors involved in the negotiation processes in order to achieve an understanding of what might be called the 'negotiation of negotiations'. We believe it is important to cover these issues in depth, since the Eritrean–Ethiopian conflict is not just a tragic event involving two countries, but also a sad example of the failure of the conflict prevention and resolution mechanisms brought to bear by international society and international representative organisations such as the OAU and the UN. Interest in their role is heightened by the consideration that this was the biggest war in the world in 1998–9, clearly surpassing the Kosovo war in terms of accumulated numbers of casualties (dead and wounded, about 75,000), troops involved (about 500,000) and number of displaced civilians (about 600,000).

Initial Eritrean and Ethiopian Responses

The first official statement from either party on the border dispute was issued by the Council of Ministers of Ethiopia and made public on 13 May 1998, a mere week after the armed clashes started in Badme on 6 May. The brief statement emphasised the positive development and peace endeavours undertaken by the Ethiopian government since 1991, and reassured the public that 'peaceful relations with neighbouring countries are undertaken with the conviction that border claims can be resolved through peaceful means'. Thereafter, the statement explains the failure to solve the border dispute amicably and concentrates on condemning the acts of the Eritrean government. It reads:

> On this basis we, on our part, have been trying to resolve claims relating to some localities on our borders with Eritrea peacefully and through negotiation. This being the fact, the Eritrean Government and the ruling Popular Front for Justice and Democracy have chosen to resolve the border issue by force reneging from the process of peaceful settlement of the matter.
>
> Consequently they have on the 12th of May 1998, entered Ethiopian territory which they have been claiming. They have clashed with police and local militia forces present to maintain the security of the area, and are in control of some positions. The Ethiopian Government vehemently condemns this move of the Eritrean Government and the Popular Front since it violates the sovereignty of Ethiopia and obstructs the ongoing efforts to resolve issues of claims in a peaceful manner.

The Ethiopian statement presented only one possible solution to the emerging conflict:

> Ethiopia demands that the Eritrean Government unconditionally and immediately withdraw from Ethiopian territory and cease its provocative and belligerent activity. In the event that the Eritrean Government and the Popular Front do not desist from this dangerous action and withdraw from Ethiopian territory without any precondition the Ethiopian Government will take all the necessary measures that the situation demands to safeguard the sovereignty and territorial integrity of our country.[1]

It is important to note that the Ethiopian government, already at this stage, expressed its willingness to back its demand for unconditional Eritrean withdrawal with 'all necessary measures', or armed confrontation.

The Eritrean government convened a cabinet meeting to consider the Ethiopian accusations two days later on 14 May 1998, and stated that it was 'greatly saddened by the tone and contents of these grave accusations'. Acknowledging the fact that there had been, and would continue to be, border disputes in certain locations along the Eritrean–Ethiopian border, the Eritrean government pushed the blame for the outburst of violence back to the Ethiopian side and, referring to incidents in 1997, explained that 'These problems have been instigated by the unlawful practices of the Ethiopian army, which occasionally made incursions into these Eritrean territories; dismantling the local administrative structures and committing crimes against the inhabitants.'[2] The Eritrean statement stressed that, despite these incidents, the government had worked consistently for a peaceful settlement of the dispute through bilateral negotiations, since they held a firm belief that 'the boundary between Eritrea and Ethiopia is very clear and uncontroversial'.

An important aspect to notice is that in this first statement the Eritrean government blames the Ethiopian ethnic-federal system for the existence

---

[1] Appendix 4.
[2] Appendix 5.

of the border disputes, explaining that it 'knows that the recurrent border incursions that continue to be perpetuated by Ethiopian forces basically emanate from the narrow perspectives of the Administrative Zones'. The policy of ethnic federalism in Ethiopia (*kilil* system), which gives cultural and, on paper, political autonomy to ethnic groups, has been a long-term source of dispute between EPLF and TPLF (see Chapter 3). This issue has not, however, been emphasised as the reason for the outbreak of war in later statements by the Eritrean government.

The Eritrean statement of 14 May consequently stressed Eritrea's desire to negotiate the dispute, and the Joint Border Commission was mentioned as the proper forum in which to solve the differences between the two governments. The Eritrean government was, however, of the opinion that the work of the border commission was put in jeopardy by the actions of the Ethiopian military forces:

> The Cabinet of Ministers further noted that a Joint Committee had been formed from both governments to resolve these problems and to delineate on the ground the boundary line. The Cabinet of Ministers asserted that the Government of Eritrea has been exerting all the necessary efforts to expedite the process and facilitate the work of the Joint Committee. But on Wednesday, May 8, 1998, and while the Eritrean delegation was on its way to Addis Ababa for a meeting of the Joint Committee to discuss ways and means for accelerating its work, Ethiopian army contingents that had already penetrated into Eritrean territory in the areas around Badme (south-western Eritrea) opened fire and caused grave damage on Eritrean units that attempted to approach them for dialogue. This unprovoked attack subsequently triggered a cycle of clashes in the area.

Instead of threatening Ethiopia with the use of more violence, the Eritrean statement tried to play down the differences between the two governments, emphasising the traditional friendly relations between the two peoples:

> The Government of Eritrea firmly believes that attempts to inflate the minor and temporary problem that has been created along the borders of the two sisterly countries will not serve the fundamental interests of the Eritrean and Ethiopian peoples. The Government of Eritrea pledges that it will, as ever before, spare no efforts to handle the present problem with the requisite patience and responsibility. It does not, accordingly, see any wisdom in precipitating tension through inflammatory campaigns.
>
> The Government of Eritrea therefore calls upon the Government of Ethiopia to pursue a similar path that will promote the interests and good neighbourliness of the peoples of both countries. The Cabinet of Ministers of the Government of Eritrea further reasserts its belief that the peoples of Eritrea and Ethiopia will maintain and preserve their mutual interests rooted in peace, good neighbourliness and cooperation.

The Eritrean statement, playing down the gravity of the situation, offered the following plan for solution of the dispute:

The Cabinet of Ministers reiterates its firm belief that the enduring mutual interests that exist and bind together the peoples of Eritrea and Ethiopia cannot be jeopardised by any border dispute. The Cabinet of Ministers accordingly proposes the following framework as a solution to the problem that has been made to be blown out of proportions and derailed from its path.

1 The Government of Eritrea condemns the logic of force as it firmly knows and upholds that border disputes of any kind can only be resolved through peaceful and legal means; and not through military means.

2 On the basis of this principle, each party shall publicly announce to the peoples of Eritrea, Ethiopia and the international community the territories that it claims – if any – and designate them on the political map with clear geographical coordinates. Each party shall also accept that the dispute cannot, and should not be, resolved by force but through peaceful negotiations.

3 Both parties shall agree that all negotiations and understandings that will be conducted henceforth shall be carried out in the presence and through the mediation of a Third Party. The latter will act as witness and guarantor.

4 Areas under 'dispute' shall be demilitarised temporarily and be free from the presence of armies of both countries. The enforcement of this under-standing shall be guaranteed by the Third Party.

5 If the above proposal for resolving the dispute through the involvement of a Third Party and without further complications is not acceptable, the matter to be referred to international adjudication.

In another brief statement issued the following day (15 May), the Eritrean government played down the Ethiopian accusations, and instead called for an 'independent inspection by any third party to verify the facts of the matter on the ground'.[3] These initial statements from both parties clearly illustrate the polarised and confrontational understanding of the situation which exploded in May 1998; positions which have been sustained and entrenched ever since.

The US–Rwanda Peace Plan

Soon after armed clashes broke out between Eritrea and Ethiopia, several third parties offered their services as negotiators. After the request from both parties, the United States teamed up with Rwanda (an ally of both Eritrea and Ethiopia) and started to broker the conflict in mid-May. Their objective was to 'promote a peaceful and durable settlement of this dispute and to prevent a war'.[4] On 3 June 1998 the US–Rwanda team offered the

---

[3] 'Statement of the Government of Eritrea calling for an Independent Inspection', Asmara, 15 May 1998.

[4] US Department of State, Office of the Spokesman, press statement by Spokesman James P. Rubin, 3 June 1998: 'The Dispute between Ethiopia and Eritrea'.

first third-party plan for a peace accord. The US press statement on the accord stated that

> the facilitation team listened carefully to the detailed positions of both parties. An attempt was also made to take full account of the respective perspectives and interests without making any judgement as to where the disputed border lies or what actions may have precipitated the crisis that began with the border skirmish on May 6.

Subsequently the facilitation team stated that it had identified many 'areas of commonality between the two parties'. The team presented its recommendations to both parties on 30–31 May 1998.

This public presentation of the peace accord went against Eritrea's understanding of the US–Rwanda peace initiative. Yemane Ghebreab, one of the Eritrean negotiators, and Zemereth Yohannes (deputy head of Political Affairs in PFDJ) explained to one of the authors that the Eritreans felt they were 'overrun' by the US–Rwanda delegation, and that the delegation went beyond its mandate.[5] From the Eritrean viewpoint, the US had been asked only to facilitate communication with Ethiopia, not to act as an own 'operator' in the conflict resolution process. When the US–Rwanda peace accord was presented in Addis in the beginning of June, the Eritrean side explained that this came as a surprise to them, since they, according to Yemane Ghebreab, had not seen the full proposal or been given the opportunity to comment on it.

The US–Rwandan recommendations for the peace accord are summarised as follows in the press statement:

1   Both parties should commit themselves to the following principles: resolving this and any other dispute between them by peaceful means; renouncing force as a means of imposing solutions; agreeing to undertake measures to reduce current tensions; and seeking the final disposition of their common border, on the basis of established colonial treaties and international law applicable to such treaties.

2   To reduce current tensions, and without prejudice to the territorial claims of either party: a small observer mission should be deployed at Badme. *Eritrean forces should re-deploy from Badme to positions held before May 6, 1998; the previous civilian administration should return* (authors' emphasis): and there should be an investigation into the events of May 6, 1998.

3   To achieve lasting resolution of the underlying border dispute, both parties should agree to the swift and binding delimitation and demarcation of the Eritrean–Ethiopian border. Border delimitation should be determined on the basis of established colonial treaties and international law applicable to such treaties, and the delimitation and demarcation process should be completed by a qualified technical team as soon as possible. The demarcated border should be accepted and adhered to by both parties, and, upon completion of demarcation, the legitimate authorities assume jurisdiction over their respective sovereign territories.

[5] Interviewed by Kjetil Tronvoll in Asmara, 15 and 2 October respectively.

4 Both parties should demilitarise the entire common border as soon as possible.

In brief, the two sentences emphasised in the four-point plan – i.e. unilateral Eritrean withdrawal and the restoration of Ethiopian administration in the disputed areas – were the core issues to be resolved between Eritrea and Ethiopia. Only one day after the US–Rwandan peace plan was made public, Prime Minister Meles Zenawi publicly stated that Ethiopia endorsed the proposal:

> The Ethiopian Government has been insisting from the very beginning that to resolve the crisis peacefully the Eritrean Government must first withdraw its troops from areas it forcefully occupied. In view of the fact that our Government had repeatedly stated that if the Eritrean Government adhered to this legitimate demand and withdrew from the area, that Ethiopia would be ready to reduce tensions and work towards the peaceful and legal resolution of the boundary issues; and since the proposal of the facilitators is consistent with the Ethiopian position, the Ethiopian Government fully accepts the proposal of the facilitators in the belief that the proposal would lay a firm foundation for the peaceful resolution of the crisis.[6]

Eritrea, on the other hand, was reluctant to accept the peace accord. In particular, it emphasised the bone of contention:

> The Government of Eritrea has further underlined to the Facilitators that in its view, the question of temporary administration of the civilian centres in the demilitarised areas could be handled with necessary flexibility in the interim period as the jurisdiction of the sovereign State would be reinstated as soon as the demarcation of the boundary on the basis of the established colonial treaties is completed.[7]

Nevertheless, Eritrea maintained that the facilitation team should not have come up with a conclusive peace plan at that point in time; the US–Rwanda team ought to have continued the negotiations in order to clarify certain important issues:

> The four-point recommendations that have evolved in the facilitation process address the paramount issues that the Government of Eritrea has been raising and are, therefore, not controversial at all to the Government of Eritrea. At the same time, the Government of Eritrea believes that the facilitation process has not been consummated and that there are still serious issues of detail and implementation that need to be worked out in the period ahead.

The Eritrean reluctance to accept the full peace plan was regretted by the US and Rwanda, and exploited by the Ethiopian government to delegitimise the Eritrean position. Officially, Eritrea was sceptical towards the credibility of the Ethiopian will to peaceful negotiations, and the Eritrean government stated that 'while the facilitation process has gone a long way in creating grounds for a non-violent and legal solution, the

---

[6] Address by Prime Minister Meles Zenawi, 4 June 1998.
[7] The Government of Eritrea, 5 June 1998.

Government of Ethiopia, which has stated its acceptance of the recommendations, is still bent on an all-out war'. This position reflected Meles Zenawi's official statement on the previous day:

> Although the Ethiopian Government maintains its stand for peace and supports the compromise proposal presented by the Governments of the United States and Rwanda even now, the continued aggression of the Eritrean Government has exhausted our patience. *Therefore, the Defence Forces of Ethiopia have been directed to take all necessary measures against the repeated aggressions of the Eritrean Government and to safeguard the territorial integrity of the country.* [...] The situation demands that while the Ethiopian people continue with their peaceful efforts, every necessary measure to safeguard the country's territorial integrity be taken. I therefore call upon all the peoples of Ethiopia to take all the actions necessary for the safeguarding of our country according to directives to be issued by organs of the Government and the Defence Forces of Ethiopia [authors' emphasis].'[8]

Ethiopia's seeming duplicity in simultaneously accepting the peace plan *and* ordering the country's armed forces to prepare for military action – operationalised on 5 June when the Ethiopian air force initiated a first-strike bombing sortie on Asmara airport – might to some extent explain the Eritrean position. But probably just as important is the context of the negotiations as such, and the role played by the US delegation. PFDJ representatives who explained their view of the peace accord to one of the authors visiting Eritrea at the time remarked critically not only on the conduct of the proposal but also on how the negotiation process was carried out. When this view is elaborated, a picture emerges in which the Eritreans view themselves as 'sacrificed' and misunderstood by the international community.

The head of the US delegation was Ms Susan Rice, an under-secretary of the State Department in charge of African affairs. Both Eritreans and Ethiopians have commented that by sending a relatively young and inexperienced woman as head of the delegation the US had implicitly characterised the dispute as unimportant and given it low priority. But the Eritreans were also surprised by how the US delegation worked and argued in their meetings with them. According to Yemane Ghebreab, the US was expected only to facilitate communication with Ethiopia, and not to launch its 'own' plan as such. But from the first meeting onwards, according to high-ranking PFDJ cadres, the Americans were trying to persuade the Eritreans to give concessions and accept a unilateral withdrawal of Eritrean forces out of disputed territories. The US delegation argued that Eritrea should consider Meles Zenawi's weak position within the party and government; that he was being challenged by a 'hard-line' TPLF faction which wanted to pursue a tougher line towards Eritrea; and that if these 'hard-liners' were to assume power, they would put Eritrea in

---

[8] Meles Zenawi, 4 June 1998.

an even more dire situation.[9] An Eritrean representative explained to one of the authors that they rejected this kind of argument, emphasising the need to view Ethiopia as one coherent party in this conflict rather than speculating on internal divisions and factions within TPLF or EPRDF. As the war has developed, however, the Eritrean government itself seems to have done all it can to depict the TPLF as the oppressors of other government coalition partners.

Yemane Ghebreab emphasised that he did not believe that the US delegation had instructions from their superiors to pursue such a line; in his view certain members of the delegation took control of the situation and 'went beyond their mandate'. The fact that the US delegation included a person with a long-term and close personal relationship with Meles Zenawi and top TPLF cadres also helps one to understand Eritrea's hesitation and reluctance.

Concurrently with the announcement of the peace plan, Ethiopia escalated the conflict by initiating air bombing of Asmara airport on Friday 5 June. The same afternoon, Eritrea retaliated by bombing Mekelle, hitting a school full of children. Because the evacuation of US personnel from Asmara started the day before the bombing, and all other embassies were warned to follow suit, the Eritreans believe that the US had prior knowledge of the planned Ethiopian air attack on Asmara. This created a mistrust about the intentions and posture of the US in the conflict.

The US–Rwanda proposal was formulated and presented in a manner that put the blame for the conflict on one of the parties only, or, at least, it was perceived as such. Since all subsequent negotiation attempts build on the US/Rwanda peace plan, this cemented the positions of the parties, making it even more difficult to create a space for the two governments to manoeuvre within.

The OAU Initiative

The Eritrean–Ethiopian border conflict was one of the major preoccupations of the 68th Ordinary Session of the OAU Council of Ministers and the 34th Ordinary Session of the Assembly of Heads of State and Government held in Ouagadougou, Burkina Faso, from 1 to 10 June 1998. The OAU and its member states were particularly concerned about the escalation of

---

[9] This hypothesis about internal disagreement within the TPLF leadership has flourished in Ethiopia since the outbreak of the war. It is claimed that the 'old gang of four', composed of Meles Zenawi, Tewolde Woldemariam, Alemseged Gebreamlak and Kinfe Gebremedhin, is challenged by the 'new gang of four', composed of Abay Tsehaye, Seyoum Mesfin, Seye Abraha and Gebru Asrat. How much credibility this hypothesis should carry, however, is difficult to assess, given the covert nature of TPLF leadership.

the dispute and the use of air strikes,[10] and the meeting issued the following statement:

> Having heard the report of the facilitators on the evolution of the situation between Ethiopia and Eritrea. Having listened to the interventions of the two parties. Paying tribute to the work of the facilitators and requesting them to continue. Considering the gravity of the situation and the loss of lives. Urgently appeals to the two parties to, at the same time and simultaneously, put an end to all hostilities, accept and implement the recommendations of the facilitators. Recommends to the Heads of State and Government to be immediately seized with the matter.[11]

Immediately after the close of the OAU session, it was decided that a High-Level Delegation, comprised of the Burkina Faso, Djibouti, Zimbabwe and Rwanda heads of states and the OAU chairman, should visit the two countries to hear the views of the conflicting parties. The delegation made its visit on 18–19 June, when Ethiopia confirmed its acceptance of the US–Rwanda facilitation plan. Eritrea, on the other hand, repeated its views on the US–Rwanda plan and preferred to view the OAU effort as a new initiative. Thus no new headway was made by the OAU High-Level Delegation, but it was decided that an ambassador committee should follow up and continue its work.

The mandate of the Ambassador Committee was, *inter alia*, to investigate and collect information about the development of the crisis and the status of the disputed area of Badme. Eritrea protested at the singling out of the disputed area of Badme, and called for a full investigation of the other disputed areas, in particular of Adi Murug and the events taking place in that area in July 1997. After conducting the mission from 29 June to 9 July, the Ambassador Committee submitted a comprehensive report to the foreign ministers of the High-Level Delegation, who met in Burkina Faso on 1–2 August 1998. The ministerial meeting endorsed the report and a set of recommendations for conflict resolution was developed and approved, building on all relevant material gathered from the two parties by the OAU. In a separate 'Introductory Note' read to the foreign ministers of Eritrea and Ethiopia, the OAU Ministerial Committee referred to the two parties' understanding of the conflict as follows:

> For the Eritrean Party, the crisis between Eritrea and Ethiopia has its origin in the violation by Ethiopia of the colonial borders of Eritrea and the occupation of some parts of its territory by force. According to it, it is a border dispute which can be settled by technical and legal means (demarcation, and in case of controversy, arbitration). All other issues, including that of Badme, are aimed, according to it, at creating diversion. … The Ethiopian side considers that there are two distinct issues involved in the present conflict. First, there is what it considers as the act of aggression perpetrated by Eritrea which, according to

---

[10] Soon afterwards, the USA brokered an air moratorium that put a temporary stop to the use of warplanes until Ethiopia resumed the air war in February 1999.

[11] OAU, Ouagadougou, 10 June 1998.

Ethiopia, must be undone and not rewarded. Then, there is the problem of the border dispute which must be considered once Eritrea will have withdrawn its forces from Badme and its environs.[12]

The note also states that the OAU is of the opinion that Ethiopia administered the disputed area of Badme before 12 May, when Eritrean forces established control of the area. The report emphasises, however, that 'this conclusion does not obviously prejudge the final status of that area which will be determined at the end of the delimitation and demarcation process and, if necessary, through arbitration'. The note acknowledges Eritrea's reservation that the 'administration of Badme in itself was not valid if the process by which that administration had been established was illegal', and the issue that the incidents in Badme in May 1998 must be seen in the context of Ethiopia's border incursions in Adi Murug in July 1997. The OAU Ministerial Committee notes that it 'understands the viewpoint of Eritrea on the origin of the conflict and notes, in this connection, its concerns about the incidents which would have taken place at other places on the common border in July 1997'. Nevertheless, the Ministerial Committee concludes that:

> It is, nevertheless, of the view that what happened in Badme between 6 and 12 May constitutes a fundamental element in the crisis. Consequently, the challenge to be taken up is to find a solution to that particular problem within the framework of a comprehensive settlement of the conflict in all its dimensions.

The Eritrean Foreign Minister, in reaction to the 'Introductory Note', praised the work of the Ambassadors Committee and the fair and impartial handling of the matter by the Ministerial Committee. But Eritrea protested against the sole focus on Badme, termed this a 'prejudgement', and rejected the characterisation of the events in Badme during 6–12 May 1998 as a fundamental element in the crisis. The Ethiopian Foreign Minister, on the other hand, expressed his satisfaction with treatment of the Badme question in the 'Introductory Note'. In that regard, Ethiopia stressed the need to ensure the return to the *status quo ante*, 'because without movement on that issue, there will be no movement in the overall search for peace'.[13]

The OAU Ministerial Meeting in Ouagadougou at the beginning of August came to the conclusion that there was no noticeable breakthrough in the stalemate, or movement in the positions of the parties. The ministers agreed that more political work was required before reaching any further conclusions, and that it was premature to submit recommendations to the parties, since that fell under the mandate of the OAU High-Level Delegation.[14]

---

[12] 'Introductory Note', Ministerial Committee, OAU, Ouagadougou, 2 August 1998.
[13] See also press releases from the Ethiopian Foreign Ministry, 4 August 1998, and from the Eritrean Foreign Ministry, 5 August 1998.
[14] See communiqué issued on 2 August 1998 by the Ministerial Committee.

The High-Level Delegation had its next meeting on 7–8 November 1998. Present in Ouagadougou were both President Issaias Afwerki and Prime Minister Meles Zenawi, who held separate talks with the Delegation. The High-Level Delegation had prepared a statement that was delivered to both parties. The crux of the statement, however, was as before:

> In our reflection we have drawn the conclusion that the events which took place between 6 and 12 May 1998 were a fundamental element of the crisis that evolved between the two countries. ... We have also been led to the conclusion that the events prior to those of 6–12 May 1998 contributed to the gradual deterioration of the relations between the two countries.[15]

In other words, Eritrea's position had been rejected by the High-Level Delegation, which instead tried to emphasise commonalities in the positions of the warring parties:

> Apart from the divergent views of the two Parties on the origin and nature of the conflict, it should be pointed out that there is a general agreement on the modalities for the settlement of the border dispute based on the delimitation and demarcation of their common border. This convergence of views is not, however, translated into reality due to the difference that continues to exist between the two Parties regarding the approach. While the Ethiopian side demands the prior withdrawal of Eritrean forces from Badme and its environs and the restoration of the *status quo ante*, the Eritrean side proposes the demilitarisation of the common border through the simultaneous withdrawal of the forces of the two Parties. Our major concern has been and still is to know how to reconcile these two positions. We sincerely believe that a comprehensive solution based on the redeployment of the forces present in Badme and its environs to the positions before 6 May 1998 which would be monitored by a Group of Observers and followed by the demilitarisation of the entire common border is an approach which deserves to be considered by the two Parties.

In a separate set of proposals for a Framework Agreement for a peaceful settlement of the dispute, the High-Level Delegation also repeated the controversial demand that a military observer group be deployed at Badme 'and that such group will also assist in the reinstatement of Civilian Administration and in the maintenance of law and order during the interim period'.[16]

Prime Minister Meles Zenawi asked for clarification concerning paragraphs 3 and 4 of the peace proposal: the unilateral withdrawal of Eritrean forces from all territories occupied after 6 May 1998 (and not only from Badme and its environs); and the reinstatement of the Ethiopian civilian administration in the occupied territories with 'all necessary organs to protect law and order except the army'. When the OAU, as Ethiopia

---

[15] Statement given to Eritrea and Ethiopia by the OAU High-Level Delegation, Ouagadougou, 7 November 1998.

[16] Article 4 in 'Set of Proposals' given to Eritrea and Ethiopia by the OAU High-Level Delegation, Ouagadougou, 7 November 1998.

claims, confirmed these clarifications, Meles Zenawi recommended the peace agreement to the Ethiopian government and received its full endorsement of the set of proposals.[17] President Issaias Afwerki stressed once more the need of a formal ceasefire agreement in order for both sides to 'commit themselves to the cardinal principle of the rejection of the use of force to resolve the dispute'.[18] Eritrea was of the opinion that 'a cessation of hostilities is certainly a sufficient condition for the deployment of an observer force and for carrying out an expeditious demarcation', a position which sidetracked the crucial differences of opinion between the two parties which had locked the peace process, in order to 'kick-start' the negotiations. Ethiopia was firm on its stand, however, rejecting a ceasefire agreement before Eritrean withdrawal from Badme.

The High-Level Delegation was in agreement that the submission of the proposals to both parties was itself a major achievement, and that it was now up to the warring parties to react on the proposals and to communicate a definitive response to the proposals submitted to them. The High-Level Delegation thus offered its good services to the parties if necessary, meanwhile submitting a final report on its efforts to the Central Organ of the OAU Mechanism for Conflict Prevention, Management and Resolution, to be addressed at its next session at Summit level on 18–19 December 1998.[19] After the meeting, the High-Level Delegation chairman separately briefed the UN and EU representatives in Ouagadougou, which led to separate statements from both the EU and the UN Security Council giving full support to the OAU process and the set of proposals for a Framework Agreement.[20]

Before the OAU Central Organ meeting was convened, Secretary General Salim A. Salim met with Issaias Afwerki in Asmara on 12 December 1998. At this meeting the Eritrean President presented the Secretary General with a letter explaining Eritrea's reluctance to endorse the proposals for a Framework Agreement, emphasising *inter alia* that:

> Indeed, while Eritrea had made it clear that the [US–Rwanda] facilitation process was over and it regarded the OAU initiative as a new one, the recommendations by the Committee of Ambassadors revolved around the same parameters that had led to the failure of the facilitation process.[21]

---

[17] See press release issued by the Office of the Spokesperson, 9 November 1998 and letter from Meles Zenawi to Chairman Blaise Compaore, President of Burkina Faso, 12 November 1998. See below for formal clarification by OAU on this issue in their response to Eritrea's points of clarification, 29 January 1999.

[18] See Eritrean Foreign Ministry press release on the OAU Meeting at Ouagadougou, 9 November 1998.

[19] OAU press communiqué, 8 November 1998.

[20] See EU statement of 13 November 1998 and statement by the President of the UN Security Council of 13 November 1998.

[21] 'Document handed over to the Secretary General during the Meeting with the President of Eritrea in Asmara, 12 December 1998'.

The Eritrean government nevertheless recognised the 'positive elements' in the proposals for a Framework Agreement and in order to give their 'full and definite opinion' on the proposals, they submitted to the Secretary General of the OAU a list of questions needing further clarification before acceptance of the proposals could be confirmed.[22] The central issues raised were the exact geographical location of Badme in relation to the international border and what was meant by 'Badme and its environs' in the Framework Agreement; redeployment and the justification for unilateral Eritrean withdrawal; and the reinstatement of civilian administration in contested areas before a demarcation of the borders. Answers to the Eritrean inquiries were not given before the OAU Central Organ meeting the following week.

Prime Minister Meles Zenawi addressed the OAU Central Organ meeting on 17 December 1998 and gave the latest Ethiopian views on the dispute. In his address, he repeated the Ethiopian demand for unilateral Eritrean withdrawal, based on the principle that 'what was done by force must be undone'. Ethiopia demanded a return to the *status quo ante*:

> The Eritrean forces must withdraw from the areas they have occupied and the duly constituted administration which was on the ground and which was Ethiopian administration when the Eritrean tanks rolled over into Ethiopia, must be reinstated.

Meles Zenawi backed his demand by drawing the picture of an aggressive and violent Eritrean state, based on her gloomy history of border disputes:

> In five years, four of Eritrea's five neighbours had been assaulted, attacked. The only neighbour which so far has not been assaulted is Saudi Arabia. It is anybody's guess when and if this is going to happen. So Your Excellencies, there is a pattern of behaviour here; Ethiopia was attacked as part of that pattern of behaviour. This is not a freak event. This is a pattern of behaviour of openly flaunting and openly rejecting the core principles of civilised conduct among nations; of shooting first and talking later; of undue and exaggerated belief in one's military might and invincibility; of belief in might is right.[23]

Meles Zenawi also asserted that Issaias Afwerki had a habit of attacking third parties engaged in negotiating the conflict – here he referred to the Eritrean accusations against Rwanda, Djibouti and OAU's Secretary General, amounting to an 'unacceptable pattern of behaviour which is a source of continued instability in the region'.

President Issaias Afwerki, in his statement to the OAU Central Organ, dismissed the Ethiopian accusations portraying Eritrea as 'worshipping the gun' as baseless and explained that 'Ethiopia's shrill and offensive language

---

[22] See Appendix 8 for a full version of the list of inquiries.

[23] Transcribed impromptu statement given by H. E. Prime Minister Meles Zenawi, to the Fourth OAU Central Organ Summit, 17 December 1998, Ouagadougou, issued by the Office of the Spokesperson.

is designed to drown the facts in a sea of accusations'.[24] He gave credit to the OAU's efforts to solve the dispute, and said he understood its difficulties in passing judgement when facing opposing versions of the events leading to the crisis. He then concentrated on explaining Eritrea's crucial points of disagreement with the OAU's proposal for Framework Agreement:

> I am sure Your Excellencies will agree with me that the issues of redeployment and administration are closely linked with the location of the areas under consideration, whether they are in Eritrea or Ethiopia; and also with the causes of the conflict, that is, who used force, where and when. Since these vital questions have not been determined by an investigation, which Eritrea has been requesting for the past six months, any proposals for redeployment and administration need to take that fact into account. In regard to redeployment, Eritrea holds that, with a ceasefire in place and military observers on the ground, demarcation can be done expeditiously without the complicated and time-consuming disengagement of hundreds of thousands of troops. Eritrea, however, has no objection in principle to redeployment in the framework of demilitarisation. On the question of administration, Eritrea has repeatedly stated that, like all sovereign nations, it cannot countenance alien administration of its own territory and over its own population. Indeed, the question of administration cannot be separated from the issue of inherited colonial borders. Therefore for reasons of principle and the interest of not complicating and prolonging the conflict and practicality (since we are talking about a short period of six months), the suggestion of administration should be dropped altogether and focus placed on an expedited demarcation of the border, which will automatically solve the question of administration.

The OAU Central Organ took note of the respective positions of the two parties on the proposals, but nevertheless unconditionally endorsed the proposals for the Framework Agreement as an 'appropriate framework for the resolution of the dispute between Ethiopia and Eritrea'. Further, the Central Organ called on the two parties to 'continue to cooperate with the [High-Level] Delegation with a view to creating the necessary conditions for the speedy implementation of the Framework Agreement'.[25] The OAU Central Organ thus dismissed Eritrea's reservations on the Framework Agreement and the suggestions for improving it put forward by Issaias Afwerki. Neither had they as yet responded to Issaias Afwerki's 31-point request for clarification of the Framework Agreement. The net result of the OAU process at the end of the year 1998 was thus that no progress had been made on the crucial issue raised by Eritrea at the very start of the facilitation process at the beginning of June 1998: that the conflict had to be analysed against the background of the incidents of July–August 1997 when, as the Eritrean government claims, Eritrean territories were occupied by Ethiopian forces. Thus, in essence, all

---

[24] President Issaias Afwerki's speech to the OAU Central Organ meeting, Ouagadougou, 17 December 1998 (distributed by the Information Officer, Embassy of Eritrea to the US).

[25] Statement of the OAU Central Organ on the 'dispute between Ethiopia and Eritrea', Ouagadougou, 17–18 December 1998.

negotiation attempts had failed and the conflict was in deadlock.

The new year commenced with increasing signs of a possible full-scale war between the two parties. Eritrea issued a press statement on 12 January 1999 accusing Ethiopia of planning to 'launch an attack against Eritrea', an accusation denounced by Ethiopia. Eritrea later backed this accusation by reporting that similar information on Ethiopia's war preparations had been passed on to them by Western intelligence sources.[26]

At the end of January, the Eritrean government received a response from the OAU to their request for clarification of the Framework Agreement (see Appendix 9 for a full version). The OAU response received little attention at this time, however, since both parties were engaged in mutual accusations of war preparations and in responding to the UN Security Council's sudden new interest in the conflict. The UN had so far maintained a low profile in the conflict, leaving the negotiation initiative to the OAU. We shall return to the OAU initiative, but at this point need to consider UN responses to the conflict.

UN Security Council Resolutions and the UN Envoy's Initiative

The OAU process received broad international support from its inception. The UN Security Council swiftly extended its sanction. Its resolution 1177 of 26 June 1998 reads, in part:

> Commending the efforts of the OAU and of others, in cooperation with the OAU, to achieve a peaceful settlement of the conflict,

> 1 Condemns the use of force and demands that both parties immediately cease hostilities and refrain from further use of force;

> 2 Welcomes the commitment of the parties to a moratorium on the threat of and use of air-strikes;

> 3 Urges the parties to exhaust all means to achieve a peaceful settlement of the dispute;

> 4 Expresses its strong support for the decision of the Assembly of the Heads of State and Government of the OAU on 10 June 1998 (S/1998/494) as well as for the mission and efforts of the Heads of State of the OAU and urges the OAU to follow up as quickly as possible;

> 5 Calls upon the parties to cooperate fully with the OAU.

During the rest of the summer and autumn of 1998 neither the UN Security Council nor its Secretary General engaged themselves directly in the ongoing conflict resolution process.[27] Although the Eritrean and Ethiopian

---

[26] See press statements issued by the Eritrean Ministry of Foreign Affairs, 12 and 15 January 1999, and by the Ethiopian Ministry of Foreign Affairs, 14 January 1999.

[27] Two other UN agencies, UN High Commissioner of Human Rights and UNDP, Asmara, issued statements on the situation of Eritrean deportees from Ethiopia on 1 July and 22 July 1999 respectively.

ambassadors to UN both addressed the conflict in General Assembly plenary sessions,[28] the UN Security Council did not involve itself in the conflict until the beginning of the new year. Resolution 1226 (1999), adopted by the Security Council on 29 January 1999, reconfirmed strong support of the OAU initiative and its proposal for a Framework Agreement, and 'affirms that the OAU Framework Agreement provides the best hope for peace between the two parties' (paragraph 1). The resolution also endorsed the decision by the Secretary General to send a special envoy to the Horn in order to strengthen the OAU negotiation initiative. Ethiopia's acceptance of the agreement was welcomed, and the resolution noted the fact that Eritrea had received answers from OAU on their points of clarifications and thus 'strongly urges Eritrea to accept the Framework Agreement as the basis for peaceful resolution … without delay' (paragraph 5). The resolution called on both parties to work for a reduction in tensions between them and it 'strongly urges Ethiopia and Eritrea to maintain their commitment to a peaceful resolution … and to exercise maximum restraint and to refrain from taking any military action' (paragraph 7).

Eritrea reacted quickly to the UNSC resolution, responding in a letter the same day to the President of the Security Council which stressed that 'Eritrea is fully engaged in the peace process because it understands and realises full well that the framework is not a "take it or leave it" offer'.[29] The Eritrean government thus emphasised the procedural aspects of the negotiations, and its continuing unwillingness to accept the unamended Framework Agreement. Notably, it did not mention receipt of the OAU response on the points of clarification. Ethiopia, on the other hand, welcomed the UNSC resolution which 'left no ambiguity with regard to what is expected from whom'.[30] The fact that Eritrea was dragging its feet over acceptance of the OAU Framework Agreement clearly provoked the Ethiopian government, and thus it explicitly repeated that 'the OAU Proposals do not leave open the possibility for misinterpretation and misrepresentation'.

Shortly after the UN Security Council meeting, the UN envoy Mohamed Sahnoun flew to the region to start talks with the parties. While he was actively engaged in preparing the negotiations, the first major military offensive since June 1998 commenced in the first week of February 1999. The air moratorium was also broken, and Ethiopia intensified the offensive with the use of air bombardment. This time the UN Security Council reacted immediately: its second resolution in two weeks on the conflict condemned the use of force by the parties and demanded an

[28] See 'Extract from General Assembly Plenary Press Release GA/9478, 36th Meeting (PM), 12 October 1998'.
[29] 'Eritrean UN Mission Letter to the UN Security Council', 29 January 1999.
[30] Press release by the FDRE Ministry of Foreign Affairs, 2 February 1999.

immediate halt to the hostilities.[31] Resolution 1227 also strongly urged 'all States to end immediately all sales of arms and munitions to Ethiopia and Eritrea', thus encouraging an international weapons embargo on the two warring parties. The reactions from the parties to the resolution were immediate and predictable. Eritrea claimed that it did not start the offensive and had not broken the air moratorium. It was also surprised to notice the weapons embargo and noted that this would only lead to regional imbalance.[32] Ethiopia, on the other hand, accused Eritrea of initiating the offensive with an air raid on the northern Ethiopian town of Adigrat on 5 February and explained that it had a legitimate right to self-defence.[33] Although Ethiopia welcomed the fact that the Council once again urged Eritrea to accept the OAU Framework Agreement, they regarded the weapon embargo imposed on them as extremely provocative. In a comment on the draft resolution made on 10 February, the Ethiopian ambassador to the UN drew a direct parallel between the current weapons embargo and the way Ethiopia was treated by the League of Nations in 1936 when 'the Organisation imposed an arms embargo on both Fascist Italy and Ethiopia knowing full well that Fascist Italy, the aggressor, was self-sufficient in arms while Ethiopia, a poor country, was trying to defend its sovereignty'.[34] The very issue of the UN arms embargo can be seen as a turning point in Ethiopia's relations with the international community over conflict resolution. Later, the Ethiopian parliament passed a separate resolution on the issue, condemning the UNSC resolution in strong terms:

> Expresses, on behalf of the people of the Federal Democratic Republic of Ethiopia, its deep anger at the injustice done to Ethiopia by the Security Council through its adoption of Resolution No. 1227, which was unjust and totally inappropriate;

> Deplores the attempt to deny Ethiopia, the victim of aggression, which in that capacity should, at the minimum, have been accorded the understanding and the sympathy of the Security Council, the right of self-defence which is enshrined in the UN Charter and sanctioned by international law.[35]

We do not have any of our own information validating either of the parties' claims that their adversary attacked them. International observers and journalists, however, have judged it plausible that it was Ethiopia who

---

[31] Resolution 1227 (1999), 10 February 1999.

[32] 'Statement of the Government of Eritrea on Security Council Resolution 1227 (1999)', 11 February 1999.

[33] 'Eritrea Bombs Adigrat', press release issued by the Office of the Government Spokesperson, FDRE, 5 February 1999.

[34] Statement by H.E. Ambassador Duri Mohammed before the adoption of the Draft Resolution 1227 (1999), 10 February 1999.

[35] Resolution 01/1999 of the House of People's Representatives, FDRE, 'On the War of Aggression by Eritrea against Ethiopia and on the Resolution of the United Nations Security Council No. 1227/1999'.

started the offensive on 5 February, falsely announcing an Eritrean air attack on Adigrat in order to 'retaliate'. This position can also be read into the statement by President Clinton on the resumption of the conflict, in which he argues his concern on 'the recent use of air power which escalates the conflict and violates the agreed air strike moratorium. I urge the Ethiopian government to refrain from further use of its aircraft as currently employed along the border.'[36]

Eritrea and the OAU

In the past, Eritrea has been lukewarm towards the OAU. In the current situation, this attitude backfired, weakening its position and credibility. Issaias Afwerki has belittled and criticised the OAU and its bureaucracy repeatedly as incompetent and corrupt, not doing any good nor producing anything of value for its member states. The historical relationship between Ethiopia and the OAU is also an issue that affects the current situation. The bare issue of access to the OAU system and decision-makers is also unfavourable to Eritrea, since the OAU headquarters is located in Addis Ababa.

The OAU initiative is also weakened, in the eyes of Eritrea, by the presence of Djibouti on the High-Level Delegation, the Ministerial Com-mittee and the Ambassador Committee. Eritrea has accused Djibouti of assisting Ethiopia in its war preparations, since Ethiopia received war supplies through the Djibouti port. The accusation led to Djibouti's decision to break diplomatic relations with Eritrea, which Eritrea interprets as taking sides with Ethiopia in the border conflict.[37] It is also worth mentioning that Eritrea and Djibouti had armed border clashes in the spring of 1996 over a so-called disputed area, a point unlikely to strengthen the trust Eritrea has in the efforts of the OAU and the High-Level Delegation as long as Djibouti forms an integral part of this initiative.[38]

Eritrea views the OAU initiative as an abortive attempt since it did not manage to clear the deck after the US–Rwanda proposals: 'Indeed, while Eritrea had made it clear that the facilitation process was over [US–

---

[36] Statement by the United States President, 10 February 1999.

[37] See press releases by the Djibouti Ministry of Foreign Affairs and International Co-operation, 10 November and 18 November 1998, and by the Eritrean Ministry of Foreign Affairs, 19 November 1998. See also an interview with President Hassan Gouled of Djibouti in which he strongly criticises Issaias Afwerki, calling him a 'nuisance to his neigh-bours' and characterising his regime as follows: 'If we look back at Issaias' seven-year rule of Eritrea, we find that creating instability is the distinctive feature of the system.' *Effoyita* (a monthly Amharic magazine), 12 November 1998.

[38] See also the formulation in the Eritrean 'Document Handed over to the Secretary General of OAU during the Meeting with the President of Eritrea in Asmara', 12 December 1998.

Rwanda initiative] and it regarded the OAU initiative as a new one, the recommendations by the Committee of Ambassadors revolved around the same parameters that had led to the failure of the facilitation process.'[39]

With the resumption of the fighting in February, Ethiopia started to lose some of its diplomatic legitimacy and standing, since most observers drew the conclusion that it had initiated the offensive. Ethiopia, on the other hand, felt that it had been betrayed by the international community in general, and the USA in particular, over the imposition of the UN arms embargo and the criticism of its breach of the air moratorium.[40] This escalation of the conflict and Ethiopian criticism of US statements terminated a US negotiation initiative that for some time had worked in parallel with the OAU initiative. Before we return to the OAU process, let us briefly recapitulate the role of the USA after its aborted peace initiative in June 1998.

The Second US Initiative

After the failed US–Rwanda proposal of 4 June 1998, the US kept a low profile for some time in order to give the OAU a chance to find a solution. By September 1998, however, the US was again ready to be engaged. At that time Eritrea was critical of the renewed US interest and issued a press release exposing its reluctance to support this new initiative:

> As it may be recalled, the prospects of an early and peaceful solution to the border conflict between Eritrea and Ethiopia were curtailed due to the interference of the US team that was entrusted with the task of facilitating communication between the two parties. Continued and unwarranted interference of these officials in the subsequent period has further contributed to negatively influence the OAU initiative underway and to limit its positive contribution.
>
> The US Government has now stated, through personal communication made to the Eritrean President on Wednesday, 16 September 1998, its desire to launch a new initiative. The US delegation will be led by Mr Anthony Lake, the former National Security Advisor. He is expected to visit Asmara and Addis Ababa.
>
> President Issaias has underlined the reservations of the Eritrean Government while expressing its readiness to receive the US envoy.[41]

The US government did not issue any statement explaining why Anthony Lake had replaced Susan Rice as head of a new delegation. The

---

[39] 'Document Handed over to the Secretary General of OAU during the Meeting with the President of Eritrea in Asmara', 12 December 1998.

[40] See for instance the statement 'A New Twist in Eritrea's Campaign of Lies and Prevarication', issued by the FDRE Office of the Government Spokesperson, 5 March 1999.

[41] Statement by the Ministry of Foreign Affairs, Asmara, 18 September 1998.

Anthony Lake delegation carried out four visits to the region during October–January 1999, yet very little information was offered on the rationale of his initiative, nor was the specific mandate of his mission made public. It is clear, however, that America was concerned that if a full-scale war between Eritrea and Ethiopia should erupt, this would create an opportunity for groups advocating political Islam to broaden their activities in the region. Such a scenario would have a negative impact on US economic and political interests not only in the Horn of Africa, but also in the Red Sea and Indian Ocean regions. One must assume that its vital geo-political interests provided at least one element of the rationale for US re-engagement in conflict resolution.[42]

Based on the scant information available, it is difficult to assess the implementation and impact of the Anthony Lake initiative. It is worth noting, however, that the Eritrean attitude towards the initiative changed during its course. High-ranking Eritrean officials told one of the authors that after Anthony Lake's first visit to the region, they had much more confidence in his initiative than they had had in Susan Rice and her delegation. Anthony Lake's last visit was in mid-January 1999, when he met both heads of state. Nothing materialised from his visit, however, and soon thereafter the war recommenced.

Resumption of Full War and the Failure of OAU Diplomacy

In a briefing to the African diplomatic community on 27 January 1999, Prime Minister Meles Zenawi gave what has been interpreted subsequently as a forewarning of the coming resumption of war activities. In the last section of a long statement, he asked:

> So what do we expect from the OAU? Not a whole lot, because the OAU has done what is expected of it. What we expect from member states of the OAU, however, is quite different. We expect member states of the OAU not only to be loyal to the decisions of the OAU … but we are going to ask you to exert all the pressure that you can possibly exert, directly and indirectly, to see to it that the OAU decision is implemented. Furthermore, we would expect all our brothers in Africa to understand that if some amongst us decide to play poker

---

[42] A private newspaper in Ethiopia (*Tomar*, 9 December 1998), referring to informed sources, stated that the US delegation had raised two major points beyond the territorial question in the process of the ongoing peace negotiations between the two countries. First, Ethiopia must be guaranteed access to the sea: thus the entire services of the Port of Assab should be made available to them. Second, the currencies of both countries should circulate on an equal footing in the markets of the two countries. The newspaper reported, however, that there was no indication as to whether Ethiopia would give parts of its territory to Eritrea in exchange for the port of Assab. As a carrot for the parties to accept these proposals, it is claimed that the US government had pledged multi-faceted support to the two countries.

with the rule of law as exemplified by the OAU, if those very same forces have nothing but contempt for our collective decisions and continue to occupy the territory of a member nation, we would not ask you to come to our rescue and fight our wars. That request could be feasible, but we believe unnecessary. That request would be fair, but we believe unnecessary. But we would expect you to fully understand and defend our right to defend ourselves.[43]

After initial air raids on 5 February, the large-scale offensive started the following day on the Badme–Shiraro front along the western section of the Eritrean–Ethiopian border. The conflict escalated rapidly into what has been estimated to be the biggest battle on African soil since the expulsion of Nazi forces from Egypt during the Second World War. The Secretary General of the OAU issued a statement soon after the resumption of the war, expressing his concern and urging the parties to refrain from further military action. He also acknowledged the Framework Agreement as the only viable instrument to achieve a peaceful settlement, and in this regard reminded the Eritreans that 'in order to advance the peace process, the OAU High-Level Delegation awaits the response which the Eritrean side undertook to communicate to it after receiving the clarifications sought on the elements of the Framework Agreement'.[44] By mid-February, while the military clashes continued, the OAU High-Level Delegation issued a statement that it was still seeking a breakthrough; the following week they visited both capitals to negotiate with the two governments. Foreign Minister Seyoum Mesfin, on behalf of the Ethiopian government, reconfirmed its commitment to the OAU Framework Agreement when receiving the delegation, and made it clear that the cessation of hostilities 'will be realised when Eritrea joins Ethiopia in accepting the OAU Framework Agreement'.[45]

After an intensive Ethiopian offensive against the Eritrean positions at Badme towards the end of February, the Ethiopian army managed to break through the Eritrean trenches. Over 40,000 Eritrean troops were deployed in the area, but Ethiopia, using a 'wave' strategy of pouring thousands of men against the Eritrean positions during the three-day battle of 23–26 February, managed to drive the Eritrean army out of Badme town and the surrounding Badme plains. The victory was won at great cost, and conservative estimates suggest that Ethiopian casualties at Badme

[43] 'Verbatim Briefing to the African Diplomatic Community by Prime Minister Meles Zenawi, 27 January 1999', issued by the FDRE Office of the Government Spokesperson, 30 January 1999.

[44] 'Statement by the Secretary General of the OAU on the Current Situation between Eritrea and Ethiopia', Addis Ababa, 8 February 1999.

[45] 'H.E. Seyoum Mesfin, Minister of Foreign Affairs of the Federal Democratic Republic of Ethiopia, received the OAU High-Level Delegation Ambassadorial Committee on Feb. 19, 1999 and exchanged views with them on the current hostilities between Ethiopia and Eritrea', statement issued by the FDRE Office of the Government Spokesperson, 21 February 1999.

reached 10,000, whereas Eritrea probably had a lower casualty rate since they were in defensive positions.[46]

The loss of Badme to Ethiopia was a terrible blow for the Eritrean army and for the prestige of President Issaias Afwerki. Some months earlier he had said that 'expecting Eritrea to withdraw is as unlikely as the sun never rising again'. This Eritrean military arrogance greatly provoked the Tigrean military, inspiring them to name the Badme offensive 'Operation Sunset'.

The day after the defeat at Badme, the Eritrean government announced its acceptance of the OAU Framework Agreement. On the same day, 27 February, the President of the UN Security Council made a statement welcoming Eritrean acceptance of the Framework, demanding an immediate halt to all hostilities, and calling on the parties to refrain from further use of force.[47] In the aftermath of Badme, some confusion arose over Eritrea's acceptance of the Framework Agreement – although the Eritrean government conveyed this to the UN immediately, as the President of the Security Council confirmed in his announcement on 27 February. In a press release from the Eritrean Ministry of Defence from 1 March quoted by the government-owned Eritrean News Agency, however, military spokesmen claimed that

> We [Eritrea] have left our position with our forces intact and have taken up new positions.... They [Ethiopia] are obviously prepared to sacrifice their men for what can only be short term gain, but they have not changed the military balance at all. That is what is important. Territory can change hands.[48]

Neither did the Ethiopian government seem to be aware of Eritrean acceptance of the Framework Agreement at this early stage. In its press release of 1 March, the Ethiopian Government Spokesperson's Office condemned Eritrea for its arrogance towards the OAU, and asked rhetorically: 'Why does President Issaias and the EPLF clique in Asmara have such a disdainful attitude towards the OAU and the strenuous efforts to find a peaceful solution to the conflict?'[49]

Only days after the Eritrean acceptance of the OAU Framework

---

[46] In a statement issued by the Eritrean defence forces on 27 February 1999 they claimed that in the four-day Badme offensive 'a total of 9,000 TPLF soldiers were killed, 12,000 wounded, 170 including a battalion commander captured'. The Eritrean statement does not mention the exact number of its own casualties, stating only that they were 'minimal'. The Ethiopian press release after the battle, 'Total Victory for Operation Sunset', states that the Ethiopian defence forces 'captured, killed and wounded tens of thousands of enemy army personnel' (issued by the FDRE Office of the Government Spokesperson on 28 February 1999). It does not say anything about its own casualty rates.

[47] 'Ethiopia–Eritrea: Statement by the President of the Security Council' (S/PRST/1999/9), 27 February 1999.

[48] *Eritrean News Agency Update*, 1 March 1999.

[49] 'Ethiopia Seeks Lasting Peace in the Region', statement issued by the FDRE Office of the Government Spokesperson, 1 March 1999.

Agreement, the situation was not progressing towards negotiations, but degenerating instead into the now-habitual mutual accusations of subversive activities and distrust. Thus an Eritrean Foreign Ministry statement of 2 March claimed to have exposed Ethiopia's acceptance of the Framework Agreement as a bluff, since it had not ceased its military offensive. Indeed, the Eritrean authorities now aimed to expose what they claimed had been the main reason for the war all along, as the statement explains: 'Many may have thought that this was a simple border dispute that has gone beyond proportions. But now it is becoming clearer that Ethiopia's agenda encompasses expansionist territorial ambition on its sovereign neighbour and subversion of its government.'[50] Soon thereafter, representatives of the OAU High-Level Delegation visited Asmara, held discussions with the Eritrean government and received their reassurance that Eritrea fully accepted the agreement and welcomed an immediate ceasefire and cessation of hostilities.[51] Ethiopia, on the other hand, instead of embracing the victory at Badme and accepting Eritrea's approval of the Framework Agreement, questioned the new position Eritrea had taken and rejected its approval of the peace agreement as a purely tactical move:

> The statements of Eritrean officials and the actions of the Eritrean army on the ground thus prove that so far there has been no change of heart. The Eritrean government is not trying to cut its losses after its humiliating defeat in Badme. It is simply trying to buy time to regroup and reorganise in order to retain the Ethiopian territories that it continues to occupy to this day and regain Badme.[52]

When we analyse, from an outsider's perspective, the steps taken by the warring parties and by the OAU negotiator in the aftermath of Eritrea's acceptance of the Framework Agreement, we are left with a feeling of puzzlement. As the war on the ground continued, the parties became engaged in a semantic exercise over the interpretation of the conditions of withdrawal outlined in the Framework Agreement. The focal point of discussion was whether Eritrea needed to withdraw from all occupied territories in order to confirm the acceptance of the agreement, as argued by Ethiopia. An Ethiopian government communication of 12 November 1998 referred to a clarification given by the OAU High-Level Delegation:

> It is … to be noted that the High-Level Delegation underscored in its clarification, that with regard to Article 3 [in the Framework Agreement], the Eritrean forces are to withdraw from all Ethiopian territories that they have occupied since May 6, 1998. Accordingly, as underlined in no uncertain terms by its Prime Minister, the demand that Eritrea must withdraw from all occupied Ethiopian territories for peace to be achieved between Ethiopia and

---

[50] 'Ethiopia is Intent on Waging War: Peace Was Never on its Agenda', statement by the Eritrean Ministry of Foreign Affairs, Asmara, 2 March 1999.

[51] 'OAU Delegation Visit', press release, Ministry of Foreign Affairs, Asmara, 5 March 1999.

[52] 'A New Twist in Eritrea's Campaign of Lies and Prevarication', statement issued by the FDRE Office of the Government Spokesperson, 5 March 1999.

Eritrea has been a firm Ethiopian position and a fundamental and irreducible minimum condition....[53]

The Eritrean government, however, referred to the points of clarification given by the OAU the 26 January 1999 to its list of questions submitted to the High-Level Delegation on 12 December 1998.[54] On the issue of redeployment of forces in the Framework Agreement the clarification states that 'the redeployment is of Eritrean troops from Badme Town and its environs' (paragraph 2c) and that 'environs refer to the area surrounding Badme Town' (paragraph 1b). Eritrea rejected Ethiopia's claim that they have to redeploy from all disputed territories (including Zalambesssa and Alientena) before the implementation of a ceasefire, and referred again to the OAU's clarification of the Framework Agreement. Eritrea asked: 'According to Ethiopia, "Badme and environs" means "all Ethiopian border territories occupied by Eritrea since May 6, 1998", what are the OAU's views?' And the OAU responded: 'See paragraph 36 in the Report on the efforts of the OAU High-Level Delegation, presented to the Fourth Ordinary Session of the Central Organ, meeting at Heads of State Level, which states: "the High-Level Delegation took note of the position of Prime Minister Meles Zenawi. There was, however, no further discussion on the issue" (paragraph 1c).' Obviously, Eritrea interpreted this as a rejection of Ethiopia's claim for Eritrean withdrawal from all occupied territories.

It is plausible to believe that Eritrea accepted the Framework Agreement on the same day as their defeat at Badme was announced, since at that time the precondition in the agreement was, *de facto*, met: Eritrean forces no longer controlled 'Badme and its environs'. Eritrea at that stage had nothing to lose, in terms of military withdrawal, by accepting the agreement, since they had been forced out of Badme. On the contrary, they had everything to gain by accepting the agreement, since it stated that Badme should be a demilitarised zone, even if Ethiopian civilian administration was supposed to be restored. This implied that Ethiopia should actually withdraw its military forces from Badme and its environs, and give up the territory that it had won by sacrificing thousands of its soldiers! This was, of course, impossible for Ethiopia to accept. In an interview given on 2 March 1999 to one of the authors by Yemane ('Jamaica') Kidane, a high-ranking Ethiopian government official and party cadre, this view was confirmed. He stated quite explicitly that: 'The rationale of the Framework Agreement was to avoid a war. Now that the war has erupted and we have won back Badme, the Framework Agreement

---

[53] 'Ethiopia Was, Is and Will Always Be Loyal to the OAU Framework Agreement', statement issued by the Foreign Ministry, Addis Ababa, 10 March 1999.

[54] See letter of 12 March 1999 sent to the President of the UN Security Council by the Eritrean Permanent Representative to the UN.

is nothing! The conditions on the ground have changed, and if the OAU process shall continue, they have to start over again to clarify the principles on the ground.'[55]

The OAU was, and still is, reluctant to clarify the matters and principles in the Framework Agreement and to 'enforce' both sides' compliance with it. There might be two reasons for this: it does not have the institutional capacity to do it; and it dare not openly challenge Ethiopia. Consequently, during the spring the parties continued the war on the ground as well as the war of semantics. The issue of the interpretation of the practical implementation of the Framework Agreement was addressed regularly, without any consensus being reached. The parties raised the issue before both the OAU and the UN, without receiving any decisive answers or action in response.

The terrible and devastating warfare between Eritrea and Ethiopia continued in March and April, with a lull in fighting in May and at the beginning of June, and then a major new offensive at the Badme–Mereb front towards the end of June. How many casualties the two parties have sustained is difficult to estimate, since both sides exaggerate the numbers of casualties inflicted upon the enemy and minimise their own losses. With the start of the rainy season in July, however, the fighting ceased and the two sides used the opportunity to regroup their forces and to recruit thousands more troops to their training centres.

On 11 July 1999 African leaders gathered in Algeria for the last OAU summit of the century. Immediately prior to the sumit, Libya's Muammar Gaddafi had tried to bring Issaias Afwerki and Meles Zenawi to Tripoli for negotiations, but failed. Thus the Eritrean–Ethiopian war dominated discussions at the OAU session. Algerian President Abdelaziz Bouteflika took over the chairmanship of the OAU, and many had hoped that this would create a new momentum in the peace negotiations between the two warring countries. The OAU summit endorsed a new document, 'Modalities for the Implementation of the OAU Framework Agreement', which was worked out by the OAU High-Level Delegation and presented to Eritrea and Ethiopia on 12 July. The Modalities agreement called for the two parties to reaffirm 'their commitment to the principle of the non-use of force to settle disputes' and 'their acceptance of the Framework Agreement and commit themselves to implement it in good faith'.[56] The agreement further stated that:

> The Eritrean Government commits itself to redeploy its forces outside the territories they occupied after 6 May 1998.

[55] Interviewed by Kjetil Tronvoll, Addis Ababa, 2 March 1999.
[56] 'Modalities for the Implementation of the OAU Framework Agreement on the Settlement of the Dispute between Ethiopia and Eritrea', presented 12 July 1999. See Appendix 13 for a full version of the document.

The Ethiopian Government commits itself to redeploy, thereafter, its forces from positions taken after 6 February 1999 and which were not under Ethiopian administration before 6 May 1998.

The redeployment of forces would not prejudice the final status of the territories concerned, which would be determined at the end of the border delimitation and demarcation. The document also stated that the 'modalities for the re-establishment of the civilian Administration and population in the concerned territories shall be worked out after the cessation of hostilites'. Moreover, the implementation of the agreement was to be supervised by a group of military observers deployed by the OAU in cooperation with the UN.

At the closing session of the OAU summit, Issaias Afwerki announced Eritrea's acceptance of the Modalities agreement and a formal letter of confirmation was delivered to the OAU Chairman. In accepting the agreement, however, Eritrea observed that, 'undoing the damage done by the conflict does not only require redeployment but, more importantly, addressing the humanitarian dimensions of the conflict. In this regard, it is imperative to fully compensate the deportees, if not for the irreparable harm done to them, at least for expropriated property.'[57] Prime Minister Meles Zenawi's statement at the end of the summit also focused on the Modalities agreement, but he did not confirm Ethiopia's acceptance of it. Rather, he stressed the ambiguity of Eritrea's acceptance, since Issaias Afwerki had put forward new criteria for the modalities as a condition of Eritrea's acceptance. Meles explained that:

> We cannot accept that modality by emasculating it, gutting the substance out of it, bringing in totally new substance and then say we accept it. That is not acceptable. That is rejection. We will not engage in such a subterfuge. If we accept the package, Your excellencies, we will tell you so. No ifs, no buts.[58]

The Modalities agreement was brought back to Ethiopia for further discussions and analysis, and on 20 July 1999 the Council of Ministers issued a statement accepting the proposals put forward in the agreement, since, as they pointed out, 'the proposals reflect the position taken by Ethiopia since the beginning of the conflict'. But, the Ethiopian government continued to warn that Eritrea was 'putting up various preconditions in order to oppose the peace proposals':

> The Ethiopian Government, therefore, does not believe that the EPLF will accept and implement proposals aimed at the peaceful resolution of the conflict. Since it understands that the Issayas regime will not refrain from continuing the war, the Ethiopian Government will not lessen its vigilance. In

[57] 'Eritrea Formally Accepts OAU Peace Formula', press release, Ministry of Foreign Affairs, Asmara, 15 July 1999.
[58] Statement made by Prime Minister Meles Zenawi on the OAU summit in Algiers, 14 July 1999.

this regard, the heroic Defense Forces must continue their unyielding effort to ensure that the sovereignty of our country is respected. The entire people of Ethiopia must redouble their efforts to enhance the significant contributions they have already made to ensure the respect of our sovereignty.[59]

Thus just as the two parties accepted the Modalities agreement, the process was once more derailed and stalled. The facilitators believed they had created a true momentum for negotiations, and both the UN Security Council and the US issued press statements which praised the acceptance of the Modalities, without understanding the complications already created by Eritrea's preconditions. The United States also dispatched their special envoy Anthony Lake to the region to follow up on the implementation of the agreement. After a week of shuttle diplomacy between Asmara and Addis, Lake went back to the US and 'diplomatic officials' were making unsubstantiated claims that 'great progress' had been achieved.[60] By the end of July representatives from Algeria, the OAU, the US and the UN were meeting in Algiers in order to start to work out the technical details of a ceasefire agreement between Eritrea and Ethiopia.[61] During the weekend of 7–8 August an OAU team submitted the 'Technical Arrangements for the Implementation of the Framework Agreement and Modalities' to Eritrea and Ethiopia. This agreement itemised and outlined an elaborate plan of action for the implementation of the two foregoing agreements – the Framework Agreement and the Modalities. No new issues were supposed to be introduced into the Technical Arrangements and the document was final: no amendments to the plan were possible.[62] After considering the content of the Technical Arrangements, Eritrea officially notified the OAU Chairman's Special Envoy of its acceptance of the arrangements. Ethiopia, for its part, welcomed the submission of the Technical Arrangements and reiterated its will to contribute to a peaceful resolution to the conflict. Ethiopia also 'expressed the wish to seek some clarification on some aspects of the arrangements', however, and thus no confirmation of acceptance was given to the Special Envoy upon his visit to Addis Ababa.[63] The following week, the Ethiopian Government Spokesperson issued a statement elaborating on the reasons why Ethiopia had felt it necessary to seek clarifications from the OAU concerning the Technical Arrangements, and thus 'to ensure that the *status quo ante* is

---

[59] 'Statement of the Council of Ministers of the Federal Democratic Republic of Ethiopia', 20 July 1999, Addis Ababa.

[60] BBC World News, 'Optimism over Horn Negotiations', 26 July 1999.

[61] See press news from Reuters, 'Experts Meet on Ceasefire between Ethiopia, Eritrea', 29 July 1999, and AP News Service, 'Talks on Peace Plan Open in Algeria', 31 July 1999.

[62] See Appendix 14 for full version of the Technical Arrangements.

[63] See OAU press release, 'Technical Arrangements for the Implementation of the Framework Agreement and Modalities Presented to Eritrea and Ethiopia', Addis Ababa and Algiers, 11 August 1999.

restored, the Technical Arrangements must leave absolutely no loopholes for President Issaias to have a chance to wreak havoc with their interpretation'.[64] But when the Ethiopian government was putting Eritrea's acceptance of the Technicalities in doubt, President Issaias Afwerki visited the US and expressed cautious optimism that a successful peace agreement would be forthcoming.[65]

The Ethiopian government presented an elaborate list of issues to the OAU for clarification of what it regarded as inconsistencies with the original Framework Agreement and Modalities.[66] The 'cardinal principle' not accommodated in the Technicalities from the Ethiopian point of view, however, was that 'aggression cannot be rewarded'. This was, according to Ethiopia, dealt with in an unsatisfactory manner in the provisions relating to the restoration of the *status quo ante*.[67] The second major point of disagreement centred on the issue of a peacekeeping force in the area. The Framework Agreement stated that an OAU Military Observer Group in cooperation with the UN was supposed to be established in the border areas, while the Technicalities presupposed that a UN peacekeeping force would be deployed. Another issue raised by Ethiopia was the lack of clarity about the restoration of civilian administration, including an armed militia, in the disputed areas.

The OAU responded to the Ethiopian inquiries to the Technical Arrangements in writing on 23 August 1999.[68] Basically, the OAU stressed the need to see all three documents – the Framework Agreement, the Modalities and the Technical Arrangements – as a whole, constituting one broad settlement plan. Detailed semantic studies on the coherence between the documents were seen as inappropriate and the OAU response to Ethiopia simply elaborated on the provisions outlined in the Technical Arrangements without making any reformulations. In its conclusion, the OAU repeated the fact that the Technical Arrangements were not open to amendment and that the response would 'pave the way to acceptance of the settlement plan (including Technical Arrangements) and to the rapid implementation of a peaceful and lasting solution to the conflict'.[69]

During the weeks and months following the presentation of the Technical Arrangements, the two governments intensified their propaganda efforts

[64] 'Lasting and Durable Peace', press release, Office of the Government Spokesperson, Addis Ababa, 16 August 1999.

[65] See Reuters, 'Eritrea Optimistic on Peace with Ethiopia', Washington, 16 August 1999, and Associated Press, 'Eritrean Leader: Peace Prospects Good', Washington, 16 August 1999.

[66] See Appendix 15 for full list of issues raised by Ethiopia.

[67] See 'Statement on the Current Situation in the Ethio-Eritrean Conflict', Ministry of Foreign Affairs, Addis Ababa, 4 September 1999.

[68] See Appendix 16 for the full document.

[69] See 'Clarifications of the OAU in Response to the Questions Raised by Ethiopia Relating to the Technical Arrangements'.

to justify their own positions, and to denounce the other side. Thus an Eritrean Foreign Ministry official stated that 'Ethiopia is holding peace hostage'.[70] Ethiopia, on the other hand, pointed to Eritrea's sudden shift of position from initial rejection of the Framework Agreement to full acceptance of the OAU peace accords, and explained that the Eritreans were 'simply spewing the kind of rhetoric they know the international community wants to hear. Either way, the Eritrean government cannot be trusted.'[71] In the midst of mutual accusations, the OAU kept quiet and a US delegation composed of Susan Rice, architect of the first US–Rwanda peace plan, and the envoy Anthony Lake returned to the region in order to try to push the peace process forward. The trip was fruitless and they went back to Washington without brokering Ethiopian acceptance of the Technical Arrangements.

Without any seeming success the Ethiopian government tried during the autumn to explain its principled stand against endorsement of the Technical Arrangements.[72] No new points of argument were presented, and it is difficult to understand why it was impossible to accept the Technicalities as long as they endorsed the Framework and Modalities agreements. To enter into a discussion of semantics, as the Ethiopian government did, while several hundreds of thousands of troops are standing by to engage in combat, is somewhat incomprehensible to the international community. No matter the gravity of the situation, the process takes on the appearance of a farce: Ethiopia asks for clarifications of details and language while Eritrea calls for the international community to put pressure on Ethiopia to sign the agreement. Just ten months earlier, the situation had been the other way around: Eritrea delayed acceptance of the Framework Agreement, while Ethiopia called for sanctions and international pressure!

At the beginning of December Prime Minister Meles Zenawi explained in an extensive interview with Ethiopian television that following the OAU clarifications on the Technical Arrangements, 'it was no longer a question of whether the document was clear or not but a question of whether it was adequate or not'.[73] The Ethiopian government subsequently submitted a 14-page document to the OAU detailing its problems with the Technicalities and Ethiopia's position in that regard. As the situation stood at the end of

[70] See ERINA, 'Clarifications Received: Still No Response from Addis', Asmara, 26 August 1999.

[71] See 'Eritrea on the Issue of Withdrawal: Then and Now', press release, Office of the Government Spokesperson, Addis Ababa, 31 August 1999.

[72] See for instance, 'Ethiopia's Bottom Line: Aggression Must Be Reversed', statement by the Ministry of Foreign Affairs, Addis Ababa, 14 September 1999; and 'Status Quo Ante: The Reversal of Eritrea's Aggression', statement by the Office of the Government Spokesperson, Addis Ababa, 9 November 1999.

[73] The interview was screened on Ethi TV, 6 December 1999. It has been translated and transcribed by Walta Information Centre, and is available at: http://www.telecom.net.et/~walta/.

1999, the OAU had not given any public response to the Ethiopian document of inquiry. What happens next will depend on the OAU's willingness to amend the Technical Arrangements, which in principle were not amendable. To put even more pressure on the OAU, Tekeda Alemu, Ethiopia's Deputy Minister of Foreign Affairs, confirmed in an interview on 14 December 1999 that since 'the Technical Arrangements fail to be consistent with the two basic documents and accordingly they fail to ensure the full return of the *status quo ante*, Ethiopia finds it absolutely difficult to accept the Technical Arrangements'.[74]

The Failure of Diplomacy

The Eritrean–Ethiopian war is not only a case of the failure to establish mechanisms of peaceful inter-state relationship between the new state of Eritrea and its old 'coloniser', Ethiopia. It is also an illuminating example of the failure of regional and international diplomacy, in which once again the OAU has shown its inability to cope with conflict prevention and resolution in Africa. The role of the UN in the conflict should also be a reminder of how differently the international community responds to conflicts and crisis in Africa compared with similar events elsewhere in the world. If only a fraction of the resources put into resolving the Kosovo crisis had been devoted to conflict resolution in the Eritrean–Ethiopian war, accord would probably have been achieved. This was admitted by the UN Secretary General's envoy to the region, Mohamed Sahnoun, in a press briefing after his visit in late January and early February 1999. According to the official minutes, Sahnoun said that

> the United Nations should be given more means to address such issues and that the international community should be more involved. It was not enough to pass a resolution and forget about the issue. There should be strong bilateral actions and a warning of sanctions to be imposed if the conflict severely affected civilians.[75]

Obviously, the main responsibility for the repeated breakdown in diplomatic efforts rests with the warring parties themselves. Both governments have shown a lack of political maturity during the escalation and consolidation of the crisis. Choosing violence as a political strategy comes easily to two former resistance movements, whose leaders have been socialised in warfare since their early twenties. Sadly, it seems to be more difficult to govern states in peace than to run battle-hardened guerilla movements in war.

[74] See 'Exclusive interview to Walta Information Centre (WIC)', 14 December 1999, http://www.telecom.net.et/~walta/.

[75] 'Press Briefing by Special Envoy of Secretary General in Africa', 10 February 1999.

The main cause of the inadequate diplomacy we have seen from the OAU, the UN, the US and the warring parties is the fact that no one is willing to address the deeper causes of the conflict. As we have tried to demonstrate in this book, this war is not a border conflict. The territorial issues are merely the expression of deeper levels of conflict between the EPLF and the TPLF of which the international actors are ignorant and which the parties have not been willing to disclose. Our following concluding chapter will highlight some of these core issues.

8 From Border War to Total War

On 18 December 1998 the OAU High-Level Delegation recommended that the Eritrean armed forces then in Badme town and its environs be redeployed to the positions they held before 6 May 1998, without prejudging the final status of the area concerned. The OAU proposal – the Framework Agreement – further recommended the redeployment be supervised by a group of military observers to be deployed by the OAU with the support of the UN.

The OAU proposal was indeed very similar to the US–Rwanda recommendations of June 1998 in its description of the immediate cause of the conflict, but also differed markedly from the earlier document in many important aspects. The OAU High-Level Delegation had more time in which to collect all the relevant facts presented to it by the parties in conflict, and presented a report that was unanimously agreed by the member states that were entrusted with the task.

The recommendations of the OAU High-Level Delegation were actually made known in August 1998. The Ambassadors Committee had completed its fact-finding mission and reached the conclusions which were later adopted and stamped with the approval of the High-Level Delegation. Thus after August 1998 observers of the conflict, as well as the parties to it, could with certainty predict the final pronouncement which, however, had to await the OAU High-Level Delegation meeting on 17–18 November 1998.

The reaction of Eritrea to the OAU's Framework was predictable. Although Eritrea did not reject the Framework in an outright manner, as with the US–Rwanda proposal, it nonetheless adopted a strategy of indefinite postponement. As a veteran observer of the region described it, Eritrea adopted a strategy of diplomatic filibustering, again and again demanding explanations on various points of the proposals set forward.

Meanwhile, Eritrea persistently called for a ceasefire and immediate demarcation of the boundaries. Such appeals, quite expectedly, were rejected by Ethiopia, whose position was further strengthened by the Framework.

From 10 June 1998 until 6 February 1999 there was no serious military confrontation between the two countries. Officially, the Ethiopians hoped that the OAU mediation efforts would bring the Eritrean government to its senses; at the same time it spared neither effort nor money in rebuilding an army big enough to defeat the 'Eritrean aggressors'. Eritrea, as one observer noted, instead of exploiting the *de facto* ceasefire (from 18 November to 6 February), continued to question the details of the Framework while at the same time calling for an official declaration of ceasefire on the part of Ethiopia.

The most intriguing question is why the Eritrean government did not accept the Framework Agreement, even though it undoubtedly would have meant a certain loss of prestige for the Eritrean leadership *vis-à-vis* its neighbours and also, perhaps, in the eyes of some Eritrean citizens. Acceptance would have also meant that Eritrea would have to begin the frustrating process of picking up negotiations with its Ethiopian counterpart in most fields of Eritrean–Ethiopian relations. Yet we believe that acceptance would not have threatened the position of President Issaias Afwerki in any significant manner.

A veteran observer suggested that two closely interrelated processes conditioned the actions of the Eritrean leadership. The first was the suspicion that Eritrean withdrawal would lead the Ethiopians to demand concessions in exchange for border negotiations. The second factor was that sheer intransigence, nurtured by arrogance and feelings of superiority, did not allow the Eritrean government to implicitly admit having made a mistake. If there is some truth in such an analysis, then one has to deduce the conception and use of power in the present Eritrean state system.

We have directed the question to Eritrea – why did it reject both the US–Rwanda plan and the OAU Framework? – because it was Eritrea that occupied by force a contested area previously administered by Ethiopia. Nonetheless, in view of the declared commitment of the Ethiopian government to peace and development, it is legitimate to direct the question to both parties. Whereas the position of the Ethiopian government as the aggrieved party has been stated repeatedly, public opinion within Ethiopia has at least the opportunity to raise and discuss other options. Views ranging from the need to withstand a total war of annihilation to Ethiopia's role in the creation of the conflict are widely discussed without, however, appearing to influence the official position of the Ethiopian government. According to the government, the country is prepared to go to war until all the areas occupied by Eritrea revert to it.

How far is Ethiopia prepared to go in order to reverse Eritrea's forceful occupation of a few villages whose history and economy are so closely entwined with the latter? The Ethiopian government knows quite well that Eritrea sooner or later has to negotiate, as it stands to lose more from the economic blockade. Why did the Ethiopian government pursue the strategy of rearmament, spending hundreds of millions of dollars in the purchase of arms? According to some estimates the Ethiopian government may have purchased arms to the tune of one billion US dollars. Are such huge expenses justifiable in view of the severe famine that looms over the country? Why didn't the Ethiopian government continue with the policy of magnanimity *vis-à-vis* Eritrea which it showed in the early 1990s? Why did the Ethiopian government choose to draw parallels, which are to say the least highly tenuous, between 'Eritrean aggression' and the Italian invasion of Ethiopia in the 1930s? There can be no denying the fact that a great deal of precious time for defusing the conflict (from June 1998 to 6 February 1999) was lost.

On the 27 February 1999 the Eritrean government announced that it had accepted the OAU Framework for peaceful resolution of the border dispute. The timing as well as the motives for Eritrean acceptance have been subjects of discussion and speculation. The Ethiopian government reacted by stating that the Eritrean acceptance was a strategy for gaining time so as to recover from the heavy defeat it suffered during the successful Operation Sunset. Ethiopia attempted to prove that the Eritrean government was maintaining its belligerent attitudes and that Eritrea was rebuilding its military might for a continued war of aggression and destabilisation.[1] The Eritrean government stated that its acceptance of the Framework had nothing to do with the reoccupation of Badme by the Ethiopian forces. Moreover, its withdrawal from Badme was motivated by its concern for the lives of its soldiers rather by reasons of military setback.[2]

The US, through its Anthony Lake mission, had tried to bring the parties to the negotiating table. The timid efforts of the European Union, Italy and the UN did not appear to have any clout behind them and were rejected unceremoniously by both parties. Anthony Lake's shuttle diplomacy (he reportedly travelled to Asmara and Addis Ababa four times between September 1998 and January 1999) failed, his mission remains the most enigmatic. So far, nothing of consequence has been leaked or

---

[1] See the website of the Ethiopian Government Spokesperson from February 1999 onwards: http://www.ethiospokes.net/.

[2] Such was the theme repeatedly stressed by the official media (*Eritrea Profile* and the Tigrinya tri-weekly *Hadas Eretra*) between 27 February and June 1999. Since June 1999 the Eritrean media have dwelt more on the extent of its victory against the Ethiopian forces at the battle of Tsorona in June 1999. Cf. Tesfagiorgis 1999, p. 164.

made public.[3] Why did the conflict that the Eritrean government described as a border dispute until the end of 1999 prove to be so difficult to
resolve? Although it is possible to dwell on the existing conspiratorial
explanations as well as to come up with new ones, it is not certain that
such explanations would bring us any closer to understanding a conflict
that at first glance appears to be so enticingly simple. In reality neither the
Eritrean nor the Ethiopian government is keen to limit the conflict to what
they both continue to describe as a border dispute. We believe that there
are at least three reasons for this underlying and persistent hostility.

War of Annihilation

The first reason is that each country is convinced that the other is out to
destroy it. The Ethiopian government, for example, has suggested
repeatedly that Eritrea provoked the war on the assumption that it would
trigger a military uprising of the opposition groups in Ethiopia (mainly the
Oromo and the Somalis). The objective of Eritrean aggression is to
dismember Ethiopia. No doubt this is a conspiracy theory developed and
elaborated by the Ethiopian side, and as such one ought to be ready to set
it aside when better explanations are available. There may not have been
too much substance to such a conspiracy theory at the beginning of the
conflict. In the aftermath of the occupation of Badme the position of the
Eritrean government was contradictory, but not as inflexible as it later
became. At one time the Eritrean government stated that it would never
withdraw from Badme; at another time it ridiculed the importance which
the Ethiopian government attached to Eritrean withdrawal by describing
Badme and other contested territories as barren and marginal areas. The
Eritrean government called for direct negotiations on border and other
issues of common interest. There is indeed good reason to believe that in
so far as the Eritrean government had a precise motive for occupying
Badme, it was to speed up the boundary demarcation process as well as to
force the EPRDF government to review its economic policies *vis-à-vis*
Eritrea.

It is tempting to argue that, since it has accepted the entire OAU
Framework Eritrea is now ready to initiate the long process of demarcating borders and normalising relations with Ethiopia. Unfortunately,
however, we believe that ample scope for doubt remains. While pointing
an accusing finger at Ethiopia as the party which has refused to accept the
Framework fully, Eritrea has not in any way diminished its propaganda

---

[3] It would indeed be very interesting to know what went on in these meetings. Let us hope
that Anthony Lake's mission is properly documented. Undoubtedly future historians
would have great use for such material.

warfare against Ethiopia. Eritrea's daily broadcasts in Tigrinya, Amharic and Oromo beamed to Ethiopia are all designed to arouse rebellion against what Eritrea defines as the Woyane minority regime in Ethiopia. Although we cannot substantiate such claims with hard and credible evidence, Eritrean support to Somali and Oromo armed combatants is regularly reported by observers of the Horn.[4] Not only is Ethiopia convinced that Eritrea supports Somali and Oromo terrorists (and Ethiopian perceptions, like Eritrean ones, are very important factors to take into account), but the US government is also on record regarding Eritrea's supply of arms to factions in Somalia.[5]

The refusal of the Ethiopian government to hold direct negotiations before the formal and complete withdrawal of Eritrean forces from Badme, coupled with massive deportations of Eritreans from Ethiopia, might have led to a redefinition of the underlying reasons for the conflict. It is indeed highly indicative of the economic role of the Eritreans in Ethiopia that the Eritrean government considered their deportation a far worse action than the actual war itself. Although it is difficult to date the change of policy clearly, the introduction of special programmes in Amharic beamed to Ethiopia from Asmara in August 1998 could be taken as a step in the policy of destabilisation. A similar programme has been beamed to the Oromo people since September 1998. It is also from the beginning of August 1998 that the Eritrean government newspapers began to describe the Ethiopian government as a purely TPLF (Woyane) government and no longer as a coalition government. The government papers mince no words (in English or Tigrinya) in exhorting the Ethiopian people to rise up against the Woyane minority group that is oppressing and leading them to war.

Though initially evidence was lacking, the Ethiopian government accused Eritrea of arming the Oromo Liberation Front (OLF) and Somali factions inside Ethiopia and in Somalia. Quite naturally, the Ethiopian government interpreted Eritrean armed support to opposition groups as additional evidence of Eritrea's long-term policy of dismembering Ethiopia. Although the amount and extent of support to the OLF remains unsubstantiated, Eritrean support to the Somali factions appears to have been confirmed. Susan Rice, the US under-secretary for African Affairs, recently testified to the US Senate that Eritrea was supplying arms to Somali factions.[6] Lara Santoro of the *Christian Science Monitor,* reporting from Mogadishu, wrote in no uncertain terms that Eritrean personnel and military supplies were made available to Oromo

---

[4] See for instance Gilkes and Plaut 1999, p. 74. The authors appear to be convinced about Eritrea's destabilising activities, although they do not reveal their sources.

[5] US State Department, see Appendix 12.

[6] *Ibid.*

and Somali factions in southern Somalia.[7]

The resumption of the war early in February 1999, the forced withdrawal of the Eritrean army from Badme on 26 February and the heavy casualties which both sides suffered in the intense battles in March and April appear to have contributed further to the hardening of the Eritrean position. The messages put out in the Eritrean government newspapers and in their information bulletin on the Internet lead us to believe that the Eritrean government has lost hope of resolving the conflict by means other than war. The manner in which the Eritrean media portray the conflict, its casualties and the Ethiopian government strongly indicates that the Eritrean government has very little interest in a peaceful resolution.

In their turn the Eritreans have argued ever since May 1998 that Ethiopian expansionist ambitions lay behind the war. At first these ambitions were explained and defined with reference to the border areas. But after the fighting in May–June 1998, the Eritrean media projected the view both inside the country and abroad that TPLF (Woyane) was using Ethiopia and its resources for the expansion of the province of Tigray. The Eritrean media repeatedly reminded the Ethiopian people that one day the 'TPLF ruling clique' would dump the rest of Ethiopia after establishing and consolidating an expanded Tigray. The message was that Eritrea and the rest of Ethiopia would have to do something to put an end to such minority politics. These views gained prominence from August 1998 onwards.

The more the Eritrean media tried to depict Ethiopia as a country ruled by an oppressive minority which looked first and foremost after its own narrow regional and ethnic interest, the more determined the Ethiopian government became not only to push Eritrea out of the occupied territories but also to bring down the EPLF government in Asmara. By September 1998 the strategy of the Ethiopian government was either to topple the government of Issaias Afwerki or to weaken him so badly that he would cease to threaten Ethiopia's northern border. There was a serious intent behind the rhetoric that was repeated *ad nauseam* by the Ethiopian media. Military expenditures and military recruitment were initiated on a scale out of all proportion to the initial issue of the conflict. Ethiopia began to organise and finance Eritrean groups ready to fight against the Eritrean army or to liberate their region from the oppressive rule of the dictatorial regime of EPLF.

It is very possible that the Eritrean government and army may have talked themselves into believing that the armed conflict which picked up in intensity after February 1999 would not end until either the Ethiopians had achieved their goal or the Eritreans had succeeded in defeating them.

[7] Lara Santoro, *Christian Science Monitor*, 22 July 1999.

It is also possible that the Ethiopian government had reached the point of no return when Eritrea's supply of arms to Somali and Oromo opposition groups began to make a difference to the scale of conflict inside Ethiopia.

At this juncture it is worth mentioning the role of the electronic media and the impact of huge losses in both armies on the conduct of the war. Unlike the old thirty-year war of independence, when news from the front was supplied randomly and not interactively, the current conflict is carried out as much on the Internet as on the ground. Public participation on both sides has been actively solicited; and, to judge from the amount of material that is pouring out of all the websites, there appears to be a tremendous response. In this war daily events reach the public via cyberspace the moment they occur. The information is censored, of course, but whatever the government in question wishes to communicate can be dispatched in a very short period of time. Information technology has brought those who have access to it very close to policy and to decision makers. Likewise, views on the conflict from any quarter of the world, authored by virtually anybody, can likewise reach Ethiopia and Eritrea as soon as they are formulated. The Internet allows individuals and small groups of people to convey their views in ways which did not exist just a decade ago. We have neither the capacity nor the space to examine further the implications of the wide use of information technology on the conduct of the war and on policy formation. We are, however, of the opinion that the role of the electronic media in the conflict merits closer scrutiny.

The impact of the huge human losses that both armies suffered could affect the future conduct of the war. Since February 1999, the Eritrean side estimates that up to 40,000 Ethiopian enemy soldiers may have been killed and a good number wounded. According to the estimates put out by the Ethiopian government, the Eritrean armed forces may have suffered an equal number of losses. One pre-May 2000 count put the total figure from both sides close to 100,000 deaths, while Eritrea claims that Ethiopia alone may have lost up to 70,000 men. Even if we slash the figures supplied by both countries by half, we have to concede that the losses so far incurred are so considerable that they could affect the policy options available to both countries. Lately the Eritrean media and some European journalists have argued that the huge losses that Ethiopia suffered at the battle of Tsorona in March and April 1999 would compel her either to accept a humiliating ceasefire or to continue the war. As sooner or later both countries will have to account for most if not all of their losses to their citizens, it is plausible to argue that a ceasefire on the part of Ethiopia prior to Eritrean withdrawal from forcefully occupied territories would send the wrong signal. While so much might be conceded by way of explaining Ethiopia's intransigent position, the same question can be asked as to the impact of losses on the Eritrean side. Like their Ethiopian counterparts, the Eritrean government media only tell us how much damage has been imposed on enemy forces. But surely Eritrea has also lost tens of thousands of soldiers in the war? How is the loss of so many lives helping to decide the issue of redeployment and withdrawal? If the losses were considerable, what effect would this have if both states were at this stage to accept the OAU Framework? These are questions that at this moment can only be posed. While the interplay or connection between losses and the continuation of war raises issues which require specialised expertise that we do not possess, it is clear enough that *some* impact is inevitable.

Persistence of Historical Links

We believe that the second reason for the transformation of the war from what was ostensibly a border dispute into a total war involving up to a quarter of a million soldiers on each side of the border has to do with the persistence of the historical links between the Eritrean and Ethiopian peoples. Here we wish to enter a strong *caveat*. Although the leaders of both countries have affirmed repeatedly the fraternity of the Eritrean and Ethiopian peoples, they have not in a clearly discernible way interpreted either the cause or the goal of the war in the manner we shall presently attempt. It is possible that we are stretching our imaginations too far in searching for a fuller explanation of the conflict. Our main assumption is that if the conflict had been over a contested border, neither the Eritrean nor the Ethiopian government would have jeopardised the well-being of its citizens by resorting to total mobilisation or a huge purchase of arms. If both countries, as they repeatedly state, were tired of war – and admittedly they have had plenty of it – they would have resolved issues of demarcation in some other way. We also wish to point out that we are engaged in a highly conjectural discourse which will, we hope, at least enhance understanding of a conflict which otherwise ought to be described as criminally foolish.

Let us begin by outlining the policies of the Eritrean government on Ethiopia. Soon after the independence of Eritrea in 1993, Eritrean political leaders took the initiative in defining the relations between the two countries. The Eritrean government raised the issue of confederation but failed to elicit a warm response from Ethiopian quarters. The wide-ranging protocol agreements that were signed between the two countries were designed to lead eventually to economic and political integration. The repeated endeavours of the Eritreans to persuade their Ethiopian counterparts to open up both countries to joint investment opportunities can also be interpreted as favouring integrated coexistence. The commitment of the Eritrean leadership towards some form of union with Ethiopia was expressed clearly by the President of Eritrea and his ambassador to Ethiopia towards the end of 1996.

Once established and internationally recognised, political states tend to survive, although the survival chances of many states in Africa have become slimmer with the end of the Cold War. In this context, Eritrean overtures on political and economic integration were certainly not designed to lead to the dissolution of the state of Eritrea. These statements simply reflected and recognised the extent of the economic and social links between Eritrea and Ethiopia.

Relations between the two countries began to deteriorate seriously from early 1997. They began to accuse each other of creating obstacles to the free flow of trade and investment. The decision of the Eritrean government to issue its own currency, its expectation that this new currency would function at parity level with Ethiopia's, and the latter's refusal to go along with this expectation created what the Eritrean government described as an unacceptable situation. The Eritrean government went even further in its rejection of Ethiopia's trade policy; Ethiopia's policy, it threatened, could lead to undesirable consequences. It is worth remembering that trade and currency negotiations between the two countries had virtually broken down before the famous letter of President Issaias Afwerki to Prime Minister Meles Zenawi on the border issues (July 1997) was sent. As we can read from the long interview that President Issaias gave in March– April 1998, Eritrea felt rejected, expelled from the Ethiopian landscape. It was in this interview that Issaias reminded his readers that culture, history and geography bind the Eritrean and the Ethiopian peoples, and that their destinies are entwined.

President Issaias intimated in the aforementioned interview that the then-current state of affairs – Ethiopia's decision to conduct its trade with Eritrea in hard currency, and the non-convertibility of the two currencies – ought not to continue for unlimited time. He expected the Ethiopian government to take into account his government's views on the nature of the relations between the two countries. As Professor Tekie Fessehazion put it,

> Eritrea was not just another country.... History, location and happenstance have contributed to the creation of an economic region that traverses political boundaries, so much so that economically northern Ethiopia and Eritrea are like two Siamese twins joined at the back and naturally looking in opposite directions.[8]

We would certainly agree with such an analogy, but we would question

---

[8] Tekie Fessehazion, 'Eritrean and Ethiopian State of Economic Relations: a Nakfa/Birr/ LC Analysis', Internet material from Dehai post, accessed 29 June 1999.

the opposite direction that Eritrea was deemed to follow. If one recent study of ethnicity in northern Ethiopia is anything to go by, the great majority of the Tigrinya-speaking population in Eritrea share primordial sentiments with the people of northern Ethiopia.[9] In other words the Tigrinya-speakers in Eritrea and Ethiopia feel that they belong to the same 'nationality', however such a concept is defined.

Although we would still maintain that the occupation of Badme might not have been designed with the intention of either ousting EPRDF (read TPLF) from power or balkanising Ethiopia, it is possible to argue that it was almost certainly aimed at bringing pressure on the Ethiopian government. Eritrea rejected Ethiopia's trade policy on the grounds that such a policy was discriminatory and excluded Eritrea from the Ethiopian economy. Ethiopia's policies were contrary to the goals and ambitions of economic and eventually political integration. Thus the presence of a huge Eritrean army can also be seen as determination on the part of Eritrea to bring about a favourable balance in its future (integrative) relations with Ethiopia.

We may thus draw the following conclusions about why the Eritrean government had amassed up to a quarter of a million soldiers along the border. First, by threat of force Eritrea expected to bring Ethiopia to a negotiating position. Secondly, Eritrea adopted from the outset an 'over-kill' approach in order to bring about a quick end to the confrontation.

The Ethiopian response can likewise be explained in terms of the persistence of historical links. By skilful exploitation of the US–Rwanda and OAU peace initiatives, the Ethiopian government bought the time it needed to rearm itself. But all along, as we learn later, the border dispute was only a pretext for dealing with several unresolved issues. The first and rather intractable issue was the intricate links that brought the Eritrean community and the Eritrean state within the sphere of the Ethiopian economy. In Ethiopia it was widely perceived that Eritrea was part of and separate from Ethiopia, all at the same time. The second issue was the deep resentment in many parts of the society, but especially in the urban areas, of the independence of Eritrea. Many Ethiopians felt that their Eritrean brothers and sisters rejected them. Such resentment was expressed by a relentless campaign that began soon after the declaration of independence by Eritrea to send all Eritreans home or to curtail their privileges. Such a campaign had actually never ceased. Towards the end of 1996 both the government in Addis Ababa and the articulate public in the capital city were convinced that economic relations between the two countries were skewed in favour of Eritrea at the expense of Ethiopia.

[9] Alemseged Abbay, 'Identity Jilted or Re-Imagining Identity? The Divergent Paths of the Eritrean and Tigrayan Nationalist Struggles', 1998.

In addition to favouring Eritrea, the Ethiopian government was also accused by some of subordinating national interests to ethnic and regional goals. Depicted as a government dominated by a single ethnic group, the Ethiopian government was under pressure to prove to its critics that it had the interest of the nation at heart.

The opportunity for solving what one might call the Eritrean question arose in May 1998. By August 1998 the Ethiopian government had made it quite clear that its ultimate objective was to create or recreate conditions in Eritrea which would not threaten Ethiopia. The intensive support given to Eritrean opposition groups of all kinds, and at the same time the daily litany affirming the fraternity of the Eritrean and Ethiopian people, leads us to believe that the current war has most of the characteristics of a civil war between one people spread out in two countries. In this context it is indeed quite correct to describe the position of the Ethiopian government as either expansionist or hegemonistic. But such an analysis would be correct if we assume that the great majority of the citizens of both countries accept the borders established a century ago. Although the opposition organisations who aspire to break away from Ethiopia either supported Eritrean independence (the Oromo and Somali factions, for example) or remained neutral, the majority of the Ethiopian literati, and in particular the Amhara and the Tigreans (about 35 per cent of the population), are not at all convinced that there were good reasons why Eritrea 'seceded from Ethiopia'. Yet it was basically the government in power that sanctioned the independence of Eritrea. Ethiopia's intransigent position and the determination with which the war is being planned and conducted makes us believe that, somewhere along the line, the objective is to change the relations between Eritrea and Ethiopia fundamentally.

The Ethiopian government clearly knows what it does not like in the Eritrean–Ethiopian relations that prevailed up to the time of the border dispute. Equally clearly, Ethiopia has been ready since September 1998 to defeat the Eritrean state and its army. After such a victory, the Ethiopian government hopes that the Eritrean and Ethiopian people will live in peace. If and when the Ethiopian army succeeds in defeating Eritrea, it is anybody's guess what would ensue from a Pax Ethiopica. It can be foreseen, however, that the military victory of either side would unleash forces that could lead to a reconfiguration of borders and a realignment of ethnic or national groups.

Meanwhile the Ethiopian government, like that of Eritrea, is diverting scarce resources for arms purchase and in the process exposing an already vulnerable population to famine and starvation. It is a tragic war in which common history and the deleterious impact of colonialism are having a significant say.

TPLF, Ethiopia and Eritrea

One third reason has to do with the role that TPLF is made to play with regard to Ethiopia and Eritrea. TPLF as an organisation did indeed recognise and support the right of the Eritrean liberation organisations to fight for their independence. But neither TPLF nor the people of Tigray have accepted the colonial thesis: that Eritrea was a colony of Ethiopia, or that Eritreans have a different identity because of Italian colonialism. The strenuous efforts of the Eritrean political leadership to the contrary, most ordinary Eritreans (here reference is made to the Tigrinya-speakers who constitute at least 60 per cent of the population) believe they are one and the same with the people of Tigray. They speak the same language, and they have the same history and tradition.

TPLF, as the most important member of the EPRDF coalition government, had for several years found itself squeezed between Eritrea and the rest of Ethiopia. On the one hand it attempted to create structures for smooth relations between Eritrea and Ethiopia. On the other hand, it could not completely ignore the intensive accusations of ethnicity and ethnic favouritism originating from the urban élite. Finally, the TPLF had two not always compatible functions. It was a dominant part of the coalition government: the Prime Minster, the Minister of Security and the Minister of Foreign Affairs are all from TPLF. And, at its home base in Tigray, TPLF is the only party in power entrusted with the development of the region.

It was in connection with TPLF's development strategy that conflict emerged in the relations between the two countries. As we mentioned earlier, the development of Tigray was partly premissed on the control or curtailment of Eritrean exports to Ethiopia. This was largely because of the fact that Eritrean exports (textiles, beverages, and finished products) could as well be produced in Tigray. Competition between Eritrea and Tigray over access to the Ethiopian market has indeed been a factor in the making of the conflict. That is why it is understandable that the Eritrean media continuously insist that Eritrea has no enemy among the other regions and peoples of Ethiopia, but only in the ranks of the TPLF clique.

TPLF has reacted very strongly to Eritrea's accusations. Although bearers of a considerable portion of Ethiopia's ancient and medieval history, the Tigray people have been marginalised throughout most of the twentieth century. Encircled by Eritrea in the north and completely ignored by Addis Ababa, the Tigray remained one of the least developed regions of the country. Tigray barely survived as a transit for goods and services between Eritrea and the rest of the country. Moreover, it constructed an image of itself as a producer of cheap labour for Eritrea.

95

Earlier governments in Ethiopia (imperial, 1941–74 and military, 1974–91) had partly by design and partly by the logic of their visions of development ignored Tigray. As Ethiopia's exportable products were in the south and southwest of the country, large parts of the Amhara region and Tigray were essentially left on their own. Moreover, earlier governments did not appear to lament the languishing state of development in Tigray because of a historical fear that a strong Tigray would contend for political power.

The coming to power of TPLF as the leading member of the EPRDF coalition was bound to change the priorities of the government in power. The Tigray region can no longer be ignored by government policy. It has to be recalled that TPLF conducted its protracted armed struggle to develop Tigray either within a newly constituted Ethiopia or outside of Ethiopia. As long as Ethiopia continues to survive with its current boundaries intact, and as long as the present EPRDF coalition continues to hold, TPLF is bound to balance the pressure originating from its two constituencies.

As a member of the EPRDF coalition, TPLF had not only to accommodate pressures from other regions but also to further enhance the economic well-being of the entire nation. It had to take into account the views and opinions of the major ethnic groups and coalitions on Ethiopia's relations with its neighbours. The OLF's position – that the Eritrean–Ethiopian conflict was an internal war among and between Abyssinians, and thus has nothing to do with the Oromos – certainly has a great deal of truth. TPLF must be aware that the continuity of the EPRDF coalition is greatly dependent on how much the coalition is seen as performing in the interests of the country as a whole.

In Tigray, on the other hand, the demands of the constituency are primarily those initiated and developed by TPLF itself. The objective of TPLF is to integrate Tigray more fully into the Ethiopian economy through, among other things, the development of the manufacturing sector. Compared with the southern regions of the country, Tigray has less potential as an exporter of agricultural products. Competing with Eritrea or replacing Eritrean exports to Ethiopia were central elements in the development strategy of the TPLF. It is thus no wonder that the Eritrean government continues to identify its chief enemy as TPLF and not its coalition partners.

9 Pre-Modern Wars in Post-Modern Times

The battle that led to the Ethiopian recapture of Badme has been likened to a re-run of the First World War. The Eritrean–Ethiopian war has also been described as the largest war, surpassing Kosovo, in today's world. Couched in modernist terms – the defence of territorial sovereignty – the Eritrean–Ethiopian war is being carried out as if there were no international safeguards defending nations whose territories have been transgressed. The total neglect of the Eritrea–Ethiopia war by the European Union and the UN (apart from innocuous resolutions) and NATO's deep involvement in the Kosovo affair are a diptych which fails to raise the eyebrows of the international community. Globalisation does not after all appear to include the concept of equal concern over humanitarian issues wherever they might occur.

The Internet has made its presence felt in a big way in the Eritrea–Ethiopia war, by creating possibilities for the participation of people from all corners of the world. Whether its potent force can be harnessed towards meaningful communication, peace and development, or whether it will spawn a plethora of views and options that confuse rather than enlighten, remains to be seen.

Neither Ethiopian nor Eritrean borders have assumed the contours that one would expect to find in modern state systems. The federal constitution of Ethiopia, which allows nations and nationalities the right of self-determination up to and including secession, may be a harbinger for the emergence of several states within the modern map of Ethiopia.[1] Some are already on record demanding such a right. Neighbouring Somalia has by its disintegration made a valuable contribution to our knowledge of state systems, namely the concept of the 'non-state state'. The war of

[1] Kjetil Tronvoll, *Ethiopia: A New Start?*, Minority Rights Group International, London, 2000.

annihilation that both countries appear so keen to pursue includes the organisation and provision of arms to opposition groups. Eritrea is actively engaged in supplying arms to the internal enemies of the EPRDF government. Likewise, Ethiopia supports Eritrean opposition groups. At least in the diaspora, the efforts of the Eritrean government appear to have met with some success in identifying groups who are prepared to collaborate with Eritrea to oust the EPRDF government in Addis Ababa.

In Ethiopia, as time goes by, the rhetoric of Eritrea as the aggressor nation is ceasing to appeal to the civilian population. Although the Ethiopian government is now reputed to have a seasoned army of about four hundred thousand men and thus no longer resorts heavily to forced recruitment, the continuation of the war can only lead to its weakening. Corruption and mismangement of public affairs cannot be fought vigorously so long as the country remains on a war footing.

Moreover, there are recent indications that the daily programmes beamed from Eritrea to Ethiopia are progressively undermining the power base of the EPRDF government in Addis Ababa. The political organisation of the country along ethnic lines[2] and the policy of allocating government positions on the basis of ethnic quotas (the Achilles heel of the Ethiopian government) are being skilfully used by the Eritrean radio broadcasts beamed to Ethiopia. Sooner or later the Ethiopian government must feel the undermining impact and react either by disallowing the ethnification of politics or by pursuing an even more belligerent attitude *vis-à-vis* Eritrea, or by a combination of the two options.

The Ethiopian government is also facing new pressure from the international community, especially after Eritrea's unconditional acceptance of the entire package of the OAU Framework in July 1999. Ethiopia's reservations on the Technical Arrangements and its provisions have so far gained her no sympathy. Eritrea, as the Ethiopian government alleges, may have accepted the Framework only in order to placate the hitherto critical international community. Be that as it may, there are strong indications that Ethiopia is being pressured to accept the Framework, including the Technical Arrangements. International pressure on Ethiopia is likely to increase as the famine that has already affected the southern and eastern parts of the country unfolds further in the forthcoming months. The Ethiopian government cannot continue with the war *and* effectively prevent the spread of famine.

In Eritrea, too, the fate of the country as a nation state now hangs in the balance. A small rupture of relations along the Eritrea–Ethiopia border, let alone a conflict of this nature, is bound to make waves in Asmara and its environs. The shortness of the distance from northern parts of Ethiopia to Asmara and the non-existence of linguistic or cultural

---

[2] See Tronvell 2000 on the issue of the workings of the ethnic federal system.

barriers make that border extremely sensitive. The policy of destabilisation financed and coordinated from Ethiopia may in the long run lead to the break-up of Eritrea.

Now in its second year, the Eritrean–Ethiopian war, which does not seem to abate, has already brought great damage to the future relations between the two countries. The loss in human lives is estimated to be in the range of 50,000–80,000 men and women. The deportation of Eritreans and Ethiopians of Eritrean origin from Ethiopia, and of Ethiopians from Eritrea, is bound to leave a deep scar that will take many years to heal, even given a mutual spirit of reconciliation. Millions of dollars are being siphoned off daily to the purchase of arms and to maintain up to half a million armed soldiers on both sides of the long border. An equal number of people have been displaced to make way for the soldiers along the border and the entire area has been turned into a minefield. Meanwhile, the civilians of both countries are facing daily real and structural famine on a scale reminiscent of 1984–5.

The heyday of maintaining political states simply because they are states appears to be over with the end of the Cold War and the collapse of the Soviet Union. Now left alone, Africa appears to pick up threads that were either broken or left untied by the colonial interlude. A veritable process of nation building is taking place in several parts of Africa. And what we are witnessing in the Horn may be similar to the process that Europe went through some two hundred and fifty years ago.[3]

As the armed conflict approaches its third year both countries are feeling the impact of the state of war on their economies. Moreover, both countries are beginning to realise that neither the patience nor the resources of their civilian populations are unlimited. The economy of Eritrea, especially its export sector, is hard hit and the country has so far managed to maintain a state of normalcy only by the remarkable ability of its government to galvanise the support of Eritreans abroad. Organised around an appealing slogan of 'one dollar a day keeps the Woyane away', the government of Eritrea has been able to access a considerable amount of foreign currency. It has also been able to use such support to reassure its own population inside Eritrea.[4] We believe that in the long run the involvement of Eritreans in the diaspora in the current conflict through direct measures and regular monetary contribution to the war is neither desirable nor sustainable. The presence of diaspora Eritreans could very well circumscribe the options available for the government as it has to take into account the financial muscle that the former are able to provide, and

---

[3] See the insightful remarks of Hugh Seton-Watson, 1977.
[4] A standing item in the Tigrinya tri-weekly newspaper (*Hadas Eretra*) deals with the amount of money collected by the various Eritrean communities all over the world as well statements from abroad in support of the position of the government.

the citizens of the Horn of Africa in the diaspora tend to entertain extremist positions. It is also worth pointing out that the monetary contribution of the Eritreans in the diaspora (this applies to all diaspora groups) will in a decade or so tend to decline owing to demographic factors and the already discernible gap between the various age groups within the diaspora population. Commitment is highest among those who left Eritrea during the war of liberation (1961–91). Unless Eritrea is able to shed thousands of new refugees to Europe and North America (and it is quite hard to imagine a realistic scenario), one must assume that the revenue from the diaspora will decline in the long run (and perhaps within a couple of decades).

Its ostensible causes notwithstanding, the Eritrea–Ethiopia war can indeed be seen as a continuation of the internal politics of the region of the late nineteenth century. It is ironic that thousands of soldiers are pitched along the border not so much to defend the border but essentially to reconfigure it. Eritrea hopes to achieve peaceful coexistence once TPLF is either defeated by EPLF or by the combined forces of Oromo, Amhara, Somali and other disgruntled groups in the country. Likewise, the EPRDF government in Addis Ababa and TPLF in Tigray are eager to assist the Eritrean people to form a government that would suit both Addis Ababa and Tigray.

Gauging the political and emotional climate as best we can, we hold the opinion that the definition of the conflict as arising from a border dispute misses the essential point: economic and historical relations between the two states. The two countries share a complementary economic basis. Eritrea needs access to the Ethiopian market and resources, while Ethiopia, especially northern Ethiopia, stands to benefit from active economic interaction with Eritrea. Moreover, although Ethiopia seems to have succeeded admirably well in rerouting its trade via Djibouti, the usefulness of Massawa and Assab for northern Ethiopia remains of great importance.

The war has created hard feelings between the brotherly populations, but we do not share the view that all is lost. Both governments still stress the cultural, historical and economic links that bind the Eritrean and Ethiopian peoples, in spite of the recorded violations of human rights in connection with the deportations. We believe that it is important to capitalise on the existing fund of shared culture and history, and to use this fund to explore the landscape of post-conflict relations.

Yet the future does not seem to augur well for Ethio-Eritrean relations. The main actors in the war are the core armies and cadres of EPLF, in the case of Eritrea, and TPLF, in the case of Ethiopia. These are seasoned guerilla soldiers who in adverse circumstances could quite easily revert to guerilla warfare. The war of destabilisation that each is waging against the other is unlikely to result in the defeat of either of the core armies.

Increased Somali and Oromo pressure may succeed in wrenching large parts of Ethiopia free of the control of EPRDF. But such an unlikely scenario would not necessarily weaken the hard-core TPLF army. Likewise, Ethiopian victories against Eritrean garrisons may be envisaged, but it is unlikely that such victories would lead to the collapse of EPLF. The two armies facing each other can always fall back on the option of returning to the 'jungle' to continue guerilla warfare.

Appendices

We have tried to minimise the number of appendices, since many of the official statements are easily available elsewhere. However, we have felt it necessary for documentary purposes to include in full the main documents and statements given by the warring parties (Ethiopia and Eritrea), and the negotiators (the OAU, the UN and the US–Rwanda team).

The appendices covering the minutes of meetings on bilateral affairs between Eritrea and Ethiopia (1993–6) were given to Tekeste Negash by the Ethiopian Foreign Ministry during his visit to Addis Ababa in September 1998. The minutes were written in English and were copied by hand by Tekeste Negash.

The appendices covering the letters exchanged between President Issaias Afwerki and Prime Minister Meles Zenawi on the incidents happening in Adi Murug and Badme in July–August 1997 were given to Kjetil Tronvoll by the PFDJ during his visit to Asmara in October–November 1998.

Appendices

APPENDIX 1
Joint Communiqué of the First Round-Table Meeting of the Ethio-Eritrea Joint Ministerial Commission, 22–27 September 1993, Asmara

The JMC meeting took place in accordance with the provision of the agreement of friendship and cooperation signed between the two governments on July 30, 1993 in Addis Ababa.

In view of the very high value attached to the advancement and promotion of cooperative relations between the two countries, the two sides expressed their profound satisfaction with the establishment of a JHMC. The JHMC is composed of the prime minister of TGE and the minister of local government of the government of Eritrea as co-chairmen. Foreign ministers of the two countries and the ambassadors of the two countries to each other, as the supreme body entrusted with the task of preserving and building upon the achievements already made, facilitate the implementation of the agreements signed and identify and promote further areas of cooperation.

The JHMC formed three joint committees: political, economic and social affairs which held extensive discussions and consultations in their specific areas.

The discussions were conducted in the spirit of brotherhood, mutual trust and understanding reflecting the close and friendly relations between the peoples of the two countries and led to the signing of 25 protocol agreements aimed at reinforcing and further expanding fields of cooperation which would contribute towards promoting mutual interests.

In the fields of economic cooperation it was decided to work together and to coordinate development strategies and policies of the two countries. In this connection, a protocol agreement on harmonisation of economic policies between the two countries has been signed, covering the issues of fiscal, monetary, trade and investment policies. On the sectoral level specific cooperation agreements were signed on industry, transport and communication, agriculture, natural resources development and environmental protection, mining and energy, construction and tourism.

The two governments have reaffirmed their commitment to vigorously continue their efforts to further expand their cooperation in various areas of mutual interest. The JHMC and the three joint committees are entrusted with the task of following-up, coordinating and expanding the implementation of agreements reached in the political, economic and social fields.

Tamrat Layne, Romedan M. Nur
Asmara, 27 September 1993.

APPENDIX 2
Extract from Final Report of the Joint Review
Committee on the Implementation
of the Ethio-Eritrea Economic Agreements,
Addis Ababa, 1 January 1997

Table of Contents

The following notes were made under the following points:

2.1.5. Harmonisation of Economic Policies

A protocol on harmonisation of economic policies signed on September 27, 1993 included, among other things, several provisions on the harmonisation of macro-economic policies which are summarised below.

a) to harmonise exchange rate policies and interest rate structures;
b) to work out a mechanism for making the growth of the money stock consistent with inflation objectives of the two countries;
c) to work out a scheme to synchronise policies related to foreign exchange surrender requirements, allocation of foreign exchange to importers, capital flows and external debt management;
d) to gradually harmonise policies regarding tariffs, sales tax, excise tax and profit taxes;
e) to harmonise their investment policies;
f) to provide national investors of both countries the same and equal treatment in each other's territories.

2.1.3. Transport and communication agreements

In the transport and communication fields the agreements concluded by the two countries include Transport and Communication Protocol agreement, the commercial road transport services agreement, and port and transit services agreement, all of which were signed on September 27, 1993. Since problems raised with respect to commercial road transport services are few and largely administrative, only highlights of port and transit services agreements are summarised.

Port and transit agreement

a) Assab and Massawa shall serve as transit ports for Ethiopia; speedy movement of goods in transit shall be expedited and transit documentation and procedures shall be simplified and harmonised.
b) Ethiopian goods transiting through Assab and Massawa shall be free of taxes and customs duties.
c) Eritrea shall provide all necessary port handling and agency services to ships owned by Ethiopia and cargo destined to or originating from Ethiopia.
d) Payments for services rendered to Ethiopian ships and cargo shall be effected in Birr except where the handling costs were paid for by the shipper or consignee in hard currency.
e) Payment for Eritrean freight cargo loaded on Ethiopian ships shall be effected in Birr and the rate of payment shall be according to the agreed governing International freight rate.
f) Food aid cargoes and materials which serve the immediate human need shall be free of port dues and storage penalty charges.
g) Port services regulations and tariffs used by Eritrea shall be given to the Ethiopian government and when Eritrea intends to make changes of these regulations and tariffs it shall notify the Ethiopian government 60 working days in advance.

2.1.1. Trade agreement

On September 27, 1993 the Transitional Government of Ethiopia and the State of Eritrea concluded a trade agreement and protocol in order to promote and expand trade between the two countries. The agreement included the following main provisions.

a) There shall be free movement of goods and services between the two countries for local consumption except those that are in short supply.
b) Goods imported from a third country shall be re-exported freely subject to the laws and regulations of the two countries.
c) Goods and services originating in a member country cannot be re-exported to a third country.
d) A uniform standardisation system shall be established for the goods and services traded between the two countries.
e) Trade and service transactions between the two countries shall be made in Birr.
f) A joint trade committee shall be established to review the implementation of the agreement.

A memorandum of understanding signed on October 7, 1994 by the Ministers of the two countries further liberalised trade between the two countries making the following provisions.
a) No additional intermediate and local payment should be imposed on goods and services traded between the two countries.
b) The two parties agree to establish a joint customs committee to monitor day to day activities and give solutions to problems arising during implementation.
c) Both parties agree that free movement of goods and services should not be distracted by 'short supply'.
d) Transit goods shall be checked at end check points if the proper authorised documents are presented.

On April 3, 1995 the Government of the state of Eritrea and the Transitional government of Ethiopia further agreed to form a free trade area (FTA) as a first stage in the process of economic integration. The main provisions of the agreements are the following:
a) Removal of tariff and non-tariff barriers on all goods and services produced and exchanged by the two countries.
b) Periodic review to include new products and services produced and exchanged between the two countries.
c) Harmonisation and simplification of customs documents and procedures, introduction of common classification of goods (based on SITC method), common instruments for data collection and a system of exchange of trade data.

2.2. Implementation status and underlying constraints.

As can be gathered from the above summaries of the main elements of the sectoral and macroeconomic agreements signed by the two countries, the agreements have opened up at least on paper a wide door for economic cooperation between the two countries. But realisation of the economic and social benefits to be derived depends on the extent of implementation of the agreements. The degree of implementation in turn depends on the fulfilment of prerequisites for successful implementation and on whether the set of agreed upon actions to be taken within a given time frame to translate the agreements into practice have been taken or not. The prerequisites against which the implementation of the agreements has to be judged are the following:

a)   The degree to which agreements signed are in harmony or out of tune with the domestic economic and social policies of the two countries.

b)   Whether the gains expected by both parties from the agreements outweigh the sacrifices of independent policy making.

c)   Whether the independently followed economic policies of the two countries were converging or diverging over the implementation period.

d)   The degree of complementarity or competitiveness of the structures of domestic output of the two countries.

e)   The adequacy of the institutional mechanism set up to monitor the implementation of the agreements.

f)   Whether the substance of the agreements is fully communicated to those who are responsible for their implementation at various levels.

g)   Whether the agreements are stated in a manner that does not give rise to misinterpretations or differences in interpretation during implementation.

2.2.1. *Trade and customs*

… But as will be seen in the section on identified implementation problems the removal of tariff barriers is less than total because an important provision of the agreement, which in effect says that no additional local and intermediate payment should be imposed on goods and services traded between the two countries, has not been fully implemented. Besides, the payment of profit taxes at customs posts is a practice which can be regarded as a tariff barrier on trade.

With respect to the removal of non-tariff barriers, on the other hand, as noted by the Eritrean side, very little has been done since important provisions of the agreement with respect to this are still encountering implementation problems. Eritrea has been facing restrictions and outright prohibitions on its imports of Ethiopia's exportable products throughout the implementation period. The practice of multiple checks in between origin and destination is still going on contrary to the agreement which says that goods and services moving between Eritrea and Ethiopia with the appropriate documents shall be examined at point of origin and destination only. Ethiopia's decision to prohibit franco-valuta imports is a measure which can totally block re-export trade between the two countries and also can be a cause for the further intensification of illegal trade along the borders of the two countries. Differences in licensing requirements of the two countries are still acting as further obstacles to trade.

The Ethiopian side indicated that the agreements signed in the area of trade and customs have significantly contributed to the growing trade transactions between the two countries. However, the current practice of charging sales and excise tax on the basis of differences in tax rates of the two countries is not in line with the customs agreement.

The Ethiopian side further indicated that the restriction of exportable goods is in conformity with the trade agreements. Moreover, the prohibition of franco-valuta imports which is aimed to address problems which are associated with the operation of such importing procedures is consistent with article II:2 of the trade agreement signed on September 1993.

Although the two countries have entered into an agreement to combat illegal trade, no cooperative action has been taken so far. In fact, discussion with customs officers at Zalenbessa border post revealed that coffee is being smuggled to Eritrea.

With respect to the request by Eritrean customs officers for overtime payment, the Ethiopian side regards such practice as a barrier to trade since such additional costs among other things, raise the final price to customers.

Moreover, it has been noted that Ethiopian traders are often requested to either present import–export licences or rent import–export licences from Eritrean traders in their sales or purchase of goods from Eritrea, which is believed to inhibit the free flow of goods between the two countries.

A broad conclusion that can be drawn from the above brief assessment of the implementation of various articles of the agreements is that the overall progress achieved in implementing the trade and customs agreements is not fully satisfactory. The underlying constraints which have impeded the implementation of the trade and customs agreements are mainly:

a) divergences in economic policies of the two countries;
b) differences in their trade regulatory systems;
c) differences in the interpretation of various articles of the agreements;
d) gaps in the agreements which provide loopholes for maintaining or introducing tariff and non-tariff barriers; and
e) failure to establish in time the institutional mechanisms for following up the
   implementation of the agreements.

2.2.4. Macroeconomic policy harmonisation

Despite the protocol agreement of macroeconomic policy harmonisation little practical measure has been taken by the two countries to harmonise their macro-economic policies due to the absence of the prerequisite of fully developed banking, transport and communication system and other institutional mechanisms required for full coordination within the framework of their cooperation agreements. Indeed new investment codes, tariff regimes, and exchange and interest rates have been put in place by the two countries independently since the cooperative agreements were signed. In the case of Ethiopia, the investment policy and interest rates were revised for the second time and tariff rates for the third time after the two countries signed the economic cooperation agreements. Although it is not the result of the joint efforts to harmonise the macroeconomic policies of the two countries, the divergence between the investment policies and tariff regimes of the two countries is narrower now than it was the case immediately after the signing of the cooperation agreements.

Full harmonisation of economic policies and particularly the macroeconomic policies of the two countries is a stage in the process of economic integration which can be reached only after successful implementation of the less demanding integration schemes of free trade and customs union.

Thus it could be argued that harmonisation of macroeconomic policies is an issue which must be pragmatically addressed at a proper time in the future after the two countries have reached a high stage of cooperation particularly in the area of trade, transport and communications, banking, investment and institutional mechanisms for cooperation.

On the other hand, Ethiopia and Eritrea have on a number of occasions expressed their commitments to regional and sub-regional economic integration. And these commitments in most cases call for the difficult task of harmonisation and coordination of macroeconomic policies. Given the common currency (though the introduction of a new currency in Eritrea is imminent), the relatively high level of cross border trade, the use of common ports, to mention but a few, Ethiopia and Eritrea are in a better position than most African countries to move into economic integration in a relatively short time.

2.2.5. Investment

A comparison of the investment policies of the two countries shows that there are more areas for investment open to a foreign investor in Eritrea than can be found in Ethiopia. Citing these and other differences in investment policy, the authorities of both countries have on a number of occasions sought clarification as to how to implement the protocol agreement.

One thing has been made clear, however, by the latest investment code of Ethiopia. Eritrean nationals residing in Ethiopia can enjoy the privileges of a domestic investor. The question of whether Eritreans – residing in Ethiopia or not – can be granted investment licences in areas reserved for Ethiopian nationals was the subject of discussion both at previous technical meetings as well as at the fourth JHMC meeting held in Addis Ababa in August 1996. Although not included in the original terms of reference of the joint review committee, it was learned from the Minutes of Understanding of the JMC (this reached the Joint Review Committee two months after the start of the review exercise) that the JRC has to study the implications of opening investment areas reserved for Ethiopian nationals to Eritrean nationals who would like to invest in Ethiopia and vice versa and come up with recommendations to the JMC.

The Eritrean investment law, on the other hand, makes no distinction between a foreign and a domestic investor, except in the trade sector which requires a bilateral agreement of reciprocity.

4. Analysis of Identified Problems and Proposed Measures

2. *Restrictions on Eritrea's imports of Ethiopia's exportable products.*
   Overtime payment to Eritrean customs personnel by Ethiopian traders.
4. *Implementation of free trade agreement.* It is proposed that the ministries of both countries closely monitor and set deadlines for the assignments of the various parts of the agreement.
5. *Lack of adequate institutional mechanisms.*
6. *Illegal trade.* Until the divergences in policies are harmonised, the two countries had entered an agreement to combat illegal trade. But so far no concrete action has been taken.
7. *Joint committee on trade.* As a result of the absence of a joint trade committee to follow up the implementation of the agreement, many problems that could

have been solved at lower levels have become a national issue.

10. *Differences in licensing systems.* Eritrean traders who have only general import/export licences are required to have additional letters of support for their purchase of commodities like coffee, hides, skins, wood etc. from Ethiopia. The time and cost involved in trying to secure a licence for every commodity one wants to trade in separately is very discouraging and a cause of delays and missed opportunities to many traders and may be regarded as a non-tariff barrier. It is suggested that Ethiopia's intended shift to the general licence system be expedited. The Ethiopian side, on the other hand, indicated that differences in licensing system were a problem requiring serious attention and proposed that steps be taken to include a provision which can address such problems in the ongoing revision of the Ethiopian licensing system.

12. *Local charges and intermediate payments.* It was pointed out by the Eritrean side that various levies made by the zonal and local authorities were becoming tariff barriers to trade between the two countries. In order to enable trade between the two countries to be conducted with minimum barriers, it is necessary to make provisions which enable the trade agreement to supersede zonal and local laws and regulations.

The Ethiopian side, however, explained that the power to tax import/export trade rests with the central government only and, therefore, the question of local tax on trade between the two countries does not arise. The question of non-tax intermediate payments charged by regional governments be adequately dealt with in the next round of customs agreement negotiations.

14. *Prohibition of franco-valuta goods.* The Eritrean side stated the prohibition of franco-valuta imports by Ethiopia is a measure that amounts to a total ban on Eritrea's re-exports to Ethiopia with considerable negative impact on the Eritrean economy. Since the Birr is a common currency of both countries and all trade transactions between the two countries are conducted in Birr the prohibition of franco-valuta imports means that Eritrea can not have legal re-export trade with Ethiopia. This move by the Ethiopian side is a violation of article II:2 and article V of the 1993 trade agreement. This move is a reversal of the progress achieved so far in the expansion of trade between the two countries. Therefore, the trade and other relevant agreements should be revised to take account of this new development.

The Ethiopian side, on the other hand, indicated that the new regulation regarding the prohibition of franco-valuta imports is aimed at addressing problems of proliferation of the black market and unfair trade practices which are associated with the operation of such importing procedures. Furthermore, it was noted that the new regulation is consistent with article II:2 of the trade agreement signed between the two countries in September 1993.

4.6. Investment and business licensing

Both countries should implement what they already allow in their investment laws. In the case of Eritrea, Ethiopian nationals must be allowed to invest in those areas where the Eritrean investment law does not restrict foreign investment such as custom clearing.

Likewise, in accordance with the new investment code of Ethiopia – which provides for Eritreans residing in Ethiopia to invest in all areas except in banking insurance, electric power supply and air transport services – Eritrean nationals residing in Ethiopia should be granted investment licences in the areas not reserved for Ethiopians only.

The Eritrean side believes that such investment and licensing demands of the nationals of either country can only be fully satisfied when the existing disparities in the investment laws and practices of the two countries are reconciled through bilateral investment promotion and protection agreement. Addressing the issue of treatment of resident nationals alone will leave the issue of the treatment of non-resident nationals unsolved which is in fact the main source of current demands for investment licensing. Besides, determining who is a resident national of either country would require having an agreed definition of residence in order to ensure a fair reciprocal treatment. Thus, the Eritrean side proposes that the issue of investment be dealt with in a comprehensive bilateral investment promotion and protection agreement which delineates the areas of investment which would open to the nationals of both countries irrespective of whether they are residents or non-residents.

5. Summary and Conclusions

3. Several agreements were signed on the basis of the objective reality prevailing prior to the formulation and introduction of its macroeconomic policy, in the case of Eritrea, and prior to the launching of its economic reform programme, in the case of Ethiopia. Significant changes in macroeconomic policy and institutional arrangements (such as the restructuring of port administration) have taken place in both countries since the agreements were signed. These developments have rendered the agreements somehow outdated. In some cases, field officers, under strict orders from their headquarters to adhere to directives, find that provisions of the agreement are sometimes contradictory with current laws and regulations.

8. Lack of investment agreement delineating areas of economic activity which would be open to investment by the government and nationals of either country: for example, Ethiopian nationals and enterprises are repeatedly requesting to operate transit, clearing and forwarding and banking services in Eritrea and similarly, Eritrean enterprises have indicated their desire to start up banking and transport businesses in Ethiopia, but they can not obtain a positive response in the absence of an investment agreement.

9. The similar production structure of the economies of the two countries is also a constraint which forces them to look for most of their import needs especially with respect to development inputs from third countries. This together with the use of the Birr as a common currency for both countries has led Ethiopia to restrict exportables from entering the Eritrean market.

10. The above constraint is reinforced by the lack of a provision in the trade agreement on how trade surpluses and deficits are to be settled periodically. Accumulated surpluses on one side means interest free loan to the deficit side and no incentive to reduce one's deficit by expanding exports to the other side.

Having analysed the above problems and issues associated with them, the JRC has come up with proposals which call for measures including:

a) A thorough revision of the existing agreements in areas of trade, customs, transport, port and transit services and macreconomic harmonisation and conclusion of new agreements in the areas of banking, investment promotion and protection and institutional set-ups for cooperation.

b) Provision of clear instructions and guidelines for those responsible for the implementation of the agreements both at the operational and supervisory levels.

c) Ensuring that all concerned have clear and timely information on the provisions of the agreements, procedures and new developments that affect established norms.

Finally, the JRC believes that, with the implementation of the proposed measures, a strong foundation and a conducive environment for an all round cooperation between the two countries will be created.

APPENDIX 3
Extracts from letters exchanged between
President Issaias Afwerki &
Prime Minister Meles Zenawi,
July–August 1997

**Letter from President Issaias Afwerki to Prime Minister Meles Zenawi,
16 August 1997, protesting the forcible occupation of Adi Murug in Badi by
the Ethiopian army**

Comrade Melles,

Greetings.

I have been compelled to write to you to day because of the preoccupying situation prevailing in the areas around Bada.

It cannot be said that the border between our two countries is demarcated clearly although it is known traditionally. And we had not given the issue much attention in view of our present and fiuture ties. Moreover, I do not believe that this will be a cause of much concern and controversy even in the future.

Be this as it may, there have been intermittent disputes in the border areas arising from different and minor causes. Local officials have been striving to defuse and solve these problems amicably. However, the forcible occupation of Adi-Murug by your army in the past few days is truly saddening.

There was no justification for resorting to force as it would not have been at all difficult to settle the matter amicably even if it was deemed important and warranting immediate attention. It would also be possible to quietly and without haste demarcate the boundaries in case that this is felt to be necessary.

I, therefore, urge you to personally take the necessary prudent action so that the measure that has been taken will not trigger unnecessary conflict.

Best Regards
Your comrade
Issaias Afwerki
16/08/97

• • •

Response of Prime Minister Meles to the Letter of President Issaias Afwerki of 16 August 1997 (the letter also addresses other bilateral issues which are not included here)

Comrade Issaias,

Greetings.

I have seen the letter you sent me. I had also heard that the situation in the border areas does not look good. I was also informed that the matter was discussed between your colleagues (*Yemane*), who had come here, and ours (*Tewolde*). We did not imagine that what happened in Bada could create problems. Because the areas our comrades are controlling were not controversial before and we believed that prior consultation was only necessary for disputed areas. We moved to the area to pursue the remnants of Ougugume (*Afar opposition*) who were obstructing our peace efforts from positions there. We believe we can ease the tension concerning the borders on the basis of the understanding reached previously between your team and our colleagues (*Tewolde*). Perhaps, it is also necessary to settle the border demarcation issue after the necessary preparations are carried out by both sides.

• • •

Second letter from President Issaias Afwerki to Prime Minister Meles Zenawi (the letter contains material on other bilateral business which is not included here)

Cornrade Melles,

Greetings.

Regarding the situation in the border areas, my information establishes that the measures taken at Adi-Murug were not in areas that are undisputed but in our own areas and by expelling our officials and dismantling the existing administration. Concerning the Ougugume, your action (*in Adi-Murug*) came as our Defence was preparing to cooperate on the basis of the request from your Army. Moreover, similar measures have been taken in the Badme area.

As I had indicated to you, these measures are unjustified. In order to expediently check any further deterioration and pave the way for a final solution, we have assigned on our part three officials (*Defence Minister Sebhat Ephrem; PFDJ Head of Political Affairs, Yemane Ghebreab; and National Security Advisor, Abraha Kassa*). I suggest that you also similarly (or in ways you think best) assign officials so that both sides can meet as soon as possible to look into these matters. I await your thoughts.

Best Regards
Your Comrade
Issaias Afwerki
25/08/97

APPENDIX 4
Statement of the Council of Ministers of the Federal Democratic Republic of Ethiopia on the Dispute with Eritrea, 13 May 1998

The Government of the Federal Democratic Republic of Ethiopia and all the peoples of our country have been making strenuous efforts to ensure the prevalence of a durable peace within Ethiopia and in the sub-region. To this end we have not only striven to build peace within the country, but we have deployed ourselves to the same degree in making unrelenting efforts to develop relations with neighboring countries on the basis of respect for equality and sovereignty. In the conviction that the peoples of our neighborhood will be the beneficiaries from the development of neighborly relations based on peace and mutual benefit, we have stood steadfastly for peace. Our stand in support of regional peace will continue to be maintained in the future.

The endeavors of the Government of the Federal Democratic Republic of Ethiopia and all the peoples of our country to ensure peaceful relations with neighboring countries are undertaken with the conviction that border claims can be resolved through peaceful means. On this basis we, on our part, have been trying to resolve claims relating to some localities on our borders with Eritrea peacefully and through negotiation.

This being the fact, the Eritrean Government and the ruling Popular Front for Justice and Democracy have chosen to resolve the border issue by force reneging from the process of peaceful settlement of the matter.

Consequently they have on the 12th of May 1998, entered Ethiopian territory which they have been claiming. They have clashed with police and local militia forces present to maintain the security of the area, and are in control of some positions.

The Ethiopian Government vehemently condemns this move of the Eritrean Government and the Popular Front since it violates the sovereignty of Ethiopia and obstructs the ongoing efforts to resolve issues of claims in a peaceful manner. Furthermore, Ethiopia demands that the Eritrean Government unconditionally and immediately withdraw from Ethiopian territory and cease its provocative and belligerent activity. In the event that the Eritrean Government and the Popular Front do not desist from this dangerous action and withdraw from Ethiopian territory without any precondition the Ethiopian Government will take all the necessary measures that the situation demands to safeguard the sovereignty and territorial integrity of our country.

The Council of Ministers,
Federal Democratic Republic of Ethiopia
May 13, 1998

APPENDIX 5
Statement of the Cabinet of Ministers of the Government of Eritrea on the Dispute with Ethiopia, 14 May 1998

The Cabinet of Ministers of the Government of Eritrea has held a meeting in Asmara today, Thursday, May 14, 1998, to consider the Statement issued by the Council of Ministers of the Federal Democratic Government of Ethiopia which accuses Eritrea for inciting conflict and hatred and pursuing a policy of territorial expansion; condemns Eritrea alleging that its army has invaded Ethiopian territory by crossing its borders; and warns that Ethiopia will take all the necessary measures to protect its territorial integrity.

The Government and people of Eritrea are greatly saddened by the tone and contents of these grave accusations.

The Cabinet of Ministers of the Government of Eritrea noted that there have been, and continue to exist, border disputes in certain localities along the common borders between Eritrea and Ethiopia. These problems have been instigated by the unlawful practices of the Ethiopian army which occasionally made incursions into these Eritrean territories; dismantling the local administrative structures and committing crimes against the inhabitants.

But despite these periodic occurrences, the Cabinet asserted that the Government of Eritrea has been consistently endeavouring to resolve these recurrent problems through bilateral negotiations with the Government of Ethiopia in a calm and patient manner; cautious for not inflating the problem out of proportions and incite animosity between the two fraternal peoples. The Government of Eritrea has opted for this course of action because it believes that the international boundary between Eritrea and Ethiopia is very clear and incontroversial. Because it knows that the recurrent border incursions that continue to be perpetuated by Ethiopian forces basically emanate from the narrow perspectives of the Administrative Zones.

The Cabinet of Ministers further noted that a Joint Committee had been formed from both governments to resolve these problems and to delineate on the ground the boundary line. The Cabinet of Ministers asserted that the Government of Eritrea has been exerting all the necessary efforts to expedite the process and facilitate the work of the Joint Committee.

But on Wednesday, May 8, 1998, and while the Eritrean delegation was on its way to Addis Abeba for a meeting of the Joint Committee to discuss ways and means for accelerating its work, Ethiopian army contingents that had already penetrated into Eritrean territory in the areas around Badme (southwestern Eritrea) opened fire and caused grave damage on Eritrean units that attempted to approach them for dialogue. This unprovoked attack subsequently triggered a cycle of clashes in the area.

Furthermore, while continued talks were underway to resolve the tension provoked by the first attack, an appalling Statement aimed at sending an unnecessary message to the peoples of both countries and the international community was issued by the Council of Ministers of the Federal Democratic Government of Ethiopia.

The Cabinet of Ministers reiterates its firm belief that the enduring mutual interests that exist and bind together the peoples of Eritrea and Ethiopia cannot be jeopardized by any border dispute. The Cabinet of Ministers accordingly proposes the following framework as a solution to the problem that has been made to be blown out of proportions and derailed from its path.

1. The Government of Eritrea condemns the logic of force as it firmly knows and upholds that border disputes of any kind can only be resolved through peaceful and legal means; and not through military means.
2. On the basis of this principle, each party shall publicly announce to the peoples of Eritrea, Ethiopia and the international community the territories that it claims – if any – and designate them on the political map with clear geographical coordinates. Each party shall also accept that the dispute cannot, and should not be, resolved by force but through peaceful negotiations.
3. Both parties shall agree that all negotiations and understandings that will be conducted henceforth shall be carried out in the presence and through the mediation of a Third Party. The latter will act as witness and guarantor.
4. Areas under 'dispute' shall be demilitarized temporarily and be free from the presence of armies of both countries. The enforcement of this understanding shall be guaranteed by the Third Party.
5. If the above proposal for resolving the dispute through the involvement of a Third Party and without further complications is not acceptable, the matter to be referred to international adjudication.

The Government of Eritrea firmly believes that attempts to inflate the minor and temporary problem that has been created along the borders of the two sisterly countries will not serve the fundamental interests of the Eritrean and Ethiopian peoples. The Government of Eritrea pledges that it will, as ever before, spare no efforts to handle the present problem with the requisite patience and responsibility. It does not, accordingly, see any wisdom in precipitating tension through inflammatory campaigns.

The Government of Eritrea therefore calls upon the Government of Ethiopia to pursue a similar path that will promote the interests and good neighbourliness of the peoples of both countries. The Cabinet of Ministers of the Government of Eritrea further reasserts its belief that the peoples of Eritrea and Ethiopia will maintain and preserve their mutual interests rooted in peace, good neighbourliness and cooperation.

Asmara, May 14, 1998

APPENDIX 6
US Press Statement
on the US–Rwanda Peace Plan

US Department of State, Office of the Spokesman, Press Statement

Press Statement by James P. Rubin, Spokesman
June 3, 1998

The Dispute Between Ethiopia and Eritrea

At the request of both parties, for more than two weeks the Governments of the United States and Rwanda have been engaged in intensive efforts to facilitate a peaceful resolution of the dispute between Eritrea and Ethiopia.

The objective of the joint American–Rwandan facilitation effort has been to promote a peaceful and durable settlement of this dispute and to prevent a war, which would cost many lives and undermine regional stability. Having excellent relations with the Governments of both Eritrea and Ethiopia, the United States and Rwanda have sought to encourage both parties to protect the peace that has taken root in the Horn of Africa since 1991. Throughout our facilitation effort, we urged both parties to exercise restraint.

The facilitation team listened carefully to the detailed positions of both parties and attempted to take full account of their respective perspectives and interests without making any judgment as to where the disputed border lies or what actions may have precipitated the crisis that began with the border skirmish on May 6.

Based on our consultations, it is clear to the United States and Rwanda that there are many areas of commonality between the two parties and that there exists a practical, principled basis for peaceful resolution of this conflict. Thus, the facilitators presented recommendations to both parties on May 30–31 and asked each party to confirm their acceptance of these recommendation.

The US–Rwandan recommendations are summarized as follows:

1) Both parties should commit themselves to the following principles: resolving this and any other dispute between them by peaceful means; renouncing force as a means of imposing solutions; agreeing to undertake measures to reduce current tensions; and seeking the final disposition of their common border, on the basis of established colonial treaties and international law applicable to such treaties.

2) To reduce current tensions, and without prejudice to the territorial claims of either party: a small observer mission should be deployed to Badme; Eritrean forces should redeploy from Badme to positions held before May 6, 1998; the

previous civilian administration should return; and there should be an investigation into the events of May 6, 1998.

3) To achieve lasting resolution of the underlying border dispute, both parties should agree to the swift and binding delimitation and demarcation of the Eritrea–Ethiopia border. Border delimitation should be determined on the basis of established colonial treaties and international law applicable to such treaties, and the delimitation and demarcation process should be completed by a qualified technical team as soon as possible. The demarcated border should be accepted and adhered to by both parties, and, upon completion of demarcation, the legitimate authorities assume jurisdiction over their respective sovereign territories.

4) Both parties should demilitarize the entire common border as soon as possible.

Finally, the facilitators presented both sides with a detailed implementation plan and recommended that each party convey, in a legal and binding manner, their acceptance of the above recommendations and implementation plan to the facilitators.

The United States and Rwanda regret that these recommendations have not yet been accepted by both sides as the basis for a peaceful resolution of this dispute. We are gravely concerned by the resumption of hostilities in recent days, which will render more difficult efforts to achieve a peaceful outcome.

As friends of the Government of Eritrea and Ethiopia, the United States and Rwanda call on both sides to avoid an escalation of the conflict, to reaffirm their commitment to a peaceful resolution of this dispute, to halt the fighting and to accept without delay the facilitators' recommendations as the basis for a peaceful resolution of this conflict. We remain committed to helping both sides achieve a peaceful settlement and avoid wider conflict through pursuit of further diplomatic efforts.

The Rwandan Government is issuing a statement on this important matter as well.

APPENDIX 7
OAU High-Level Delegation:
Proposals for a Framework Agreement for a Peaceful Settlement of the Dispute Between Eritrea & Ethiopia, 7–8 November 1998

We, the Heads of State and Government, mandated by the 34th Ordinary Session of the Assembly of Heads of State and Government of the Organization of African Unity, held in Ouagadougou, Burkina Faso, from 8 to 10 June 1998, to contribute towards the search for a peaceful and lasting solution to the unfortunate conflict which erupted between the brotherly countries, the State of Eritrea and the Federal Democratic Republic of Ethiopia;

Deeply affected by the outbreak of the conflict between the two countries that are united by historic links of brotherhood and a common culture;

Saddened by this conflict which occurred at a time when the Federal Democratic Republic of Ethiopia and the State of Eritrea had launched a new era of relations built on a partnership and a common vision and ideals as regards the future of their peoples, the region and the whole continent;

Noting, however, that differences had emerged between the two countries relating particularly to their common border, differences which the two countries endeavoured to resolve peacefully;

Deploring the fact that, notwithstanding those efforts, an open conflict broke out between the two brotherly countries, with which our 34th summit was seized;

Paying tribute to the commendable efforts made by friendly countries aimed at finding a peaceful solution to the conflict;

Conscious of the fact that resorting to the use of force results in loss of human lives, the destruction of property and socio-economic infrastructures as well as creating a division between the peoples, all the things which the two brotherly countries and our continent cannot afford at a time when all efforts must be channelled towards the promotion of peace and development which we greatly owe to our peoples;

Encouraged by the commitment made by the two Parties to the OAU High-Level Delegation to settle the conflict peacefully and by their positive response to its appeal to continue to observe the moratorium on air strikes and to maintain the present situation of non-hostilities;

Having considered and endorsed the Report and Recommendations of the Committee of Ambassadors, as submitted by the Ministerial Committee to the parties on 1 August 1998 in Ouagadougou, Burkina Faso;

Having listened to the two Parties and made an in-depth analysis of their respective positions, taking into account their legitimate concerns and after having thought deeply about the ways and means likely to contribute to the peaceful settlement of the crisis in a fair and objective manner;

MAKE on behalf of Africa, its peoples and leaders, a solemn and brotherly appeal to the Leaders of the State of Eritrea and the Federal Democratic Republic of Ethiopia to do everything in their power to opt for a peaceful settlement of the dispute and find a just and lasting solution to the conflict;

SUBMIT, hereunder, for the consideration of the two Parties, the elements of a Framework Agreement based on the following principles:

– resolution of the present crisis and any other dispute between them through peaceful and legal means in accordance with the principles enshrined in the Charter of the Organization of African Unity;

– rejection of the use of force as a means of imposing solutions to disputes;

– respect for the borders existing at independence as stated in Resolution AHG/Res. 16(1) adopted by the OAU Summit in Cairo in 1964 and, in this regard, determine them on the basis of pertinent colonial Treaties and applicable international law, making use, to that end, of technical means to demarcate the borders and, in the case of controversy, resort to the appropriate mechanism of arbitration.

We recommend that:

1. The two Parties commit themselves to an immediate cessation of hostilities;
2. In order to defuse tension and build confidence, the two Parties commit themselves to put an immediate end to any action and any form of expression likely to perpetrate or exacerbate the climate of hostility and tension between them thereby jeopardizing the efforts aimed at finding a peaceful solution to the conflict;
3. In order to create conditions conducive to a comprehensive and lasting settlement of the conflict through the delimitation and demarcation of the border, the armed forces presently in Badme Town and its environs, should be redeployed to the positions they held before 6 May 1998 as a mark of goodwill and consideration for our continental Organization, it being understood that this redeployment will not prejudge the final status of the area concerned, which will be determined at the end of the delimitation and demarcation of the border and, if need be, through an appropriate mechanism of arbitration;
4. This redeployment be supervised by a Group of Military Observers which will be deployed by the OAU with the support of the United Nations. The Group

of Military Observers will also assist the reinstated Civilian Administration in the maintenance of law and order during the interim period;

5. a) The redeployment be subsequently extended to all other contested areas along the common border within the framework of demilitarization of the entire common border and as a measure for defusing the tension and facilitating the delimitation and demarcation process. In effect, the demilitarization which will begin with the Mereb Setit segment, will then extend to the Bada area and the border as a whole;

   b) The demilitarization process be supervised by the Group of Military Observers;

6. a) The two Parties commit themselves to make use of the services of experts of the UN Cartographic Unit, in collaboration with the OAU and other experts agreed upon by the two Parties, to carry out the delimitation and demarcation of the border between the two countries within a time-frame of 6 months which could be extended on the recommendation of the cartographic experts;

   b) Once the entire border has been delimited and demarcated, the legitimate authority will immediately exercise full and sovereign jurisdiction over the territory which will have been recognized as belonging to them;

7. In order to determine the origins of the conflict, an investigation be carried out on the incidents of 6 May 1998 and on any other incident prior to that date which could have contributed to a misunderstanding between the two Parties regarding their common border, including the incidents of July–August 1997.

8. a) At the humanitarian level, the two Parties commit themselves to put an end to measures directed against the civilian population and refrain from any action which can cause further hardship and suffering to each other's nationals;

   b) The two Parties also commit themselves to addressing the negative socio-economic impact of the crisis on the civilian population, particularly, those persons who had been deported;

   c) In order to contribute to the establishment of a climate of confidence, the OAU, in collaboration with the United Nations, deploy a team of Human Rights Monitors in both countries;

9. a) In order to determine the modalities for the implementation of the Framework Agreement, a Follow-up Committee of the two Parties be established under the auspices of the OAU High-Level Delegation with the active participation and assistance of the United Nations;

   b) The committee begin its work as soon as the Framework Agreement is signed;

10. The OAU and the UN, working closely with the international community, particularly the European Union, endeavor to mobilize resources for the resettlement of displaced persons and the demobilization of troops currently deployed along the common border of both countries;

11. The Organization of African Unity, in close cooperation with the United Nations, will be the guarantor for the scrupulous implementation of all the provisions of the Framework Agreement, in the shortest possible time.

APPENDIX 8
Points of Clarification Raised by Eritrea on the OAU Framework Agreement

(handed over to the Secretary General of OAU during the meeting with the President of Eritrea in Asmara on 12 December 1998 as a follow-up to the Ouagadougou Meeting, 6–7 November 1998)

As we underlined at the OAU High Level meeting in Ouagadougou on November 8, Eritrea recognizes the positive elements in the paper submitted to both Parties. We had given our initial response then. In order to give our full and definitive opinion, we request clarification to the following issues (attached to this letter).

From the moment that the OAU was seized of the conflict between Eritrea and Ethiopia, we have clearly communicated our reservations on the approach taken. These reservations, which unfortunately were not taken into account, include:

In spite of its goodwill, the OAU Summit in Ouagadougou adopted the resolution on the basis of the misguided approach and report of the Facilitators Team. This has posed and remains a major handicap to the OAU initiative, severely limiting a fresh and independent approach. Indeed, while Eritrea had made it clear that the facilitation process was over and it regarded the OAU initiative as a new one, the recommendations by the committee of Ambassadors revolved around the same parameters that had led to the failure of the facilitation process.

Eritrea had emphasized from the outset that this was a test case for the OAU involving as it did the recognition and respect of colonial boundaries. In this spirit, Eritrea submitted its constructive proposals, supported by the relevant documents, on resolving this cardinal issue through demarcation. Unfortunately, the Committee has focused more on secondary issues. In particular, the Committee concentrated on the non-fundamental issue of administration of only one area while refusing to consider the more important questions of how the crisis originated and where that area lay in respect of the recognized boundary.

Eritrea was put at a disadvantage as Ethiopia had access to the workings of the Committee through the presence of Djibouti. (In contrast, Rwanda, which was mandated by the OAU Summit, withdrew so as not to bias a fresh start by the OAU Committee in view of its earlier role in the facilitation process.) The fact that the OAU Headquarters is in Addis Ababa where Eritrea has these days limited if no access was an added disadvantage.

Ethiopia has and continues to perpetrate gross violation of human rights against our citizens long-resident in that country. Ethiopia has to-date expelled more than 42,000 Eritreans in the most inhumane way while confiscating their property. Around 1500 of our citizens are languishing in the concentration camp of Blaten while an unknown number also remain detained in other prisons in Ethiopia. Sadly, the OAU has not taken appropriate measures to stop these gross violations which have a direct impact on the conflict.

The Ethiopian regime continues to reject all calls for measures to reduce the tension. It routinely issues threats and ultimatums that it will use force, particularly during periods preceding peace talks. Unfortunately, the OAU has not succeeded in at least arranging for a cessation of hostilities that would have created a conducive climate for a peaceful solution.

Issues that Require Clarification

1. Regarding Badme and environs
   - The coordinates of Badme and its location relative to the recognized boundary?
   - What is meant by environs? Which areas does it include?
   - According to Ethiopia, 'Badme and environs' means 'all Ethiopian border territories occupied by Eritrea since May 6, 1998'. What is the OAU's view?
   - Has Ethiopia submitted to the OAU the totality of its claims as had been repeatedly requested by Eritrea?

2. Regarding redeployment
   - What is the justification for unilateral Eritrean redeployment from Badme?
   - Why redeployment to positions before May 6? Where precisely are these positions?
   - What does 'the redeployment be extended within the framework of demilitarization' mean? Whose redeployment is it?

3. Regarding civilian administration
   - What is the justification for 'reinstated civilian administration': if the area under consideration is Eritrean with an Eritrean population?
   - What is the rationale for setting up an alien administration for a short time and when options exist for quick demarcation?

4. Regarding investigation
   - What is the purpose of 'an investigation on the incidents of July–August 1997 and 6 May 1998 and all incidents in between', if it has no bearing on the settlement of the dispute?
   - Why are not the incidents that occurred on May 6 and that escalated through a series of spiralling clashes until May 12 not seen as one integral act of violation? Moreover, why is May 6, 1998, seen as central? Why not July 1997?

5. Regarding colonial treaties
   - Has the OAU ascertained that both sides recognize and respect the colonial boundary between the two countries as defined by the established colonial treaties?
   - If this is the case, can this be affirmed through an agreement between the two Parties?
   - What is the meaning of the clause 'international law applicable to the colonial treaties'? What is the precise interpretation of the OAU and UN Charters concerning colonial treaties?

6. Regarding demarcation
   - What is the legal basis for demarcation?
   - What are its modalities, mechanism and time-frame?
   - What are the legal arrangements that will render the outcome binding?

7. The principle of 'the non-use of force and intimidation'
   - Has the Committee attempted to ascertain which Party has used force as a means of imposing a solution?
   - Has the Committee tried to ascertain which party resorted to force in the July 1997 incident at Adi Murug; the January 1998 incident on the Assab road and the May incidents in Badme?
   - What is the position of the Committee regarding the resolution of Ethiopia's Parliament on May 13, 1998 declaring war against Eritrea?
   - Who launched the first air attack? When?
   - Which Party imposed an air and maritime embargo; taking hostile measures to impose it?
   - What is the position of the Committee on the repetitive threats of the Ethiopian government to unleash war?
   - Who will investigate all these incidents and threats of war? Why and how is it possible to give judgment prior to these investigations?

8. Regarding the principle of peaceful solution to dispute
   - Which Party has been routinely rejecting a peaceful solution?
   - Is unconditional cessation of hostilities acceptable to both sides?
   - If the response to the above question is negative, what are the reasons and its implications?

9. Regarding the violation of basic human rights of citizens
   - Has the Committee taken stock of the basic violations committed and property illegally confiscated?
   - What will be the role of the OAU in ensuring that these violations are redressed?

10. Regarding the Central Organ of the OAU
    - What is the mandate of the Central Organ?
    - What can we expect from the forthcoming meeting of the Central Organ?

APPENDIX 9
OAU's Response of 26 January 1999 to the Points of Clarification Raised by Eritrea with the the OAU Concerning the Implementation of the Framework Agreement

OAU: Issues Raised by the Eritrean Side Requiring Clarification

1. Regarding Badme and Environs

a. On the coordinates of Badme and its location relative to the recognised boundary?

The OAU High-Level Delegation addressed the issue of the Administration of Badme. The issue of the coordinates of Badme was not raised. This is a technical matter which could be addressed during the implementation of the Framework Agreement.

b. What is meant by environs? Which areas does it include?

Environs refer to the area surrounding Badme Town.

c. According to Ethiopia, 'Badme and environs' means 'all Ethiopian border territories occupied by Eritrea since May 6, 1998'. What is the OAU's views?

See paragraph 36 in the Report on the efforts of the OAU High-Level Delegation, presented to the Fourth Ordinary Session of the Central Organ, meeting at Heads of State Level, which states: 'the High Level Delegation took note of the position of Prime Minister Meles Zenawi. There was, however, no further discussion on the issue'.

d. Has Ethiopia submitted to the OAU the totality of its claims as had been repeatedly requested by Eritrea?

Ethiopia has indicated that it will submit its claims when the issues of delimitation, demarcation and, if need be, arbitration are addressed.

2. Regarding Redeployment

a. What is the justification for unilateral Eritrean redeployment from Badme?

The OAU High-Level Delegation came to the conclusion that Badme town and its environs were administered by Ethiopia prior to the events of 6–12 May, 1998. Therefore, the troops to be redeployed are those that occupied the area between 6–12 May 1998.

b. Why redeployment to positions before May 6? Where precisely are the positions?

The incidents between 6–12 May are the fundamental issues that brought the dispute to the attention of the OAU and the International Community. The precise location of these positions are to be identified by Technical Experts during the implementation stages of the Framework Agreement with the cooperation of the two parties.

c. What does 'the redeployment to be extended within the framework of demilitarisation' mean? Whose redeployment is it?'

The redeployment is of Eritrean troops from Badme Town and its environs. This should be immediately followed by the demilitarisation of the entire border, through the redeployment of the forces of both parties along the entire border, to positions to be determined subsequently, as part of the implementation process of the Framework Agreement.

3. Regarding Civilian Administration

a. What is the justification for 'reinstated civilian administration' if the area under consideration is Eritrean with an Eritrean population?

This is based on the conclusions of the OAU High-Level Delegation on the Administration of the areas concerned prior to 6 May, 1998 and not on the population. This position is without prejudice to the final status of the areas concerned which will be determined after the processes of delimitation, demarcation and if need be, arbitration, have been concluded.

b. What is the rationale for setting up an alien administration for a short time when options exist for quick demarcation?

The administration referred to is not a new one; it is the one that was there prior to 6 May, 1998. The High-Level Delegation is of the view that this measure will contribute towards defusing tension and paving the way for the implementation of the other aspects of the Framework Agreement.

4. Regarding Investigation

a. What is the purpose of 'an investigation on the incidents of July–August 1997 and 6 May 1998 and all incidents in between', if it has no bearing on the settlement of the dispute?

The High-Level Delegation is of the view that such an investigation has a bearing on a lasting settlement of the dispute. It will provide further clarity on those events, and allow the OAU to appreciate the problem in all its dimensions. In the meantime, the recommendations on redeployment and demilitarisation are aimed at creating an enabling environment for the processes of delimitation, demarcation and arbitration.

b. Why are not the incidents that occurred on May 6 and that escalated through a series of spiralling clashes until May 12, not seen as one integral act of violation? Moreover, why is May 6, 1998 seen as central? Why not July 1997?

See response in 2(b).

5. Regarding Colonial Treaties

a. Has the OAU ascertained that both sides recognise and respect the colonial boundary between the two countries as defined by the established colonial treaties?

This is a fundamental principle of the OAU which all OAU Member States have accepted. This principle is therefore reflected in the proposals submitted by the OAU High-Level Delegation to both parties. The OAU takes it that by accepting these proposals and eventually by signing the Framework Agreement which contains this principle, the two Parties would have committed themselves to abide by this principle.

b. If this is the case, can this be affirmed through an agreement between the two Parties?

This principle is part and parcel of the Framework Agreement.

c. What is the meaning of the clause 'international law applicable to the colonial treaties'?

International laws are laws that govern the relations between States. In this particular case, international law would refer to the specific aspects of the international law relevant to the colonial Treaties.

d. What is the precise interpretation of the OAU and UN Charters concerning colonial treaties?

As far as the OAU is concerned, it is to be noted that its Charter refers to the principle of territorial integrity of its Member States. This position was further elaborated in the well-known Resolution AHG/Res. 16(1) adopted at the OAU Summit in Cairo in July 1964 which provided in its operative paragraphs as follows:

SOLEMNLY REAFFIRMS the strict respect by all Member States of the Organisation for the Principles laid down in paragraph 3 of Article III of the Charter of the Organisation of African Unity;

SOLEMNLY DECLARES that all Member States pledge themselves to respect the borders existing on their achievement of national independence.

6. Regarding Demarcation

a. What is the legal basis for demarcation?

The signing of the Framework Agreement by the two parties.

b. What are its modalities, mechanism and time-frame?

The time-frame is 6 months to be extended as provided for in the Framework Agreement (on the recommendation of the cartographic experts). The modalities and Mechanism to be worked out by the Follow-up Committee in consultation with the Experts.

c. What are the legal arrangements that will render the outcome binding?

Same response as in 6(a).

7. The principle of 'the Non-Use of Force and Intimidation'

a. Has the Committee attempted to ascertain which party has used force as a means of imposing a solution?

This will be determined by the investigations to be carried out as part of the comprehensive settlement plan.

b. Has the Committee tried to ascertain which party resorted to force in the July 1997 incident at Adi Murug, the January 1998 incident on the Assab road and the May incidents in Badme?

The July 1997 and the May 1998 incidents will be the subject of the proposed investigation. The January 1998 incident is new to the OAU, but could be covered by the investigation as proposed in the Framework Agreement where reference is made to the need to investigate other incidents that may have contributed to the present dispute.

c. What is the position of the Committee regarding the resolution of Ethiopia's Parliament on May 13, 1998 declaring war against Eritrea?

The Committee has refrained from making any judgement on Statements by the Governments and institutions in both countries. It has consistently appealed to both parties to exercise restraint and refrain from any actions and decisions which could harm the relations between the two sisterly countries and their peoples.

On the rest of the clarifications sought under 7, the Committee considered its role to be one of offering good offices to both Parties and urging them to exercise maximum restraint, as well as to opt for a peaceful settlement of their dispute.

8. Regarding the Principle of a Peaceful Solution to Disputes

a. Which Party has been routinely rejecting a peaceful solution?

Both Parties have consistently expressed to the OAU High-Level Delegation their commitment to a peaceful settlement of the current dispute.

b. Is unconditional cessation of hostilities acceptable to both sides?

The OAU High-Level Delegation did not address the issue of unconditional cessation of hostilities. It has taken the issue of cessation of hostilities within the context of the Framework Agreement submitted to both sides. In fact, the cessation of hostilities is contained in the first operative paragraph of the Framework Agreement.

9. Regarding the Violation of Basic Human Rights of Citizens

a. Has the Committee taken stock of the basic violations committed and property illegally confiscated?

See the relevant paragraph in the introductory note handed over to both parties by the Ministerial Committee in Ouagadougou (1–2 August 1998) which stated, inter alia, 'As regards the situation of Eritreans in Ethiopia. ... However, the conditions in which those deportations were carried out, the decision to extend those measures to families of the deported persons and the fate of their properties are a source of deep concern'.

b. What will be the role of the OAU in ensuring that these violations are redressed?

The OAU, with the cooperation of both parties and with the assistance of the United Nations and other relevant institutions, will help the parties to address all aspects of the dispute, including the humanitarian problems generated by the dispute.

10. Regarding the Central Organ of the OAU

a. What is the mandate of the Central Organ?

See the 1993 Cairo Declaration of the OAU Summit establishing the Mechanism for Conflict Prevention, Management and Resolution.

b. What can we expect from the forthcoming meeting of the Central Organ?

See the Communique adopted by the Central Organ at the end of its deliberations.

APPENDIX 10
Press Statement of 2 March 1999 from the Eritrean Foreign Ministry Accepting the OAU Framework Agreement & Explaining the Continuation of the War

Ethiopia Is Intent on Waging War: Peace Was Never On Its Agenda

Ethiopia's diplomatic offensive in the past months was anchored in one theme: that it will not contemplate peace unless and until the OAU Framework is accepted by Eritrea.

Eritrea's acceptance of the OAU framework has now exposed Ethiopia's bluff. Indeed, Ethiopia can no longer conceal its territorial ambitions and other larger objectives behind the facade of a framework 'which it has accepted in good faith but that remains rejected by Eritrea.'

The UN Security Council, the OAU High-Level Delegation, and the European Union, among others, have all issued statements this week urging both sides to cease hostilities immediately and unconditionally. But Ethiopia refuses to heed these calls.

Ethiopia has yesterday lashed out at the United Nations, arrogantly stating that it will not accept UN Security Council Resolution 1227. It particularly took offense at Article 2 of the resolution that 'demands an immediate halt to the hostilities, in particular the use of air strikes' and at Article 7 which 'strongly urges all states to end immediately all sales of arms and munitions to Ethiopia and Eritrea.' Ethiopia's underlying motive in rejecting these articles is too transparent to merit elaboration.

Ethiopia's larger design on Eritrea is coming to the surface in various forms. The regime has now begun to sing a new tune, calling for the 'overthrow of the Eritrean government' which it dubs as a 'threat to the region.' This was the gist of the official statement that the regime issued yesterday.

Ethiopia's territorial ambitions on Eritrea have been an open secret for a long time now. In June last year, Ethiopia's Deputy Foreign Minister openly boasted that the Addis Abeba regime will capture the Eritrean port of Assab 'within a week.' Ethiopia has amassed thousands of heavily armed troops on the Burie front, 70 kms from Assab, and hundreds of kilometers away from the 'disputed Badme area.' The Ethiopian regime recently bombed, without success, the airport of Assab and attempted to destroy the water reservoir supplying the port city.

Confirming its larger designs on Eritrea, the Ethiopian regime informed its troops on the eve of the large-scale offensive that it launched on February 6, that the objective was to take Eritrea's capital, Asmara; overthrow the present government; and install a 'transitional government' whose 'Charter' has already been drawn up in the Ethiopian capital, Addis Abeba.

Signs of Ethiopia's hidden agenda against Eritrea have been evident for quite a long time now: In July 1997, Ethiopia occupied by force, with the use of over 1,000 troops, the Adi Murug area in eastern Eritrea and escalated its incursions on the Badme area, which it had started much earlier; In October 1997, Ethiopia published a new map of the northern region of Tigray which incorporated large areas of Eritrea; In May 1998, Ethiopia provoked a series of clashes in the Badme area when its troops first attacked a small Eritrean unit, killing most of its members; Finally, on May 13, 1998, Ethiopia's 'Parliament' declared war on Eritrea. This declaration was executed through ground attacks that Ethiopia launched in late May and early June last year on all three fronts as well as the first air bombing of Asmara on June 5. And, since February 6 this year, and at a time when there was visible progress in the peace efforts, Ethiopia began to unleash the on-going large-scale offensives.

Ethiopia has violated fundamental principles of international law and accepted conventions and norms of civilized behavior in conducting its war of aggression. Indeed, it has: repeatedly resorted to the use of force, including the unleashing of the current large-scale offensive; violated international human rights conventions in its campaign of 'ethnic cleansing' of Eritreans; bombing civilians and economic targets; violated the US-brokered moratorium on air strikes without serving advance notice to the party concerned; employed mercenaries in its Air Force; broken into the premises of the Eritrean Embassy residence in Addis Abeba.

All these facts illustrate one thing. Ethiopia may have succeeded to smoke-screen its real intentions in the past. Many may have thought that this was a simple border dispute that has gone beyond proportions. But now, it is becoming clearer that Ethiopia's agenda encompasses expansionist territorial ambition on its sovereign neighbor and subversion of its government. This can only be a recipe for regional instability and insecurity.

Ministry of Foreign Affairs
Asmara, 2 March 1999

APPENDIX 11
Ethiopian Ministry of Foreign Affairs, Response of 10 March 1999 to Eritrea's Acceptance of the OAU Framework Agreement

Ethiopia Remains Committed to the OAU Framework Agreement

Statement by the Ministry of Foreign Affairs, Government of Ethiopia, March 10, 1999

Consistency and being true to principles and absolute commitment to the peaceful resolution of the conflict has been the hallmark of Ethiopia's position since the Eritrean aggression on our country in May, 1998.

Since the OAU facilitation commenced in June 1998, and the setting up of the High-Level Delegation, Ethiopia has dealt with the OAU in a forthright manner and with all due respect accorded to the Organization, to the High-Level Delegation and to its individual members.

When the High-Level Delegation finally put on the table its peace proposal, Ethiopia, through its Prime Minister, immediately accepted the Framework Agreement ad referendum after the clarifications it requested were given to its satisfaction at the summit in Ouagadougou. Its formal acceptance of the Framework was communicated subsequently through a message by Prime Minister Meles dated 12 November, 1998, addressed to the current chairman with copies to the other heads of state of the Delegation and to the Secretary-General of the Organization of African Unity.

In the communication of 12 November, 1998, referred to above, Prime Minister Meles said, inter alia, reiterating the clarification given to him at the Ouagadougou summit that 'It is ... to be noted that the High-Level Delegation underscored in its clarification, that with regard to Article 3, the Eritrean forces are to withdraw from all Ethiopian border territories that they have occupied since May 6, 1998.'

Accordingly, as underlined in no uncertain terms by its Prime Minister, the demand that Eritrea must withdraw from all occupied Ethiopian territories for peace to be achieved between Ethiopia and Eritrea has been a firm Ethiopian position and a fundamental and irreducible minimum condition and not, as alleged by Eritrea, a new element injected by Ethiopia at the eleventh hour. It would have been unthinkable for Ethiopia to have done otherwise, because that would have amounted to rewarding aggression; and not rewarding aggression has from the outset been the mainstay of the Ethiopian position on countering the madness in Eritrea. Fortunately, this has also been the conviction of the High-Level Delegation. In this regard, it must sound rather strange to expect Ethiopia to change its position now after Badme; and what the battle of Badme symbolizes cannot be lost on Eritrea. Forceful occupation is forceful occupation. It would be absurd – although anything can be expected from Asmara – and makes no sense logically and in terms of international law for an aggressor to be asked to withdraw only from a portion of part of a sovereign state it had seized by force. In any case, all this is partly a moot question because Eritrea did not withdraw from the Badme region in compliance with the OAU peace plan, but under duress when its army was routed in humiliation.

Ethiopia accepted the Framework Agreement not because all its elements were to its liking, but because it was a comprehensive package which as the Security Council affirmed later, was 'fair and balanced' and because it did not reward aggression and it did not ask for the humiliation of Ethiopia as Eritrea had wanted.

Ethiopia's acceptance of the Framework Agreement was thus not tactical, but principled. Ethiopia embraced the Framework, not because the imperative of tactical maneuver dictated acceptance by Ethiopia, but because Ethiopia's commitment to peace made it an imperative necessity.

All the more so because the Framework, to reiterate, did not reward aggression. The Framework Agreement which some later wanted to tinker with, as the Security Council tried to do in its formal meeting of 10 February as well as at its informal consultation of 24 February 1999, is the expression of OAU's commitment to principles of international law and to its resolute objection to and abhorrence of the philosophy that might is right.

Since the Eritrean debacle in Badme region which was liberated by Ethiopia with great sacrifice, Eritrea has suddenly become ostensibly a new convert in embracing the Framework Agreement. Within less than 24 hours after its occupation forces were routed from Badme, Eritrea informed the Security Council on 27 February 1999 through a convoluted letter by its president which is full of loopholes and resembling a war communique, about its acceptance of the peace plan. No sooner had the letter written by its president containing this message in which Eritrea's acceptance of the peace plan was thrown in as an afterthought reached the Security Council than an emergency meeting of the Council was convened on a weekend to celebrate this 'historic acceptance' of the peace plan by Eritrea.

What was of immense surprise to Ethiopia was not Eritrea's acceptance – which as subsequent events have shown was tactical and insincere – but the eagerness and enthusiasm demonstrated by some members of the Security Council to give legitimacy to Eritrea's attempt to use the Framework Agreement as a smokescreen for buying time.

There is now absolutely no doubt that what Eritrea wanted to do by accepting the OAU plan at the eleventh hour was to gain respite for further military preparation. This has been made clear by its various officials, including by its Foreign Minister as well as by developments on the ground. The speeded up tempo with which fortifications are being built and reinforced in still occupied Ethiopian territories and the rounding up of new recruits for yet another battle, are all indications that contradict Eritrea's professed intentions. Moreover, the Eritrean authorities are yet to inform their citizens formally of their acceptance of the Framework Agreement. What the Eritrean people are told officially is about a so-called voluntary tactical withdrawal in preparation for another offensive.

In the meantime, Eritrea, in its public relations exercise has become more Catholic than the Bishop about its commitment to the OAU peace plan – a plan which it had scoffed at as late as six days prior to the battle of Badme, telling the EU Troika that it was an unsatisfactory formula prepared by a fickle Organization. The conversion, if it was genuine, would still be good enough, regardless of the Eritrean attitude toward the OAU. But the conversion is fake.

Under these circumstances, it will be folly for Ethiopia to allow Eritrea to gain time for yet another aggression. The yardstick for Eritrea's genuine acceptance of the Framework Agreement is its immediate and unconditional withdrawal from the remaining occupied Ethiopian territory and the return of the status quo ante in full, in line with the letter and spirit of the OAU peace plan.

Furthermore, in light of the huge loss of lives, the humanitarian crisis and the destruction of property caused by the Eritrean aggression, Ethiopia will insist, as it already has done in a letter by its Prime Minister to the President of the Security Council on 8 March 1999, that Eritrea bears full responsibility for all these damages. This is the road to peace and to the successful implementation of the Framework Agreement.

Ethiopia pays homage to the OAU for having stood up for principles at a time when so few were seen practicing what they preach and at a time when those entrusted with the responsibility for international peace and security have been so eager to reward aggression. Eritrea still counts, even after Badme, that its aggression may be rewarded. If Ethiopia had not allowed this prior to Badme, it would be madness to expect that it would do this after Badme and after so many patriots died liberating part of their land from the aggressors.

APPENDIX 12
Testimony of 25 May 1999 by Assistant
Secretary of State, Ms Susan Rice, on the
Conflict in the Horn of Africa

The Ethiopian–Eritrean War: US Policy Options

Ms Susan Rice, Assistant Secretary, Bureau of African Affairs, US Department of State, on a Congressional hearing on Tuesday, May 25, 1999

Introduction

Thank you, Mr. Chairman, for inviting me to testify today on the conflict in the Horn of Africa. Much like the crisis in Sierra Leone, which I had the opportunity to discuss with your subcommittee members two months ago, the war in the Horn of Africa threatens a broad swath of Africa as well as United States' interests in the region as a whole.

The Ethiopia–Eritrea conflict, which began in May 1998, has substantially damaged the economic growth and development of Ethiopia and Eritrea and has led to humanitarian suffering on both sides of the border. Tens of thousands of lives have been lost and thousands more have been maimed.

The United States and others in the international community have consistently called for an immediate cessation of hostilities and speedy implementation of the Organization of African Unity's Framework Agreement. We continue to work with the United Nations and the Organization of African Unity to secure and implement a lasting peace.

Origins of the Conflict / Escalations of Hostilities

The origins of the war are complex. During the 1980s, two liberation fronts – the Tigray People's Liberation Front (TPLF) and the Eritrea People's Liberation Front (EPLF) – joined forces against Ethiopian dictator Mengistu Haile Mariam, although differences between the two led to occasional disputes. Mengistu's brutal Derg regime was toppled in 1991, and Eritrea gained formal independence in 1993. As a result, Ethiopia became landlocked, with a common border established almost 100 years ago between the Italian colony of Eritrea and Ethiopia never fully and precisely delineated or demarcated. It is important to note that the two new governments enjoyed such strong bilateral relations that neither they nor the international community considered formal determination of the border an immediate priority.

In the year leading to the outbreak of fighting, relations between the two former allies deteriorated, exacerbated by economic tensions. A border skirmish occurred on May 6, 1998, at Badme. A week later, Eritrea sent troops and armor into and beyond Badme into territory administered by Ethiopia. After several weeks of fighting, several areas previously administered by Ethiopia – the Badme area and areas near Zela Ambessa and Bure, south of the port of Assab – fell under Eritrean control.

As the ground fighting escalated, in June of 1998 Ethiopia launched airstrikes against Asmara airport. Eritrea made retaliatory strikes against the Ethiopian towns of Mekele and Adigrat, south of Zela Ambessa, hitting a school. Both sides then agreed to a US-brokered airstrike moratorium, and fighting decreased to occasional exchanges of artillery and small-arms fire over a nine-month period.

Both Ethiopia and Eritrea used the intervening months to acquire new military stockpiles, including state-of-the-art fighter aircraft and artillery, and to recruit, train and deploy tens of thousands of new soldiers. The United States actively discouraged suppliers to both parties, and the UN Security Council urged governments not to provide weapons to exacerbate the problem. Publicly, Ethiopia continued to demand a complete and absolute return to the status quo ante of May 6, 1998. Eritrea insisted that some of the area it occupied after May 6, 1998, was Eritrean territory.

Fighting resumed on 6 February 1999, when Ethiopian forces attacked, eventually displacing Eritrean forces from the disputed area of Badme. Ethiopia employed fighter-bombers, helicopter gunships, and reconfigured transport aircraft in tactical support of ground operations. Ethiopia later launched an unsuccessful counter-offensive on the Zela Ambessa front in mid-March. Eritrea failed to re-take Badme in subsequent fighting at the end of March. In April, Ethiopia struck an Eritrean Military training facility and other targets deep within Eritrea. A week and a half ago, Ethiopian aircraft bombed sites at Zela Ambessa, Badme, and the port of Massawa. Although there has been a lull in the ground fighting over the past few weeks, press reports from yesterday indicate there were clashes between ground forces this past weekend at Badme.

United States' Interests

The United States has significant interests in ending the war between Ethiopia and Eritrea as soon as possible. The current conflict threatens regional stability and to reverse Ethiopian and Eritrean progress in economic and political development.

The United States has important national security interests in the Horn of Africa. Ethiopia's and Eritrea's neighbor, Sudan, has long supported international terrorism, fostered the spread of Islamic extremism beyond its borders, actively worked to destabilize neighboring states, including Ethiopia and Eritrea, and perpetrated massive human rights violations against its own citizens. Since the conflict began last year, Sudan has increasingly benefited from the hostilities between its former adversaries. Eritrea recently signed an accord with Sudan to normalize relations. Ethiopia has renewed air service to Khartoum and has made overtures to Sudan for improved relations as well. Both sides have moved to reduce support to Sudanese opposition groups.

Eritrea's President Issaias has made several trips to Libya – Africa's other state sponsor of terrorism – for frequent consultations with Colonel Qadhafi, and has joined Qadhafi's Community of Saharan and Sahelian States (COMESSA).

We are very concerned by credible reports that Eritrea has delivered large quantities of weapons and munitions to self-proclaimed Somalia President Hussein Aideed for the use of a violent faction of the Oromo Liberation Front. The terrorist organization Al-Ittihad may also be an indirect recipient of these arms. Ethiopia also is shipping arms to factions in Somalia. The recent upsurge of violence in Somalia is, in part, related to these new developments.

Increased activity by a violent faction of the OLF in the south and the east has led to cross-border raids by Ethiopian security forces along its frontiers with Kenya and Somalia. These developments clearly reflect a dangerous trend.

Prior to this conflict, Ethiopia and Eritrea played a constructive role in the Great Lakes region. Their current dispute with each other has precluded them from continuing to take such a role in this volatile area and other areas of the continent where we had foreseen mutually beneficial cooperation.

The security costs of the conflict are matched, if not exceeded, by the grave humanitarian consequences of the war between Ethiopia and Eritrea. Tens of thousands of lives have been lost and hundreds of thousands displaced. Approximately 300,000 Ethiopian and 100,000–200,000 Eritrean civilians have been forced from their homes and fields near the border by the conflict. An estimated 60,000 Eritreans and Ethiopians of Eritrean descent have been deported from Ethiopia to Eritrea, and an estimated 20,000 Ethiopians have left Eritrea under duress. We have made clear that we consider the practice of deportation to be a fundamental violation of individual rights. The nature of these expulsions and the arrangements made for transfer and holding of property were clearly susceptible to abuse.

United States' Response

Immediately upon the outbreak of hostilities in May 1999, I led two interagency missions to Ethiopia and Eritrea to facilitate a peaceful resolution of the dispute. Working with the government of Rwanda, we proposed a series of steps to end the conflict in accordance with both sides' shared principles and international law. These recommendations, endorsed by the OAU and the UNSC, later informed development by the OAU of its Framework Agreement. These initial missions also resulted in agreement by the two parties to the airstrike moratorium, which remained in effect until February 6, 1999.

Beginning in October, President Clinton sent former National Security Advisor Anthony Lake and an interagency team from the State Department, the National Security Council, and the Department of Defense on four missions to Ethiopia and Eritrea, the most recent occurring in early 1999. We are grateful for Mr. Lake's tireless work on behalf of the President and the Secretary of State. His intensive efforts, which still continue, have been aimed at helping both sides find a mutually agreed basis for resolving the dispute without further loss of life. Working closely with the OAU and the UNSC, Mr. Lake and our team put forth numerous proposals to both sides consistent with the OAU Framework. In December, Ethiopia formally accepted the Framework Agreement. Eritrea did not, requesting clarification on numerous specific questions.

Fighting resumed on February 6 while UN envoy Ambassador Mohammed Sahnoun was in the region still seeking a peaceful resolution to the conflict. Following this first phase of fighting, Eritrean troops were compelled to withdraw from Badme – an important element of the draft OAU Framework Agreement. Subsequent Eritrean acceptance of the Framework was welcomed by the United States and the UNSC but was greeted with skepticism by Ethiopia. Ethiopia instead demanded Eritrea's unconditional, unilateral withdrawal from all contested areas that Ethiopia had administered prior to last May.

On April 14, Prime Minister Meles of Ethiopia offered a cease-fire in return for an explicit commitment by Eritrea to remove its forces unilaterally from contested areas. He later added that Eritrean withdrawal must occur within an undefined but 'short' period.

Eritrea continues to demand a cease-fire prior to committing to withdraw from disputed territories. Ethiopia insists that a cease-fire and implementation of the OAU Framework Agreement can only follow an explicit Eritrean commitment to withdraw from all territories occupied since the conflict erupted on May 6, 1998.

Conclusion

A Joint Organization of African Unity/United Nations effort to urge both sides to accept a cease-fire and begin implementing the framework agreement continues. The United States Government remains actively engaged, in support of the OAU, with both Eritrea and Ethiopia to secure a peace settlement.

There is a need, however, to not only end the conflict as quickly as possible but also ultimately to repair, over the long term, strained relations in the Horn. A resolution of the border war may be attainable. The task of rebuilding both countries and mending ties between Ethiopia and Eritrea to ensure long-term sustained peace and mutual security will be especially difficult. It will require due attention and support from the United States and the international community. Mr. Chairman, I look forward to continuing to work with you and other members of this Subcommittee as we continue to pursue our shared interest in forging a peaceful resolution to this tragic conflict.

APPENDIX 13
Modalities for Implementation of the OAU Framework Agreement on the Settlement of the Dispute between Ethiopia & Eritrea, 12 July 1999

(Submitted to both parties on Monday July 12, 1999 and reported to the 35th OAU Heads of State and Government Summit in Algiers on Wednesday, July 14, 1999)

The two Parties reaffirm their commitment to the principle of the non-use of force to settle disputes.

The two Parties reaffirm their acceptance of the Framework Agreement and commit themselves to implement it in good faith.

There shall be a return to positions held prior to 6 May 1998.

On the basis of these principles, the two Parties agree on the following modalities for the implementation of the Framework Agreement:

1. The Eritrean Government commits itself to redeploy its forces outside the territories they occupied after 6 May 1998.
2. The Ethiopian Government commits itself to redeploy, thereafter, its forces from positions taken after 6 February 1999 and which were not under Ethiopian administration before May 6, 1998.
3. The two Parties agree to put an end to all military activities and all forms of expression likely to sustain and exacerbate the climate of hostility and thus compromise the implementation of the Framework Agreement.
4. The redeployment of troops shall commence immediately after the cessation of hostilities. This redeployment shall not, in any way, prejudice the final status of the territories concerned, it being understood that this status will be determined at the end of the border delimitation and demarcation.
5. The modalities for the re-establishment of the civilian Administration and population in the concerned territories shall be worked out after the cessation of hostilities.
6. The two Parties accept the deployment of Military Observers by the OAU in cooperation with the United Nations. The Group of Military Observers will supervise the redeployment of troops as stipulated in the present modalities and carry out all other duties that are entrusted to it, in conformity with the relevant provisions of the Framework Agreement.
7. The two Parties commit themselves to sign a formal Ceasefire Agreement which provides for the detailed modalities for the implementation of the Framework Agreement.

APPENDIX 14
Technical Arrangements for Implementation of the OAU Framework Agreement & its Modalities

- Recalling that the Government of the State of Eritrea and the Government of the Federal Democratic Republic of Ethiopia, hereinafter referred to as the Parties, have accepted the OAU Framework Agreement and the Modalities for its implementation;

- Underlining that the OAU Framework Agreement and the Modalities have been endorsed by the 35th Ordinary Session of the Assembly of Heads of State and Government, held in Algiers, Algeria, from 12 to 14 July, 1999, as well as strongly supported by the United Nations Security Council and accepted as they are by the Parties;

- Having carefully examined the views submitted by the Parties;

- Recalling the acceptance by the Parties that any interpretation of the OAU Framework Agreement and the Modalities is the sole responsibility of the OAU and its Current Chairman;

- Noting that the present Technical Arrangements have been elaborated on the basis of the letter and spirit of the principles contained in the OAU Framework Agreement and the Modalities, in particular the respect for the borders existing at independence, as stated in Resolution AHG/Res. 16(I) adopted by the OAU Summit in Cairo in 1964, the resolution of disputes through peaceful and legal means, in accordance with the principles enshrined in the Charters of the Organization of African Unity and the United Nations, and the non-use of force to settle disputes;

- Further recalling that the present Technical Arrangements are the result of collective work of the OAU, the United Nations, the United States and other interested partners;

- Stressing that the ultimate goal of the process is to find a peaceful and lasting solution to the conflict:

  1. The Parties agree on the principles and other provisions contained in the Framework Agreement and the Modalities and accept the Technical Arrangements (which includes its four Annexes) as binding. In that regard, the Parties agree to use the Framework Agreement, the Modalities and the

Technical Arrangements as the sole basis for resolving the dispute.

The Parties will initiate separate requests to the Secretaries General of the United Nations and the OAU as necessary for assistance to implement the Framework Agreement, the Modalities and the Technical Arrangements.

2. In order to facilitate the process of implementing the Framework Agreement, the Modalities and the Technical Arrangements, including the work of the Commission which will be charged with determining the redeployment positions (referred to as the Neutral Commission in paragraph 3 and the establishment of a peacekeeping mission, the Parties agree to put an end to all military activities and all forms of expression likely to sustain and exacerbate the climate of hostility.

In particular, the Parties agree to the following:
a) cessation of all armed air and land attacks;
b) cessation of any other action that may impede the implementation of the Framework Agreement, the Modalities and the Technical Arrangements;
c) guarantee of the free movement of the peacekeeping mission and its supplies as required through and between the territories of the Parties,
d) respect and protection of the members of the peacekeeping mission, its installations and equipment;
e) respect for international humanitarian law.

3. In order to facilitate the process of redeployment of Eritrean forces as referred to in paragraph 1 of the Modalities and, thereafter, of Ethiopian forces as referred to in paragraph 2 of the Modalities, and to facilitate the full implementation of paragraph 5 of those Modalities, with a view to returning to positions held prior to 6 May 1998, a Neutral Commission shall be established by the Current Chairman of the OAU, in consultation with the Secretaries General of the United Nations and the OAU. Utilizing whatever information it deems relevant and in consultation with the Parties, the Neutral Commission will determine what those positions were.

The Parties agree to cooperate fully with the Neutral Commission.
The Neutral Commission will endeavour to complete its work and submit its report to the Current Chairman of the OAU in three weeks.
The determination of the Neutral Commission is binding on the Parties.
The determination of the Neutral Commission shall not prejudice the final status of the territories concerned, it being understood that this status will be determined at the end of the delimitation and demarcation process.

4. In order to monitor and assist with the implementation of the Framework Agreement, the Modalities and the Technical Arrangements, and verify compliance with the implementation of the Technical Arrangements, it is understood that a peacekeeping mission will be established under the authority of the United Nations Security Council and led by a Special

Representative of the UN Secretary-General. The Special Representative of the UN Secretary-General will liaise and work closely with the representative of the OAU Secretary-General. The deployment of the UN peacekeeping mission will be preceded by the deployment by the OAU, with the support of the United Nations, of liaison officers/observers. These liaison officers/observers will subsequently become members of the UN peacekeeping mission. The Parties will be consulted, as appropriate, throughout the establishment process.

5. In line with article 9 (a) of the Framework Agreement and in order to facilitate the implementation of the Framework Agreement, Modalities and Technical Arrangements, a Follow-up Commission (for political aspects) and a Military Coordination Commission (for military aspects) will be established by and under the authority of the Special Representative of the UN Secretary General.

> The Parties will each appoint a senior representative to the Follow-up Commission. The Special Representative of the UN Secretary General will appoint a UN senior representative as Chairman. Decisions will be made by the Chairman of the Follow-up Commission in consultation with the Parties.
>
> The Parties will each appoint a senior military representative to the Military Coordination Commission. The Special Representative of the UN Secretary-General will appoint a UN senior military representative as Chairman. Decisions will be made by the Chairman of the Military Coordination Commission in consultation with the Parties.
>
> In fulfilling their mandate, the Follow-up Commission and the Military Coordination Commission will coordinate and resolve issues pertaining to the implementation of the Framework Agreement, Modalities and Technical Arrangements.

6. Upon the signing of the Framework Agreement, the Modalities and the Technical Arrangements, both Parties will conduct demining activities with a view to creating the conditions necessary for the redeployment of the peacekeeping mission, the return of civilian administration and the return of population as well as the delimitation and demarcation of their common border (see Annex I).

> The Peacekeeping mission, in conjunction with the United Nations Mine Action Service, will assist the Parties' demining efforts by providing technical advice and coordination.
>
> The Parties shall, as necessary, seek additional demining assistance from the peacekeeping mission.

7. The Parties will submit detailed redeployment plans to the peacekeeping mission within 5 days of receipt of the determination of the Neutral Commission (see paragraph 3 above and Annex II).

8. The process of redeployment and restoration of civilian administration will then begin, it being understood that this process shall not prejudice the final status of the territories concerned, which will be determined at the end of the delimitation and demarcation process.

   Following approval of the redeployment plans of the Parties by the peacekeeping mission, the sequence will be as follows:

   a) Eritrea redeploys its troops within 2 weeks. This redeployment is verified by the peacekeeping mission;

   b) upon verification of Eritrea redeployment by peacekeeping mission, the peacekeeping mission observes and assists the restoration by Ethiopia of the civilian administration, including police and local militia, within 7 days, to enable the restored civilian administration to prepare for the return of the population;

   c) as soon as paragraphs 8a and 8b above are completed, Ethiopia re-deploys its troops within 2 weeks. This redeployment is verified by the peacekeeping mission;

   d) upon verification of Ethiopian redeployment by the peacekeeping mission, the peacekeeping mission observes and assists the restoration by Eritrea of the civilian administration, including police and local militia, within 7 days, to enable the restored civilian administration to prepare for the return of the population.

9. In order to enhance the security of local populations in and returning to areas where civilian administration is restored:

   a) the parties commit themselves to:
      a.1) full cooperation with the peacekeeping mission;
      a.2) close cooperation between the restored civilian administrations and the international civilian component of the peacekeeping mission, which will observe compliance by the restored civilian administrations:
         a.2.1) with prohibitions on displacement and deportation of civilian populations;
         a.2.2) with facilitation of human rights monitoring;
         a.2.3) with prohibitions of display of weapons by militia in populated areas where civilian administration is restored;

   b) the peacekeeping mission will:
      b.1) observe and assist if requested and as appropriate, police in areas where civilian administration is restored;
      b.2) establish, as necessary local liaison and grievance resolution mechanism, ensuring access by the local population to those mechanisms.

10. In order to determine the origins of the conflict, an investigation will be carried out of the incidents of 6 May 1998 and of any other incident prior to that date which could have contributed to a misunderstanding between

the Parties regarding their common border, including the incidents of July/August 1997.

The investigation will be carried out by an independent, impartial body appointed in accordance with appended (Annex IV) time-line by the Current Chairman of the OAU, in consultation with the Secretaries General of the United Nations and the OAU.

The independent body will endeavour to submit its report to the Current Chairman of the OAU within 3 to 6 months.

The Parties agree to cooperate fully with the independent body and accept its determination.

11. The Parties agree that the delimitation work on the ground will commence segment by segment, beginning with areas of redeployment, moving to other contested areas and, finally, to the remaining common border.

    Upon the acceptance by the parties of the delimitation of each segment, the binding demarcation of that segment will be carried out. Such signed acceptance shall be given to the UN Cartographic Unit within one week, unless arbitration is requested by either Party (see paragraph 13 below).

    The delimitation and demarcation process will be done on the basis of pertinent colonial treaties and applicable international law.

12. The Parties agree to demilitarize in those areas as may be required by the peacekeeping mission in order to defuse tension and facilitate the delimitation and demarcation process (see Annex III).

13. Delimitation and demarcation will be conducted by the UN Cartographic Unit, supported by other Experts the Unit may employ.

    In line with article 6(a) of the Framework Agreement, delimitation/demarcation will be carried out expeditiously and completed within 6 months, unless extended by the Special Representative of the UN Secretary-General at the request of Cartographic Experts.

    Should the need arise for arbitration over delimitation, a Boundary Commission shall be established by the United Nations Secretary-General in consultation with the OAU Current Chairman. The Commission shall decide such issues as expeditiously as possible and on the basis of pertinent colonial treaties and applicable international law.

    The Parties agree to accept the outcome of the arbitration as binding.

14. Consistent with paragraph 8(a), 8(b) and 10 of the Framework Agreement, the Parties commit themselves to addressing all humanitarian concerns, resulting from the conflict, particularly the issues of those persons who have

been deported or displaced, as well as the socio-economic consequences of the dispute.

For their part, and in accordance with the pertinent provisions of the Framework Agreement, the OAU and the United Nations, working closely with the International Community, will endeavour to mobilize resources to assist in addressing such concerns.

The Parties agree to refer any specific claim on such issues to an appropriate mechanism of arbitration for binding resolution, should efforts at negotiated settlement or mediation not succeed.

If the Parties are unable to agree on the appropriate mechanism of arbitration within a period of three months starting from the signing, the UN Secretary-General, in consultation with the OAU Secretary-General, will determine the appropriate mechanism of arbitration.

15. As the demarcation process is completed in each segment, the legitimate authority will assume full and sovereign jurisdiction over that part of territory which will have been recognized as being within its boundary.

16. The Parties agree to sign and implement in good faith the OAU Framework Agreement for the settlement of the dispute, the Modalities for the Implementation of the Framework Agreement and the Technical Arrangements for the Implementation of the Framework Agreement and its Modalities (including its Annexes listed below*).

17. The OAU and the United Nations will be the guarantors for the scrupulous implementation of all the provisions of the OAU Framework Agreement, the Modalities for the Implementation of the Framework Agreement and the Technical Arrangements for the Implementation of the Framework Agreement and its Modalities.

Annex I to the Technical Arrangements for the Implementation of the OAU Framework Agreement and its Modalities (Demining activities)

Demining activities include submission of the following to the peacekeeping mission:

- maps detailing dimension and exact location of all minefields;
- exact composition by type of mines and number of mines for each minefield;
- plan for clearing of all minefields;
- plan for marking minefields;
- plan for disposal of cleared mines;
- any other information needed for verification.

Peacekeeping mission will observe, verify and assist if necessary all demining activities.

Annex II to the Technical Arrangements for the Implementation of the OAU Framework Agreement and its Modalities (Redeployment plans)

Redeployment plans will include:
- current location of each unit to redeploy;
- size and composition of each unit;
- exact route each unit will utilize to redeploy;
- exact location each redeploying unit will redeploy to;
- start time of redeployment for each redeploying unit;
- estimated closure time for each redeploying unit;
- redeploying units are not authorized to deviate from the plan nor can they move from their new location unless approved by the peacekeeping mission;
- any other information needed to complete verification.

The Parties agree that redeployment will be completed within 14 days after the redeployment plans are approved by the peacekeeping mission.

The Parties agree to suspend any types of military flights in the vicinity of redeployment areas during the period of redeployment.

The Parties agree that the peacekeeping mission will observe and verify redeployment.

The peacekeeping mission will verify that the troops of one Party do not move into areas from which the other Party has redeployed.

Annex III to the Technical Arrangements for the Implementation of the OAU Framework Agreement and its Modalities (Local demilitarization plans)

Local demilitarization plans will include:
- current location of each unit to demilitarize;
- size and composition of each unit;
- exact route each unit will utilize to demilitarize;
- exact location each demilitarizing unit will move to;
- movement start time of demilitarization for each unit;
- estimated closure time for each demilitarizing unit;
- demilitarizing units are not authorized to deviate from the plan nor can they move from their new location unless coordinated with the peacekeeping mission;
- any other information needed to complete verification.

The Parties agree that demilitarization will be completed within 7 days after the demilitarization plans are approved by the peacekeeping mission.

Deployment to original positions will commence upon the determination of the peacekeeping mission.

The Parties agree to suspend any types of military flights in the vicinity of demilitarization areas during the period of demilitarization.

The Parties agree that the peacekeeping mission will observe and verify demilitarization.

Annex IV to the Technical Arrangements for the Implementation of the OAU Framework Agreement and its Modalities (Implementation planning timeline)

D-Day: Signing of the Framework Agreement, Modalities and Technical Arrangements.

D+2: Cessation of hostilities as provided for in paragraph 2 of the Technical Arrangements.

D+3: Neutral Commission established.

Initiation of demining activities by the Parties.

D+4: Parties forward requests to the UN Secretary General.

D+5: Commencement of the work of the UN Cartographic Unit.

D+10: Appointment of OAU Representative.

D+14: Deployment by the OAU, with the support of the United Nations, of liaison officers/observers.

The Neutral Commission begins its work on the ground.

D+25: Establishment of the Follow-up Commission and the Military Coordination Commission.

Appointment of the Special Representative of the UN Secretary General.

Parties designate chief representatives to the Follow-up Commission and

Military Coordination Commission (one from each Party for each of the Commissions).

D+35: Neutral Commission submits its determination.

D+40: Neutral Commission's report released to the Parties.

D+45: Parties submit redeployment plans to the peacekeeping mission.

D+48: Redeployment plans approved by the peacekeeping mission.

D+49: Observers in position to observe and verify redeployment.

D+50: Commencement of redeployment of Eritrean forces.

D+64: Redeployment of Eritrean forces completed and verified by peacekeeping mission.

Restoration of civilian administration by Ethiopia commences.

D+71: Restoration of civilian administration by Ethiopia completed.

Redeployment of Ethiopian forces commences.

D+85: Redeployment of Ethiopian forces completed and verified by the peacekeeping mission.

Restoration of civilian administration by Eritrea commences.

D+92: Restoration of civilian administration by Eritrea completed.

Establishment of an independent body to investigate the origins of the conflict.

D+185: Delimitation/demarcation completed unless extended at the request of the Cartographic Experts.

Return of legitimate authorities completed, unless delimitation/demarcation has been extended.

APPENDIX 15
Questions Submitted by Ethiopia to the OAU for Clarification of the Technical Arrangements for Implementation of the OAU Framework Agreement & its Modalities

1. Colonial treaties and applicable international law

The Framework Agreement makes reference to pertinent colonial treaties and applicable international law in addition to resolution AH G/Res. 16(I) adopted by the OAU Summit at Cairo in 1964. However, paragraph 5 of the preamble to the Technical Arrangements makes reference only to the Cairo Resolution. What is the reason for this omission of 'colonial treaties and applicable international law'? Does this omission have any implications for delimitation and demarcation of the boundary?

2. Cessation of hostilities and redeployment

2.1 The Modalities in paragraph 4 provide that the deployment of troops shall 'commence immediately after the cessation of hostilities'. In this connection, in my letter of July 29, 1999 to Your Excellency I had suggested that the OAU establish a team of verifiers through consultation with the parties. The team would then collect evidence and undertake consultations with them in order to arrive at an agreed list of areas from which redeployment is to take place on the basis of paragraphs 1 and 2 of the Modalities.

In my discussions with your Special Envoy I had indicated that verification of lines of redeployment can take place before cessation of hostilities. In fact, the process followed by the Committee of Ambassadors of the OAU High-Level Delegation to determine who administered Badme and its environs before May 6, 1998 can easily be followed. It will be recalled that the Committee visited both capitals, heard from both sides, collected evidence including from relevant third parties and arrived at the conclusion that Badme and its environs was administered by Ethiopia before May 6, 1998 in less than two weeks.

In my discussions with your Special Envoy I had also suggested that if the verifiers need to go to the area, full security guarantee can be obtained from both parties. Why was the option I put forth not preferred? Instead, under Annex IV to the Technical Arrangements redeployment of Eritrean troops will commence 50 days after D-day. Is this not contrary to paragraph 4 of the Modalities which provides for 'immediate' commencement of redeployment following cessation of hostilities?

2.2 The Modalities for the implementation of the Framework Agreement treats cessation of hostilities and cease-fire in paragraphs 4 and 7 respectively, the latter providing for a cease-fire agreement as the final step in the peace process. However, the Technical Arrangements deal only with cessation of hostilities. Why was the change made? What is the scope of cessation of hostilities under the Technical Arrangements?

2.3 On usage of important terms, the Technical Arrangements in article 2 use different terms like 'cessation of all military activities', 'cessation of any other action', 'cessation of all armed air and land attacks' and 'cessation of hostilities' (Annex IV). Does this add or detract from a normal cessation of hostilities? Why is there no uniform usage of terms?

3. Restoration of Civilian Administration

3.1 Article 9 (a) (2.1) provides for the prohibition of deportation from the areas where civilian administration has been restored. How does this square with the sovereign right of a state to take measures to remove any national security threat to the nation?

3.2 Paragraph 8(b) of the Technical Arrangements provides for the restoration by Ethiopia of the civilian administration including police and militia within 7 days. This is a clear recognition that police and militia are an integral part of the civilian administration as it is in the case of the rest of Ethiopia. However, the Technical Arrangements provide under article 9(a) 2.3. for the prohibition of display of weapons by militia. What does 'prohibition of display of weapons' mean? Will the militia have law enforcement functions as in the rest of Ethiopia? If so as in the past will they be allowed to bear arms?

3.3 It is provided under article 9(b) 2 that the Peace-keeping Mission 'as necessary' will establish a grievance resolution mechanism to which the local population will have access. Is this not contrary to the Framework Agreement and Modalities in which such mechanisms are nowhere mentioned? What is the reason for introducing it here? Who is going to decide when it is necessary to establish such mechanism? The parties or the 'Peace-keeping Mission'? If it is the latter would this not go beyond the mandate envisaged for the Observer Mission in the Framework Agreement? Will the mandate of the mechanism be to observe and verify the implementation of the agreements and report its findings to the competent bodies or will it have the mandate to take decisions and enforce them? If so would this not be in contravention of the sovereignty of Ethiopia?

4. Humanitarian issues – arbitration

Article 14 of the Technical Arrangements envisages arbitration on humanitarian issues and issues concerning the socio-economic consequences of the dispute if the Parties fail to settle it through bilateral negotiations or mediation. Will individuals have direct access to the arbitration mechanism or will their cases be espoused by their respective government?

Will the mechanism have the mandate to handle and decide cases concerning:

- Ethiopian property taken by the Eritrean Government at the ports of Assab and Massawa,
- destruction of public infrastructures like schools, clinics, public administration buildings, religious and cultural objects and private property of all kinds in the areas occupied by Eritrea since 6 May 1998,
- disappearances and killings of civilians in the occupied territories of Ethiopia etc.

5. Peace-Keeping Mission

5.1. This is not provided for in the Framework Agreement or Modalities. Rather, the two basic documents envisage Military Observer Mission. What is the reason for this departure from the Framework Agreement and Modalities?

Will the 'Peace-keeping Mission' be composed of military and other experts to observe and verify the implementation of the agreements or will it be made up of troops to keep the peace between Ethiopia and Eritrea? What will be the size and duration of this mission?

What is the mandate of this Mission? Is it going to be verification and observation or does it go beyond that?

5.2. Articles 29c) of the Technical Arrangements provide that the parties will guarantee the free movement of the Peace Keeping Mission and its supplies as required through and between the territories of the Parties. Will there be prior notification to the parties before the Mission's travels?

5.3. Under articles 8(b) of the Technical Arrangements the Peace-Keeping Mission performs the function of Observing and Assisting in the restoration by the parties of the civilian administration including police and militia. Is the assistance to be rendered upon request by the parties?

6. Delimitation and Demarcation

Article 11 of the Technical Arrangements provide for delimitation of the boundary segment by segment. It is further provided that disputes over delimitation will be submitted to arbitration. Will the disputes also be submitted to arbitration segment by segment? Will the parties have the right to submit their case and evidence to the Cartographic Unit and the Boundary commission?

7. Demilitarization (Annex III)

The Peace-keeping Mission is envisaged to 'approve the demilitarization plans'. What will it be deciding or approving? Is it going to do it in consultation with the parties? What criteria will it use in approving the demilitarization plans. What is meant by the term 'original positions' in paragraph 3 of Annex III?

8. Consultations on the establishment and operations of various bodies

The Technical Arrangements provide for the establishment of various bodies for the implementation of the Framework Agreement and Modalities. These are:

1) The Neutral Commission
2) The Follow-up Commission comprising the Political follow-up Commission and the Military Coordination Commission
3) The Verification Mission (Peace-keeping Mission)
4) The independent impartial body to carry out investigation into the origins of the conflict.
5) The Boundary Commission
6) The arbitration mechanism for the settlement of humanitarian issues and the socio-economic consequences of the conflict

Will there be consultations with the parties on the establishment of the above bodies? What will the scope of the consultations be? Once established will these bodies carry out their duties through full consultation with the parties? What will the scope of such consultations be?

9. Investigation into the incidents of 6 May 1998 as well as those of July/August 1997 (article 10)

Article 10 of the Technical Arrangements provides for the establishment of an independent impartial body to determine the origins of the conflict between Ethiopia and Eritrea.

What will be the scope of the determination by this body? Will the mandate of this body be limited to factual determination?

APPENDIX 16
Clarifications of the OAU in Response to the Questions Raised by Ethiopia Relating to the Technical Arrangements

Introduction

By letter of His Excellency Mr Meles Zenawi, Prime Minister, addressed, on 13 August 1999, to His Excellency Mr Abdelaziz Bouteflika, President of the People's Democratic Republic of Algeria, current Chairman of the Organization of African Unity, the Federal Democratic Republic of Ethiopia requested a series of clarifications regarding the 'Technical Arrangements for the Implementation of the OAU Framework Agreement and its Modalities'.

In this respect, it is to be recalled that the communiqué made public on 11 August 1999 by the current Chairman and the Secretary General of the OAU indicated that, 'taking into account the fact that any interpretation of the Framework Agreement, the Modalities and the Technical Arrangements falls within the exclusive competence of the OAU and considering that this request for clarification is made in a constructive spirit, the Personal Envoy assured the Ethiopian Party that the clarifications sought on the Technical Arrangements, once formally submitted, will be given a speedy reply in line with the Framework Agreement and the Modalities for its implementation'.

It is to be recalled that the drafting of the Technical Arrangements was made in response to clear requests by the two parties to the Personal Envoy during his meetings with them between the 22nd and the 25th of July 1999. This was intended to provide the practical measures necessary for the Implementation of the Framework Agreement and of the Modalities endorsed by the 35th ordinary session of the Assembly of Heads of State and Government of the OAU, strongly supported by the UN Security Council and accepted as they are by the Parties.

Finally, and as recorded in the 4th paragraph of the preamble to the document containing the Technical Arrangements, the Parties have accepted that 'any interpretation of the OAU Framework Agreement and the Modalities is the sole responsibility of the OAU and its current Chairman'.

It is in this spirit that the present clarifications are submitted, at its request, to the Government of the Federal Democratic Republic of Ethiopia. As in the preparation of the Technical Arrangements and as welcomed by the two Parties, preparation of these clarifications was conducted by experts from the OAU, in cooperation with experts from the UN and the United States of America.

Clarifications

Colonial Treaties and Applicable International Law

Two questions have been raised on this issue.

A.1. The first concerns the omission of any reference to 'colonial treaties and applicable international law' in paragraph 5 of the preamble to the Technical Arrangements, while the preamble to the Framework Agreement does so.

    A.1.1. In this regard, it is useful to underline that the preamble to the Framework Agreement sets forth both a principle and an approach.

    A.1.2. The principle set forth is that of the 'respect for the boundaries existing at independence, as stated in Resolution AHG/Res 16(I) adopted by the OAU Summit in Cairo in 1964'.

    A.1.3. The approach set forth is that of the 'determination of those borders on the basis of pertinent colonial treaties and applicable international law, making use, to that end, of technical means to demarcate the borders and, in the case of controversy, resort to the appropriate mechanism of arbitration'.

    A.1.4. The Technical Arrangements, which must be read as a whole, do not depart from the contents of the Framework Agreement on this issue.

    A.1.5. The specific basis for delimitation and demarcation of the border, as contained also in the 'Framework' and 'Modalities', are set out in paragraphs 11, 12 and 13 of the Technical Arrangements.

    A.1.6. The third sub-paragraph of paragraph 11 clearly states that 'the delimitation and demarcation process will be done on the basis of pertinent colonial treaties and applicable international law'.

A.2. The second requested clarification on this issue goes to whether 'this omission has any implications for delimitation and demarcation of the boundary'.

Cessation of Hostilities and Redeployment

B.1. The comments leading to the first question compare (a) the mission of the Committee of Ambassadors sent in 1998 by the OAU High Level Delegation to (b) the mission of the Neutral Commission provided for in paragraph 3 of the Technical Arrangements.

    B.1.1. The missions of these two bodies are different in important respects. The Committee of Ambassadors conducted discussions with the political authorities of the two Parties in their respective capitals. On the other hand, the purpose of the Neutral Commission, as stated in paragraph 3 of the Technical Arrangements, is to facilitate the full implementation of paragraph 5 of the Modalities with a view to returning to positions held prior to 6 May 1998. To do so, the Neutral Commission is mandated to determine what those positions were. In conducting its work, the Commission will, necessarily, visit the field, while utilizing whatever information it deems relevant and while consulting with the Parties. It is essential that this determination be made as swiftly as possible in order to enable the rapid, subsequent redeployment of forces, in accordance with paragraph 8 of the Technical Arrangements. The additional steps necessary to execute redeployment by the Parties, especially the redeployment of observers, must proceed concurrently with the work of the Neutral Commission in order to enable the swiftest possible redeployment and restoration of civilian administration.

B.1.2. As a practical matter, the safety of the members of the Commission as they visit an area currently a military frontline can only be assured in the context of the cessation of hostilities called for in paragraph 2 of the Technical Arrangements.

B.1.3. The establishment of the Neutral Commission and the execution of its mandate are an integral part of the implementation process as agreed and requested by the Parties.

B.1.4. In any event, the Framework Agreement, which remains the reference for the settlement process (supplemented by the Modalities), specifies under paragraph 1 that 'the two Parties commit themselves to an immediate cessation of hostilities'.

B.1.5. Similarly, the Modalities specify under paragraph 3 that 'the two Parties agree to put an end to all military activities and to all forms of expression likely to sustain and exacerbate the climate of hostility and thus compromise the implementation of the Framework Agreement'. On their acceptance of the Modalities, the two Parties thus committed themselves to this provision.

B.1.6. Thus, the cessation of hostilities committed to by both Parties on their respective acceptance of the Framework Agreement and the Modalities must come into force with the commencement of the implementation process.

B.2. The second question raised on this issue asks whether redeployment of the Eritrean troops 50 days after D-day is not contrary to paragraph 4 of the Modalities, which provides for immediate commencement of redeployment following cessation of hostilities.

B.2.1. The answer is a practical one. Paragraph 4 of the Framework Agreement specifies that 'this redeployment be supervised by a group of military observers, which will be deployed by the OAU with the support of the United Nations'. A period of time between the cessation of hostilities and the actual start of redeployment will be required. Furthermore, time must be allowed for the work of the Neutral Commission.

B.2.2. Qualified experts from the OAU and the UN have determined that a period of 50 days following signing will be required for the work of the Neutral Commission and deployment of military observers. The evaluation of this period of time must remain the prerogative of the OAU and UN, which will be determined, in consultation, of course, with the Parties.

B.2.3. It is clearly understood that acceptance of the cessation of hostilities by the Parties is an indivisible part of their acceptance of the complete Technical Arrangements, including specifically paragraph 8.

B.3. The next question on this issue concerns the absence of reference in the Technical Arrangements to a formal cease-fire (as referred to in paragraph 7 of the Modalities).

B.3.1. This is also an issue of practicality. A formal cease-fire is not required for the successful implementation of the process laid out in the Technical Arrangements, since each Party will be bound by the conditions specified in paragraph 2 of the Arrangements.

B.3.2. The confidence of the Parties in this cessation of hostilities should be reinforced by the fact that the OAU and the UN are the guarantors of the scrupulous implementation of all the provisions of the OAU Framework Agreement, the Modalities for the implementation of the Framework Agreement and the Technical Arrangements.

B.4. The next questions on this issue are related to the scope of the cessation of hostilities and to any differences in the terms used to describe cessation of hostilities in the various OAU documents, some of which are more specific than others.

B.4.1. All of the terms used are consistent with common definitions of 'cessation of hostilities' and with established practices in missions conducted by the OAU and under Chapter VI of the UN Charter.

B.4.2. As with other issues, the Technical Arrangements, in paragraph 2, provide the greatest detail on the scope of a cessation of hostilities. Of course, this provision of the Technical Arrangements does not negate the provisions of the Framework Agreement and the Modalities for its implementation. Taken together, all these provisions are consistent with the 'normal cessation of hostilities' mentioned in the question, neither adding nor detracting from it.

Restoration of Civilian Administration

C.1. The first aspect of the clarification requested under this chapter is related to the prohibition of deportations from areas where civilian administration is restored. The exact question is about the extent to which this corresponds with the sovereign right of a State to take measures to remove any national security threat to the Nation.

C.1.1. The answer to this question is clear: a reading of the Framework Agreement, the Modalities and the Technical Arrangements shows that the three documents as a whole (constituting the settlement plan) are not meant in any way to question the sovereignty and the authority of either of the two Parties over the whole of its territory, it being mutually understood that the redeployment shall not prejudice the final status of the territories concerned, which will be determined at the end of the border delimitation and demarcation process.

C.1.2. While not questioning the sovereign rights of either Party, it should be noted that, beyond the issue of defusing tension and building confidence addressed under paragraph 1 of the Framework Agreement, acceptance of the Framework Agreement ties the two Parties to humanitarian commitments specified under paragraph 8/a, which states that 'the two Parties commit themselves to put an end to measures directed against civilian population and refrain from any action which can cause further hardship and suffering to each other's nationals'.

C.1.3. The specific provision in paragraph 9 (a-2.1) of the Technical Arrangements, which is the subject of this question, is clearly limited in scope to areas where the civilian administration of each Party had been restored.

C.1.4. The ban on the displacement or deportation of the civilian population of one Party by the other Party in these areas is therefore meant as a general principle connected with the humanitarian commitments by each Party in accordance with the provisions of the Framework Agreement. It is a principle whose sovereign acceptance by each Party does not require the questioning of its national authority. Moreover, 'prohibition on displacement and deportations of civilian populations' is not intended to preclude the expulsion, subject to due process, of individuals determined to pose a specific threat to national security. It is expected that such expulsion, if any, would be conducted in a transparent fashion.

C.2. The second aspect of the clarifications requested on this issue relates to the questions concerning militia.

C.2.1. The first question raised concerns the meaning of 'prohibitions of display of weapons by the militia'. In this connection, the clarifications are as follows:

C.2.1.1. The phrase 'prohibitions of display of weapons' clearly allows that the militia will go back to the areas where the civil administration has been restored (and of which it is part) with its usual armament.

C.2.1.2. Prohibitions of the display of weapons are applicable to the militias of the two Parties in populated areas where civilian administration has been restored. This provision is therefore limited in space. This measure is set forth bearing in mind:

a. the commitment of the two Parties to defuse tension and to build confidence (paragraph 1 of the Framework Agreement); and

b. the fact that in accordance with paragraph 4 of the Framework Agreement (supplemented by paragraph 9-b1 of the Technical Arrangements) the peacekeeping mission may assist the police force, when it is requested and in the appropriate form, in the areas where civilian administration has been restored.

C.2.1.3. Without disregarding the specific mission assigned to the militia of the two countries of contributing to maintenance of law and order, it should be noted that in the climate of confidence necessary for the implementation of a specific agreement on the settlement of an armed conflict and with an international presence deployed to observe it with the mutual consent of the two parties, it is not accepted international practice in such circumstances that individuals may brandish weapons in a manner that could intimidate the population.

C.2.1.4. The spirit of this provision is to make clear that the respective governments are allowed to undertake normal, administrative functions, including law enforcement, but that – for the sake of smooth implementation of the Agreement – disruptive problems are to be prevented on both sides of the border. It represents a contribution to the peaceful implementation of the agreement, made by each of the two parties without prejudice to the attributes of each State concerned or to its own administration.

C.2.1.5. It is important to note that paragraph 9 of the Technical Arrangements provides clear assurances for the security of the local population.

C.3. A second question is about whether the militia will assume missions of law implementation in the rest of Ethiopia.

C.3.1. In response, it remains understood that the implementation of the settlement plan under international observers does not question the rules and principles applied by each of the two Parties in law enforcement. This therefore applies also to the traditional functions of the militia in the light of the provisions of article 4 of the Framework Agreement and of the provisions of paragraph 9 of the Technical Arrangements.

C.3.2. The Parties may wish to provide militia members performing police functions, under the control, authority and discipline of the police, with appropriate training on the sensitivity and importance of the situation and with instruction on their responsibilities.

C.4. A third question is about whether in this instance the militia could bear weapons.

C.4.1. The answers given immediately above address this question.

C.5. The following points respond to the questions about the peacekeeping mission and its relationship to the local liaison and grievance resolution mechanisms.

C.5.1. Regarding the local liaison and grievance resolution mechanisms, including ensuring the local population access to those mechanisms (paragraph 9 b-2), this arrangement reflects the letter and spirit of:

a. paragraph 8.a through 8.c of the Framework Agreement, which set forth the humanitarian commitments of the two parties; and

b. paragraph 6 of the Modalities, which states that 'the group of military observers will carry out any other duties that are entrusted to it, in conformity with the relevant provisions of the Framework Agreement'.

C.5.2. Thus, the possible institution of these communication channels open to the local populations in the Technical Arrangements is based on the contents of paragraph 6 of the Modalities. Its objectives are pursuant to paragraph 8.a of the Framework Agreement which states: 'At the humanitarian level, the two Parties commit themselves to put an end to measures directed against the civilian population and refrain from any actions which can cause further suffering to each other's nationals'.

C.5.3. A decision to establish such mechanisms could be made, as necessary, by the peacekeeping mission only in a consultation with the Parties as is normally the case.

C.5.4. To the specific question on the mandate for these mechanisms, the answer is clear. Their mandate will be to observe and verify the implementation of the agreements and report their findings to the competent bodies, as well as to the peacekeeping mission. They will not have a mandate to take decisions or enforce them. It is equally clear that the local administration of each of the two Parties will keep full responsibility for maintaining order and implementing law.

Humanitarian issues – Arbitration

D.1. Regarding the question of knowing whether individuals can have a direct access to the mechanism of arbitration or whether it is up to their respective Governments to plead their case, the necessary clarifications are as follows:

D.1.1. As specified under paragraph 8-b of the Framework Agreement and 14 of the Technical Arrangements, the resolution of the humanitarian issues and of the socio-economic consequences of the conflict is first of all the direct responsibility of the two Parties (and therefore of the two governments which commit themselves to address it).

D.1.2. In case of a failed negotiation or mediation in that respect, the two Parties commit themselves to agreeing to an appropriate mechanism of arbitration (paragraph 14 of the Technical Arrangements).

D.1.3. The same paragraph 14 allows that, in case the two Parties are unable to agree on a mechanism or arbitration, the Secretary General of the UN, in consultation with the Secretary General of the OAU, (and both Parties as appropriate), will institute an appropriate arbitration mechanism. The method of work of this body will be determined in the course of this process and in accordance with customary international practice.

D.2. Regarding the issues that may be referred to the arbitration mechanism, and without prejudice at this stage to the issues that can be raised by any Party, it is important to specify that:

D.2.1. The scope for this is set out in most general terms under paragaph 8-b of the Framework Agreement and under paragraph 14 of the Technical Arrangements.

D.2.2. The process of negotiation or mediation allowed for under paragraph 14 of the Technical Arrangements does not put any additional limitation to what has been stated above.

Peacekeeping Mission

E.1. The following clarifications address questions about the term 'Peacekeeping mission'.

    E.1.1. The participation of the UN, in addition to the OAU, in observing and verifying the implementation of the settlement plan is provided for in the Framework Agreement, especially in paragraph 4.

    E.1.2. The preparation for such cooperation with the UN was evident in a visit by the OAU General Secretariat, from 12 to 14 April 1999, on the invitation of the UN Peacekeeping Department (as referred to in paragraphs 70 and 71 of report of the Secretary General on the efforts of the OAU High Level Delegation (CM/2100/LXX).

    E.1.3. This collaboration is also indicated under paragraph 6 of the Modalities.

    E.1.4. The OAU remains at the centre of the process. The OAU holds the main political responsibility of implementing the settlement plan. But in practical terms, the OAU is constrained in its logistic and financial means. These are, thus, the reasons that led to the stating in paragraph 4 of the Technical Arrangements of the establishment of a UN peace-keeping mission. In doing so, the aim is to ensure the best conditions for the efficient and assured implementation of a settlement plan accepted by the two Parties. It is important that, as specified in paragraph 4 of the Technical Arrangements, the OAU will also deploy its personnel and designate its own Secretary General's representative, who will work in close cooperation with the UN peacekeeping mission.

    E.1.5. The term 'peacekeeping mission' is consistent with the terms used by the UN when this Organization acts under Chapter VI of its Charter. In this case, the peacekeeping mission is to observe and verify the implementation of the settlement plan in accordance with the terms of the Framework Agreement, the Modalities and the Technical Arrangements. It is not the peacekeeping force one would find in a Chapter VII operation.

    E.1.6. The scope of this peacekeeping mission will be determined by the United Nations in cooperation with the OAU, and in consultation with the Parties. It will be shaped to meet the tasks defined in the Frame-work Agreement and the Modalities, and specified in the Technical Arrangements.

    E.1.7. Regarding the duration of the peacekeeping mission and its supplies, which will be guaranteed by each Party through its territory, it remains understood that this will be done in cooperation with the government concerned, in accordance with an arrangement which will be concluded by the Parties with the UN, and with respect for the sovereignty of the country concerned.

E.3. As regards the assistance to be rendered by the peacekeeping mission in accordance with paragraphs 8.b and 8.d of the Technical Arrangements, it is clear that, as is the case for any assistance, a prior request by the Party (administration) concerned would be required.

Delimitation and Demarcation

F.1. The first question on this issue is whether any disputes requiring arbitration would be submitted segment by segment. The following clarification is provided.

F.1.1. The Parties accept that the delimitation and demarcation process will be done on the basis of pertinent colonial treaties and applicable international law. This may not be in dispute.

F.1.2. Under paragraph 11 of the Technical Arrangements, it is stated that 'Upon acceptance by the Parties of the delimitation of each segment, the binding demarcation of that segment will be carried out. Such signed acceptance shall be given to the UN Cartographic Unit within one week, unless arbitration is requested by either Party'.

F.1.3. Under paragraph 13 (subparagraph 3) it is specified that the Boundary Commission shall decide 'such issues' (plural), which implies that claims can involve each disputed segment. Furthermore, paragraph 15 of the Technical Arrangements specifies also that the demarcation process, too, is to be completed segment by segment.

F.1.4. Thus, it should be assumed that any requests for arbitration on any segment will be submitted in the context of that segment, so that work on other segments may proceed while that issue is being arbitrated.

F.1.5. As for the question of whether each Party will have the right to submit its case and evidence to the UN Cartographic Unit and the Boundary Commission, the answer is clearly positive. In any case, the UN Cartographic Unit in charge of delimitation and demarcation will make available any further clarification requested by either Party.

Demilitarization

G.1. With regard to questions on the provisions of Annex III on demilitarization procedures, the following clarification is made:

G.1.1. As set out under paragraph 12 of the Technical Arrangements, a possible demilitarization of some areas may prove to be necessary in order to defuse tension and facilitate the delimitation and demarcation process. This is the sole understanding of the concept of demilitarization set out in paragraph 12 and Annex III.

G.1.2. A local demilitarization may be required by the peacekeeping mission, as stated in paragraph 12 of the Technical Arrangements.

G.1.3. A local demilitarization plan would be submitted by the appropriate Party or Parties to the peacekeeping mission, which would first approve it for the technical merit and then observe and verify necessary troop movements.

G.1.4. This process will be conducted in a spirit of cooperation and will enable the peacekeeping mission to observe such movements effectively.

G.1.5. The term 'original positions' in subparagraph 3 of Annex III refers to the positions occupied at the time of the commencement of the local demilitarization. Return back to such positions, at the end of the local demilitarization, will be at the determination of the peacekeeping mission.

Consultations

H.1. A series of questions have been raised concerning the establishment and operation of a set of bodies provided for in the Technical Arrangements. These are:

The Neutral Commission

The Follow-up Commission

The Milirary Coordination Commission

The Peacekeeping mission

The independent body to investigate the origins of the conflict

The Boundary Commission

The arbitration mechanism for the settlement of humanitarian issues and the socio-economic consequences of the conflict.

The following clarifications can be provided in this regard:

H.1.1. All the bodies and mechanisms required are to be established in consultation with the Parties involved, who are expected to cooperate with such bodies and mechanisms, and, in some areas, to participate in them.

H.1.2. As they pursue their respective missions, these bodies and mechanisms are expected, as possible, to act in consultation with the Parties.

Investigation into the Origins of the Conflict

I.1. With regard to the scope of the determination by the mechanism on investigation provided for in paragraph 10 of the Technical Arrangements and the mandate of this mechanism, it should be noted that:

I.1.1. The scope of this independent investigation is set forth in paragraph 7 of the Framework Agreement and faithfully reproduced in the first subparagraph of paragraph 10 of the Technical Arrangements.

I.1.2. This investigation shall be conducted by an independent, impartial body as provided in subparagraph 2 of same.

I.1.3. Each Party should not at this stage anticipate elements it can submit to this body, but present those elements directly to it.

I.1.4. Finally, the mandate of this independent and impartial body is investigatory, as provided for in paragraph 7 of the Framework Agreement and paragraph 10 of the Technical Arrangements.

Conclusion

The OAU and its partners (the UN and the USA) wish to emphasize here their satisfaction at the progress made in the course of efforts to establish a plan to settle the conflict between Ethiopia and Eritrea, as contained in the Framework Agreement, the Modalities and the Technical Arrangements.

The OAU salutes the understanding reached by the Personal envoy of the current Chairman with His Excellency the President of the State of Eritrea and His Excellency the Prime Minister of the Federal Republic of Ethiopia, respectively, that the document containing the Technical Arrangements is not open to amendment.

The OAU hopes, that the present clarifications provided at the request of the Ethiopian Government (which, in a spirit of loyalty and transparency, will also be communicated to the Eritrean Government) will pave the way to acceptance of the settlement plan (including the Technical Arrangements) and to the rapid implementation of a peaceful and lasting solution to the conflict.

Postscript:
Towards a State of
'No War – No Peace'?

Just entering its third year, there may be hope that this devastating war will come to an end. On 18 June 2000 the Foreign Ministers of Eritrea and Ethiopia signed an OAU-negotiated agreement on the cessation of hostilities between the two countries. The agreement calls for the end to all hostilities, and for the deployment of a UN peacekeeping force in the area. The cease-fire agreement seems, however, to favour the stronger party, Ethiopia, since they are allowed to maintain their military positions in the retaken disputed area and all along the Ethiopian–Eritrean border. In brief, Ethiopian military troops are permitted to remain in the Eritrean territories they now occupy for security reasons and they do not have to withdraw until two weeks after the UN Peacekeeping Mission arrives. When the troops do withdraw, they will redeploy to positions that were under Ethiopian administration prior to 6 May 1998, including, *inter alia*, the disputed territories of Badme, Zalambessa and Bure. The Eritrean army will be positioned at least 25 km away from the Ethiopian forces, creating a 25-kilometre buffer zone (artillery range) on Eritrean territory in which the Eritrean army will not be allowed to position its own troops, despite the fact that the territory is indisputably Eritrean. Local civilian administration, including peasant militia, will be established however, in order to prepare for the return of the displaced civilian population. The UN Peacekeeping Mission will thus monitor this temporary security zone and Eritrean troops will not be allowed in these areas of Eritrean territory until the border is delimited and demarcated.

As described in a statement from the Ethiopian government's spokesperson's office of 21 June 2000, 'although these terms are clearly unfavourable to Eritrea, the government in Asmara had no choice but to accept them because the Ethiopian defence forces had, and continue to have, the military upper hand.' But how sustainable is a peace agreement forced upon the Eritrean government?

Before the signing of the agreement, both Eritrea and Ethiopia appeared to follow well-rehearsed proposals of how to end the conflict. Each government appealed repeatedly to the international community, whose nature and composition was rarely defined, to put pressure on the other. The Eritrean government and its sympathisers in the Diaspora readily believed that the international community, by a simple act of withholding development aid funds, could force Ethiopia to negotiate for peace. The Ethiopian government and its supporters (also in the Diaspora) likewise viewed the resolution of the conflict as a rather uncomplicated matter where the government of the United States could quite easily force the Eritrean government to withdraw from all areas occupied since May 1998 and to accept the Ethiopian preconditions for peace. The conflicting parties expected the international community to get itself together and put effective pressure on one or the other of the belligerent parties. Sadly, however, an Ethiopian large-scale military offensive penetrating deep inside Eritrea, was the driving force behind the final round of negotiations which resulted in the signing of the ceasefire agreement.

As this study goes to press (July 2000) it appears that the first step towards peace has been taken. Both parties seem to have become frustrated with the 'no war – no peace' situation of the first months of 2000. Though facing stiffer opposition from the nebulous international community, the Ethiopian government yet appeared confident of the possibility of persuading the OAU to modify the details of the Technical Arrangements. Meanwhile, the Eritrean government interpreted the efforts of the OAU and the US envoy Anthony Lake as a complete failure. On 25 February 2000 it became clear that Ethiopia had rejected the Technical Arrangements. There was very little that the OAU could do other than try to bring the parties, once again, to the negotiating table.

A proximity meeting was organised at Algiers for 25 March, the purpose of which, according to the Ethiopian government was to ensure consistency between the Technical Arrangements and the Framework Agreement and its Modalities. The meeting was cancelled as the Eritrean side showed up late and put the establishment of a formal ceasefire as a precondition for commencing the talks.

After that the electronic war continued unabated. The Eritrean government, in addition to its attempts to link the conflict with the famine in large parts of Ethiopia, also tried to create a better image for itself by offering the use of the port of Assab for channeling food aid to the famine-struck population of Ethiopia. Ethiopia immediately rejected the offer; the proposal had at any rate very little chance of being accepted as it was accompanied by rather humiliating conditions. For instance, the Eritrean government demanded assurances that the Ethiopian government would not divert food aid to feed its army. It is indeed interesting that the

167

Eritrean government raised the issue. Here, it is worth pointing out that the most tragic aspect of the war in the Horn of Africa is that food aid and development aid resources were diverted to the war efforts. This ethical dilemma is difficult to address, however, since both the Ethiopian and Eritrean governments, as well as donor countries and international NGOs, would like the public to believe that all assistance given is reaching its target groups.

The prospects for a peaceful resolution to the conflict appeared to have receded even further when officials of both governments stressed their readiness to use force. On 8 April 2000, Mr. Abdalla Jabir, head of organisational affairs in the People's Front for Democracy and Justice stated in an interview that the Eritreans were capable of resisting and destroying the Ethiopian military machine, as they had done before. The Eritrean official however, further warned that 'the internal situation in Ethiopia may outpace and overcome the regime and lead it into a different direction'. It is clear that he was hinting that the disintegration of Ethiopia would necessarily result in a change of power or a palace revolution. The Ethiopian government, carefully monitoring Eritrean statements, made its stand clear using all avenues at its disposal. During a session with the international press on 13 April 2000, the Ethiopian Prime Minister stressed that his government's commitment to reverse Eritrean aggression by force was a commitment of principle that was unaffected by any other emergencies.

The war has indeed taken a heavy toll in terms of human lives and economic resources; the impact of the famine that has struck some parts of Ethiopia could indeed have been lessened if the government could channel all its resources to famine prevention. Locked as it was in this protracted war – the causes of which we have attempted to unravel – Ethiopia continued throughout the spring to demand the unconditional withdrawal of Eritrean forces from the areas they occupied after 6 May 1998.

Even before the renewal of fighting in May 2000, news reports and official statements coming out of Eritrea indicated that it was already weary of the war of attrition and was willing to make peace. As a result of the war the Eritrean economy is under great strain. The situation is further complicated by the severe drought that has equally plagued the country, where up to thirty percent of the Eritrean population is in need of food aid. There were two major obstacles, though. The first was the uncompromising position that Ethiopia had chosen to pursue. The second was the seriously flawed way the Eritrean official media perceived the conflict and its resolution. On the one hand, the Eritrean media tended to trivialise the war and portrayed it as a minor episode that would be soon forgotten once the borders were demarcated. On the other, they appeared to rule out the possibility of achieving peace so long as the TPLF remained an active member in the Ethiopian political scene.

Our description of the Eritrean–Ethiopian conflict in terms of a war between brothers, we believe, captures the intractable nature of the relationship. Both parties have issued statements saying that the conflict has very little to do with border demarcation. Both governments accuse each other of using the border issue as a pretext to bring about major political changes in each other's country. The dramatic changes that took place in Ethiopia after the demise of the regime of Mengistu Haile Mariam are a recent lesson that the Eritrean government fully remembers. Likewise, Ethiopia, using its multiple registers (both as a 'unitary' state and as a protector of one its federal states), appears determined to redefine its relations with Eritrea.

On 8 May 2000 the Ethiopian Prime Minister, addressing the international diplomatic corps, restated the difficult position that his country had been facing for the last two years. He was candid enough to admit that the famine was in some way connected to the war that his country was obliged to endure. He also admitted that his country had been denied development aid as a form of punishment for a war that it did not initiate. The freezing of development aid had thus constrained his country to divert its limited resources away from food security to defence. Prime Minister Meles Zenawi then pointed out the unacceptable condition put on Ethiopia by the international community. He asked the international community to show him how to put an end to the war through peaceful means. If the international community could not persuade Eritrea to negotiate for peace, the Prime Minister stated clearly that Ethiopia could not afford to wait indefinitely. He reminded his audience that Ethiopia had to pursue the war option in order to put a final end to the war.

And few days later, on 12 May 2000 the Ethiopian government announced that it had initiated a new offensive in order to destroy the Eritrean forces of aggression. By 15 May the Ethiopian media were loudly reporting that they had driven the Eritrean forces out of the occupied areas around Badme and had penetrated deep into Eritrean territory. Five days after the initiation of renewed fighting, the Ethiopian forces said that they had surrounded the town of Barentu, which lies about 40 km inside Eritrea. On 18 May the Ethiopian forces occupied the town of Barentu. With Ethiopian forces deeply entrenched inside Eritrea it was clear that Ethiopia had a clear upper hand for the first time since the start of the war.

In an official statement, Prime Minister Zenawi underlined that Ethiopia's occupation of some parts of Eritrean territory was to weaken the Eritrean armed forces and thus force the Eritreans to withdraw from all other occupied territories. The offensive on the western front was soon followed up by an offensive on the central Zalambessa front. After only two days of intense fighting, the Eritrean forces withdrew from Zalambessa and Ethiopian forces pushed deep into the Eritrean highlands.

The military advantage the Ethiopians achieved in a few weeks in May 2000 was unlikely to be affected either by the UN embargo or a regrouping of Eritrean forces. Ethiopian officials stated that they could not care less about international sanctions, they would continue the military offensive until they had achieved their objectives.

It might have not been coincidental that the timing of the renewed fighting took place only three days before the general elections (held on 14 May) in Ethiopia. At least the Eritrean official media were quick to point out that the Ethiopian regime provoked the renewed fighting in order to bolster its position in the elections. There might be some truth in such allegations as several opposition parties had made statements prior to the elections that they had a good chance of challenging the government in power. The Ethiopian elections turned out, however, to be totally dominated by the EPRDF affiliated parties. In the few areas where there were strong opposition parties (like the Hadiya and Gedeo zones of the Southern Nation, Nationalities and Peoples Region), the EPRDF used all means possible to harass and intimidate the voters and to rig the elections in its favour.[1]

Yet if Eritrea and Ethiopia, as the president of Eritrea has argued, share the same fate by reasons of culture, history and geography, we are inclined to argue that neither of the parties took seriously the border negotiations and the documents that were the outcome of such negotiations, prior to the signing of the ceasefire agreement. First it was the Eritreans who demanded a series of clarifications. Later it was the turn of Ethiopia to delay its position on the Technical Arrangements until it finally rejected them. This reluctance, we believe, stems also from the fact that this war is not a border war. The real issues of the conflict, we believe, deal with the nature of economic relations between the Tigrinya people (in Eritrea and Tigray) and that of political influence and hegemony in the Horn of Africa.

There can be no better evidence about the real issues of the conflict than the series of statements that the Ethiopian Prime Minister issued at the end of May. The Ethiopian army, the Prime Minister said, shall stay in Eritrea until the conclusion of a peace agreement. Furthermore, Ethiopian forces would not withdraw from some parts of Eritrea until the international community could guarantee Ethiopia's future security against Eritrean aggression. He intimated further that Ethiopia would raise the issues of compensation (where, Eritrea as the aggressor, would have to

---

[1] Kjetil Tronvoll was doing research on the election process in Hadiya region, and witnessed these incidents in person.

pay) and the future size of the Eritrean army. The Ethiopian Prime Minister even went so far as to say that his victorious armed forces could function in the interest of the international community by providing Ethiopia the guarantee it deems necessary. It was indeed a strange diplomatic twist. Ethiopia, once the victim of aggression, now demanded and expected the international community to empower her to stay put in Eritrean territory so as to guarantee its own security. Ethiopian policy makers either judged the international community as a meaningless abstraction or as a highly discriminatory institution that would not, in any case, be mobilised to direct the historical processes taking place in that part of Africa. It was a political and diplomatic gamble. The Eritrean government responded in the same manner as Ethiopia did over two years ago: Eritrea would not negotiate a ceasefire until Ethiopia had unconditionally withdrawn its forces from Eritrean territory. But, as it turns out, Ethiopia won the gamble and most of their preconditions were met in the ceasefire agreement.

The commencement of the rainy season (June to September) would have in any case brought a halt to active military engagements. It is to be hoped that the respite brought about by the rainy season will open a window of opportunity for the ceasefire agreement to be properly implemented. But, considering the history of the war, we are still doubtful that we have seen the end to this conflict. A lasting and sustainable peace between Eritrea and Ethiopia is unlikely to emerge as long as the conflict is seen in terms of border demarcation, no matter how important this might be. The economic, political, cultural and historical links that bind these two states together have to be built somehow into a sustainable framework for peace. Thus, with the implementation of the ceasefire agreement, the true negotiations should start on how the relationship between Eritrea and Ethiopia should be organised from now and onwards. In this respect, bold initiatives are needed urgently. And we are convinced that the path-breaking strategies have to come from the citizens of the region.

Bibliography

Abbay, Alemseged (1998) 'Identity Jilted or Re-imagining Identity? The Divergent Paths of the Eritrean and Tigrayan Nationalist Struggles', PhD dissertation, University of California, Berkeley.

Abbay, Alemseged (1997) 'The Trans-Mareb Past in the Present', *The Journal of Modern African Studies*, 35(2): 321–34.

Abbink, Jon (1998) 'Briefing: the Eritrean–Ethiopian Border Dispute', *African Affairs*, 389(97): 551–65.

Asmerom, Ghideon Abay and Asmerom, Ogbazgy Abay (1999) 'A Study of the Evolution of the Eritrean Ethiopian Border through Treaties and Official Maps', *Eritrean Studies Review*, 3(2): 43–88.

Bozeman, Adda B. (1976) *Conflict in Africa: Concepts and Realities*, Princeton, NJ: Princeton University Press.

Brownlie, Ian (1990) *Principles of Public International Law* (fourth edition), Oxford: Clarendon Press.

Ciampi, Gabriele (1998) 'Componenti cartografiche della controversia di confine Eritreo–Etiopica', *Bollettino della Societá Geografica Italiana*, 12(3): 529–50.

Ellingson, Lloyd (1986) 'Eritrea: Separatism and Irredentism, 1941–85', PhD dissertation, East Lansing: Michigan State University.

Gayim, Eyassu (1993) *The Eritrean Question. The Conflict Between the Right of Self-Determination and the Interests of States*, Uppsala: Iustus Förelag.

Gilkes, P. and Martin Plaut (1999) *War in the Horn: the Conflict between Eritea and Ethiopia*, London: The Royal Institute of International Affairs, Discussion Paper No. 82.

Gottmann, Jean (1973) *The Significance of Territory*, Charlottesville: The University of Virginia Press.

Guazzini, Federica (1999a) *Le ragioni di un confine coloniale: Eritrea, 1898–1908*, Torino: L'Harmattan Italia.

Guazzini, Federica (1999b) 'La geografia variabile del confine Eritreo–etiopico tra passato e presente', *Africa* (Rome) 44(3): 309–48.

Hansson, Göte (1996) *Ethiopian Economy*, University of Lund.

Hertslet, Edward (1965) *The Map of Africa by Treaty* (third edition), London: Frank Cass.

Iyob, Ruth (1995) *The Eritrean Struggle for Independence: Domination, Resistance, Nationalism 1941–1993*, Cambridge: Cambridge University Press.

Killion, Thomas (1985) 'Workers Capital and the State in the Ethiopian Region', PhD dissertation, Stanford: Stanford University.

Markakis, John (1990) *National and Class Conflict in the Horn of Africa*, London: Zed Books.

Michaelsen, Scott and David E. Johnson (eds) (1997) *Border Theory: the Limits of Cultural Politics*, Minneapolis: University of Minnesota Press.

Negash, Assefa (1996) *The Pillage of Ethiopia*, Los Angeles: Adey Publishing Company.

Negash, Tekeste (1987) *Italian Colonialism in Eritrea, 1882–1941: Policies, Praxis and Impact*, Uppsala: University of Uppsala.

Negash, Tekeste (1997) *Eritrea and Ethiopia: the Federal Experience*, Uppsala: Nordic Africa Institute.

Pateman, Roy (1990) *Eritrea: Even the Stones are Burning*, Lawrenceville, NJ: Red Sea Press.

Peninou, Jean-Louis (1998) 'The Ethiopian–Eritrean Border Conflict', *Boundary and Security Bulletin*, 6(2): 46–50.

Seton-Watson, H. (1977) *Nation and States. An Inquiry into the Origin and Politics of Nationalism*, London: Methuen.

Sherman, Richard (1980) *Eritrea: the Unfinished Revolution*, New York: Praeger.

Tadesse, Medhanie (1999) *The Eritrean–Ethiopian War: Retrospect and Prospects. Reflections on the Making of Conflicts in the Horn of Africa, 1991–98*, Addis Ababa: Mega Printing Enterprise.

Tekle, Amare (1964) 'The Creation of the Ethio-Eritrean Federation. A Study in Post-War International Relations', PhD dissertation, Denver: University of Denver.

Tesfagiorgis, Gebre Hiwet (1999) 'Approaches to Resolve the Conflict between Eritrea and Ethiopia', *Eritrean Studies Review*, 3(2): 139–65.

Tronvoll, Kjetil (1998a) 'The Process of Nation-Building in Post-War Eritrea: Created from Below or Directed from Above?', *The Journal of Modern African Studies*, 36(3): 461–82.

Tronvoll, Kjetil (1998b) *Mai Weini, a Highland Village in Eritrea*, Lawrenceville, NJ: Red Sea Press.

Tronvoll, Kjetil (1999) 'Borders of Violence – Boundaries of Identity: Demarcating the Eritrean Nation-State', *Ethnic and Racial Studies*, 22(6): 1037–60.

Tronvoll, Kjetil (2000) *Ethiopia: A New Start?*, London: Minority Rights Group International.

Walta Information Center (1999) *One Year of Ethio-Eritrean Conflict*. Addis Ababa: Ministry of Information and Culture.

Young, John (1996) 'The Tigray and Eritrean Peoples Liberation Fronts: a History of Tensions and Pragmatism', *The Journal of Modern African Studies*, 34(1): 105–20.

Young, John (1997) *Peasant Revolution in Ethiopia: the Tigray People's Liberation Front, 1975–1991*, Cambridge: Cambridge University Press.

Young, John (1998) 'Regionalism and Democracy in Ethiopia', *Third World Quarterly*, 19(2): 191–204.

Zoli, Corrado (1930) *Cronache Etiopiche*, Roma: Sindacato Arti Grafiche.

Zoli, Corrado (1931) 'Un territorio contestato tra Eritrea ed etiopia. escursione nel paese degli Irob', *Bollettiono della societa geografica Italiana*, Rome, pp. 715–46.

Local Periodicals

Eritrea Profile, Hadas Eretra, Tobia, Aser, The Reporter, Effoita, Tomar.

Index